Rhetoric and Marxism

Rhetoric and Marxism

James Arnt Aune

Westview Press
Boulder • San Francisco • Oxford

Polemics Series

Published in 1994 in the United States of America by Westview Press, Inc., 5500 Central Avenue, Boulder, Colorado 80301-2877, and in the United Kingdom by Westview Press, 36 Lonsdale Road, Summertown, Oxford OX2 7EW

Library of Congress Cataloging-in-Publication Data
Aune, James Arnt.
   Rhetoric and marxism / James Arnt Aune.
      p.   cm. — (Polemics series)
   Includes bibliographical references and index.
   ISBN 0-8133-1771-1 — ISBN 0-8133-1772-X (pbk.)
   1. Rhetoric and socialism.   2. Rhetorical criticism.   I. Title.
II. Series.
HX550.R49A94   1994
335.43—dc20   94-14592
                                                                              CIP

Printed and bound in the United States of America

The paper used in this publication meets the requirements
of the American National Standard for Permanence of Paper
for Printed Library Materials Z39.48-1984.

10   9   8   7   6   5   4   3   2   1

Contents

Preface

THIS IS A BOOK ABOUT Marxism written from my vantage point as a professor of rhetoric. In *A Rhetoric of Motives,* Kenneth Burke contrasts the classical view of rhetoric as "the science of speaking well in civil questions" with that of Bentham and Marx, for whom rhetoric is "the knack of speaking ill in civil matters."[1] Marxism, like liberalism, participated in the Enlightenment project of eliminating mystification from social life—and this undertaking required a commitment to a perfectly transparent language.

Yet Marxism, as Burke has taught us, is "unsleepingly rhetorical," with much of its persuasiveness deriving from the "insistence that it is purely a science," or, in its Western forms, from the notion that it is purely a form of rational critique.[2] This book develops Burke's insight into an analysis of the contradictory role of rhetoric in the development of Marxism. Put simply, Marxism as a conceptual system has tended to ignore problems of communication; particularly, that form of strategic communication known in Western culture as "rhetoric." There is a link between Marxism's "rhetorical problem" and various pathologies of Marxism since Marx—from Stalinism to the political paralysis of academic Marxism.

Figures as diverse as Jürgen Habermas, Terry Eagleton, Joan Scott, and François Lyotard have directed our attention to the Marxist tradition's impoverished view of language and communication. Postmodernists, such as Lyotard, reject Marxism precisely for this reason. Marxist students of language and communication have tended to accept the poststructuralist critique of Marxism without analyzing the historical development of attitudes toward the production of strategic discourse. It is only by studying the shift in conceptions of rhetoric from the premodern to the modern period that an adequate Marxist account of communication processes can be developed.

My argument for the development of a rhetorical view of Marxism owes much to the work of Terry Eagleton. Where I differ, however, from Eagleton is that—based on twelve years of teaching—I know what happens to the study of rhetoric when it falls into the hands of professors of literature: *Oral* rhetoric gets ignored. Even after the concept of literature gets deconstructed, students of literature classes go on studying novels and poems rather than speeches or political campaigns. And, worst of all (although this trend is equally bad in departments of communication), students are trained to be critics rather than *advocates*.

The turn toward rhetoric—or, more frequently, toward "discourse"—has been viewed with considerable horror by more traditional Marxists such as Bryan D. Palmer. In fact, it was a reading of his book, *Descent into Discourse,* that convinced me to write this one.[3] I share Palmer's view that class is the central element of social and historical analysis. I agree with him—although strange that this should now be controversial—that there is a real world where people suffer and die because of unequal and unfair distribution of resources. My discussion of languages of class in the book, however, is intended to provide an alternative to poststructuralist views of discourse and still remain faithful to the idea that Marxism has neglected issues of language and communication.

I range rather widely across various schools of Marxism in this book. One of the more unfortunate aspects of the academization of Marxism is that there are now distinctive "schools" of academic Marxism that do not take each other into account. Literary Marxists seldom read Marxist economists, and both usually ignore the work of labor historians. The rhetorical power of Marxism once stemmed from the fact that it was the only available conceptual system that enabled academic fields in the sciences, fine arts, humanities, and social sciences to communicate with one another. This book identifies problems that need to be addressed before that rhetorical power can be regained.

A book that addresses problems of audience in Marxism needs to be explicit about its own audience. I have tried to write this book in such a way as to address the needs of three very different audiences simultaneously: students who may be interested in an advanced introduction to Marxist concepts of culture and communication; scholars of rhetoric and communication; and, finally, Marxist scholars in a number of disciplines. Those in search of inevitable contradictions in my account of the contradictions of Marxism might well begin with my own audience problems.

The greatest problem is that I am, alas, unable to present a complete *rhetoric* of Marxism, in the positive sense of that term. The audience conspicuously missing from my list is an activist one. I would have liked to have written a handbook of practical oral and written argument for such an audience. Nonetheless, the purpose of this book is to help open (or re-open) the question of *strategy* for Socialist politics after the fall of communism. Politics is *not* reducible to rhetoric, but the future of any Socialist politics depends on its coming to grips with the problematic of rhetoric.

What rhetorical analysis does is help train advocates to locate key moments of contradiction in their own and opposing positions. This book begins with a brief discussion of the implications of the fall of communism for Marxism. Chapter 1 is an analysis of certain key contradictions in Marxism, mostly having to do with questions of audience. Chapter 2 analyzes how Eduard Bernstein, Lenin, Georg Lukács, and Antonio Gramsci "solve" the contradictions of classical Marxism while developing new rhetorical problems of their own. Chapters 3 and 4 focus on Herbert Marcuse and Raymond Williams as representatives of the Lukácsian and Gramscian resolutions, respectively. Chapter 5 examines Jürgen Habermas's attempt to reconstruct historical materialism along the lines of a theory of communicative action. A brief conclusion provides a summary and a more or less programmatic statement about the implications of this book both for Marxism and for rhetorical studies.

I have focused on Marcuse, Habermas, and Williams because they have been most influential within my own field of rhetoric and communication. I would have liked to do an extensive analysis of "analytic Marxism" (the work of John Roemer, Erik Wright, and Jon Elster, for instance) or of attempts to integrate feminism and historical materialism (particularly the work of Nancy Hartsock and Catharine MacKinnon), but those tasks must be reserved for future work. I am painfully conscious of both the stridency and brevity of my comments on cultural studies in Chapter 4.

I began this study under the most helpful direction of Thomas B. Farrell. I am grateful for his and Vera Potapenko's support and hospitality over the years. Many of the arguments in this book were developed in conversation with colleagues and students at the University of Virginia. I especially thank John Rodden, Ted Smith, Fred Antczak, Joli Jensen, Mike Hogan, Eric Gander, and Mary Foertsch. I also thank my colleagues at St. Olaf, especially Lisa Baumgartner Brody, Pat Quade, Karen Peterson Wilson, Milt Thomas, Jeff Brand, and Jowane Howard. Michael Calvin McGee, J. Robert Cox, Kathleen Farrell, and Robert Hariman gave encouragement and helpful comments at crucial points in this project. My largest debt is to Mary Piccirillo Aune, who knows more than anyone what Walter Benjamin meant when he wrote, "It is only for the sake of those without hope that hope is given to us." It is to her and to our children, Nick and Daniel, that I dedicate this book.

James Arnt Aune

Introduction:
The Spirit of 1989

THE YEAR 1989 NOW JOINS other pivotal dates in the history of socialism and the labor movement: 1848, 1917, 1939, 1956, and 1968. These dates represented both ends and beginnings; 1989 seems to represent an unequivocal end. Marxism is dead. Communism is dead. Socialism is dead. Contrary to the assertion at the end of the *Communist Manifesto,* it is Marxism, not capitalism, that has produced its own gravediggers.

It is customary for someone to say a few words at a burial. Such a rhetorical action, at least since Pericles' *Funeral Oration,* reveals what a community holds most dear—its sense of virtue, character, and human possibility.[1] The arguments presented at Marxism's funeral do the same. A representative discourse is an essay by Richard Rorty, "The Intellectuals at the End of Socialism."[2] Rorty begins by identifying himself and his audience as "we American leftist intellectuals." He says that "visitors from postrevolutionary Eastern and Central Europe are going to stare at us incredulously if we continue to use the word *socialism* when we describe our political goals."[3] But it is not just that the word itself is inappropriate. There is now simply no point even in saying that capitalism is unjust, because we cannot "envisage a noncapitalist, and less unjust, society that might actually function."[4]

The primary economic lesson of the adventures of the Communist ideal is that the market is necessary to provide consumer goods and social services. This is not as strong as saying, like Hayek, Friedman, and other classical liberals, that you cannot have democracy without capitalism. We just have to learn to cope with what seems to be an inevitable ethic of greed: "Public virtues, as far as we can presently see, will continue to be parasitic upon private vices. Nothing remotely like 'new socialist man' seems likely to emerge."[5]

But there is a philosophical lesson as well as an economic one, and that lesson is familiar to readers of Rorty:

> I hope we have reached a time when we can finally get rid of the conviction common to Plato and Marx, the conviction that there just *must* be large

1

theoretical ways of finding out how to end injustice, as opposed to small experimental ways. I hope we can learn to get along without the conviction that there is something deep—such as the human soul, or human nature, or the will of God, or the shape of history—which provides a subject matter for grand, politically useful theory.[6]

Not only is Theory itself suspect, but its appeal for intellectuals is as well. Intellectuals' support for socialism was as much motivated by their hunger for political power as by their concern for the oppressed. It is time for left-ist intellectuals to do two things: "banalize" their political vocabulary and focus on developing practical reform programs. That is, we should "start talking about greed and selfishness rather than about bourgeois ideology, about starvation wages and layoffs rather than about the commodification of labor, and about differential per-pupil expenditure on schools and differential access to health care rather than about the division of society into classes."[7]

Rorty recognizes that what gets lost in all this is "the sense that we are continuing a great and noble tradition."[8] He hopes that future generations will find figures like Vaclav Havel inspiring, even though we should dream less of "spiritual renewal" than of "the same experimental, hit-or-miss, two-steps-forward-and-one-step-back reforms that have been taking place in the industrialized democracies since the French Revolution."[9]

Rorty's essay is significant both because it is representative of some general strategies for encompassing life "after the fall" and because of Rorty's own status as an American intellectual leader. He is also perhaps the only American academic intellectual who is read widely across disciplines. Only a fool would berate Rorty for "reformism." Not only is that sort of arrogance inappropriate at this point in history for someone who still wants to keep the "Marxist" label, but it perpetuates one of the worst features of Marx and Engels themselves: an inattention to the ethics of controversy. From Marx's public humiliation of the rather admirable Wilhelm Weitling down to Engels's attack on Eugen Dühring, Marx and Engels carried on the nastiest traditions of German academic vituperation.[10] Anyone who, like Rorty, is able to condemn the white middle class for believing "that it is more important to cut taxes than to immunize ghetto children against measles" does not deserve to be denigrated.[11]

This is not to say that there are no problems with Rorty's argument. For one thing, it seems mildly disingenuous for Rorty to write of "giving up" talk about bourgeois ideology or the commodification of labor. (Perhaps the original title of Rorty's magnum opus, *Philosophy and the Mirror of Nature,* was *Philosophy and the Mirror of the Mode of Production?*) But most important, Rorty concedes the argument from human nature to the Right. The tired contention that human beings are inevitably selfish and acquisitive has been a staple of reactionary politics since the eighteenth century. Accepting it (or refusing to combat it) undercuts the possibility of inspiring anyone to reject the tendencies of the present system. Put simply, Rorty's post-Marxist "postmodern bourgeois liberalism" has a rhetorical problem. If the only doctrine approaching political certainty at this point in history is the need for the Market, then what will motivate any audience to choose Solidarity over classical liberal self-interest? If Grand Theory motivates intellectuals and the masses toward Stalinism, then what will move people toward continuing the experimental, hit-or-miss steps toward reform? And what of all those deep intangibles like the nature of the human soul and the will of God that motivated the Polish Solidarity movement? Rorty's arguments work effectively as a self-binding strategy for intellectuals, but it is unclear how they translate into the purportedly banal world of politics.

This latter label is probably effectively chosen for Rorty's audience, but it already loads the conceptual dice against the idea that politics may have something to do with *eloquence* and thus unwittingly continues a bias against rhetoric that dates back to the Grand Theorist Plato. Rorty is en route to becoming a philosophical Walter Mondale or Michael Dukakis—emphasizing competence and fine-tuning domestic policy while giving up vision (and votes) to the Republicans.[12] Rorty repeats the mistake he attributes to leftist intellectuals by engaging only in *radical critique:* unmasking intellectuals' neurotic craving for certainty and power. He gives us no way of developing what his idol John Dewey asked for in 1929: "the improvement of the methods and conditions of debate, discussion and persuasion."[13]

In this book, I attempt to help provide what Dewey asked for. I also attempt to provide for Marxism what Marxism could not provide for itself: a sensitivity to rhetorical problems. My overall argument is that the classical texts of Marx and Engels wavered incoherently between positivist and romantic views of language and communication—views made possible by the decline of the rhetorical tradition as a cultural force. Western Marxism attempted to resolve the incoherence in the classical texts but did so without an accompanying theory of rhetoric and political judgment that could resolve that incoherence.

My purpose in this introductory chapter is to clarify what it means to have a "rhetorical problem," first by discussing some aspects of rhetorical method. Next, I outline the central assumptions of Marxism and then demonstrate how these assumptions create a conceptual and rhetorical gap between structural determination and popular struggle.

Rhetoric Versus Critical Discourse

In discussing the various ways Marxist theorists have attempted to fill in the gap between structure and struggle, I will document the implicit rhetorical theory of each of the positions. Although the concept of "rhetoric" often appears to be a rather massive and contradictory abstraction—

embracing a pedagogical tradition from the Sophists to the present, the theory of composition and figurative language, and the actual practice of political or even literary persuasion—it emerged in the West as a systematic reflection on practice.[14] Regardless of one's view of the Sophists, it is clear that the practice of communication in the new democratic regime of fifth-century Athens provided a ready market for the teaching of speaking and writing. It is also clear that philosophy as a distinctive discursive practice emerged during the confrontation between Plato and the proponents of the new art of rhetoric.

Various factors—including the exhaustion of the antirhetorical liberal tradition that animated both capitalist and Marxist attitudes toward communication, as well as the rise of a new form of capitalism that seems to be based more on the commodification of information than on industrial production—have put rhetoric back on the agenda of social and political theory. From Straussians like Larry Arnhart on the Right, to apolitical liberals like the Rhetoric of Inquiry group, and to leftists like Frank Lentricchia, the call for the revival of rhetoric seems to be motivated by a deep sense that something is missing from traditional accounts of political action.[15] Terry Eagleton, for instance, argues for the recovery of the rhetorical tradition as "the process of analyzing the material effects of particular uses of language in particular social conjunctures."[16] Paolo Valesio finds in the skepticism of the rhetorical tradition the natural enemy of ideological discourse and tries to develop a new Marxist linguistics and literary theory based on rhetoric.[17] Gareth Stedman Jones, while not using the term "rhetoric," proposes a new problematic for labor history in which the study of "languages of class" replaces the more traditional focus on economic structures of working-class "experience."[18] Michael Denning, in an important study of the dime novels that were widely read by the American working class in the nineteenth century, views his larger project as a study of "the *rhetoric of class,* the words, metaphors, and narratives by which people figure social cleavages."[19]

Because the study of language-in-use has been dominated by departments of literature since the late nineteenth century, it is probably not surprising that most of the people who have called for a rhetorical revival tend to collapse rhetoric into poetics. Even those who have a somewhat fuller, classical understanding of rhetoric have, under the pressures of the American academic mode of production, allowed a one-sided focus on critique. The net effect, even in American departments of speech, now fashionably renamed as departments of communication, is to emphasize training of critics rather than citizen-orators.

Marxism—and the Left in general—has more problems than a lack of rhetorical sensitivity, but that lack is certainly a significant one. If the story that this book is to tell is accurate, the current "poverty of strategy" on the

Left has something to do with the rejection of a tradition that emphasized the study and practice of strategic discourse.[20]

There are, of course, many rhetorics, but at the risk of oversimplification, I would like to define rhetoric in terms of a fundamental stance toward discourse-production, and then to distinguish different rhetorics in terms of relative emphasis on style and practical reasoning. The fundamental stance of rhetoric is best captured by Hans-Georg Gadamer's discussion of the concepts of *Bildung* (self-formation, or cultivation), *Sensus communis* (a community's traditional public values), *Judgment* (that "good sense" that derives from civic solidarity), and *Taste* (adaptation to the aesthetic sense of the community) as parts of the "humanist" tradition.[21] As John Angus Campbell writes, these concepts can be rewritten as rules for pedagogical and oratorical practice. First, speak in such a way that you embody the values of your culture in your character. Second, always adapt your discourse to the common sense of your listeners. Third, study past rhetorical situations in order to develop the virtue of prudence—a sense of judgment that will generalize to future rhetorical situations. Finally, study history, great speeches, and imaginative literature in order to develop a sense of timing and taste. As Campbell writes, the successful advocate knows these things even if they are not fundamentally reducible to a "method":

> This is practical knowledge, and it cannot even be arrived at by way of distinguishing between the true and probable. It is not a matter of applying a general principle to a given circumstance. The knowledge possessed by the speaker who has timing and a sense of the appropriate is culled from many sources but it is finally based on, directed toward, and determined by the concrete situation. The universal element in this form of knowledge is that it must grasp the circumstances in their infinite variety.[22]

Ronald Beiner demonstrates that post-Enlightenment political philosophy has neglected the art of rhetoric and in so doing has undercut the possibility of rational political judgment. He defines further the unique sort of knowledge possessed by the citizen-orator:

> The successful orator must command the following: an understanding of human character and goodness in their various forms (with a view to presenting a convincing appearance of his own personal character); an understanding of the emotions (with a view to putting the audience in a certain frame of mind); and an ability to reason logically (so as to provide acceptable proof in the body of the speech itself).[23]

These principles—in terms of both the teaching of the arts of discourse and the practice of political analysis—run directly counter to the dominant stance both of Marxism and of liberal individualism. Marxism from its inception has been implicated in the modern project Paul Ricoeur so aptly names "the hermeneutics of suspicion."[24] This project became historically possible only with the breakdown of traditional authority characteristic of the Enlighten-ment, that point at which a "culture of critical discourse" (CCD) replaced rhetoric as the dominant mode of analyzing discourse. Alvin Gouldner's CCD has a set of communicative rules that are diametrically opposed to those of rhetoric: First, make your own speech problematic and try to account for its origins—be self-reflexive and self-monitoring. Second, submit all truth-claims to a process of examination, regardless of the speaker's societal position or authority. Third, distance yourself from the common sense of the culture in which your speech occurs, since the common sense of a culture is ultimately a rationalization for that culture's relations of domination. Finally, in order to escape cultural prejudice, privilege theoretical discourse—speech that is rela-tively context-free.[25]

Lest I be misunderstood, to identify the differences between CCD and rhetoric as fundamental codes for discourse-production is not to argue that rhetoric is an inherently superior code. The preceding analysis, after all, was written largely in CCD. Further, CCD can function as a rhetoric for limited audiences, mostly intellectuals.[26] My argument is intended to en-courage an ability to switch codes. Rhetoric alone, as Plato demonstrated long ago, can degenerate into immoral manipulation. But philosophy alone, as Cicero responded, leads to the truth becoming powerless.[27]

Particular cultures, or social formations, depending on the sort of lan-guage you want to use, will vary in the extent to which they reflect self-consciously on rhetorical processes and in their dominant stance toward public discourse. Particular rhetorical practices (key political speeches, for instance) may reflect implicit rhetorical "theories" that are at variance with a culture's "official" stance toward discourse as manifested in its edu-cational institutions.[28]

Current approaches to rhetorical analysis tend to be categorized into two extremes: those that focus on practical reasoning and those that focus on figurative language or narrative. There is no necessary conflict between the two emphases—Chaim Perelman's emphasis on practical reasoning de-pends on an understanding of the way in which rhetorical figures undergird argumentation.[29] Nonetheless, approaches in which figurative language or narrative dominate often make the poetic dimension of language dominate over practical considerations such as audience. Kenneth Burke's *A Rhetoric of Motives,* for instance, analyzes mostly imaginative literature and philos-ophy rather than practical political discourse.[30] Recent rhetorical revivals, like those of Eagleton and Lentricchia, repeat the same analysis.

A model for the stance toward rhetoric emphasized in this book is Albert O. Hirschman's recent *The Rhetoric of Reaction.*[31] Hirschman seeks to iso-late broad patterns of conservative argumentation against social change from the French Revolution to the welfare state. He discovers that conser-vatives typically argue three theses.

First, the *perversity thesis:* "The attempt to push society in a certain direction will result in its moving all right, but in the opposite direction."[32] Charles Murray, for instance, "proves" that spending money to eliminate poverty in the 1960s actually increased poverty. Hirschman demonstrates that this thesis (a) is not universally true—change sometimes does occur in the direction intended, and there are even unintended *positive* consequences of social change; (b) serves a psychological function for its adherents: "Could they be embracing the perverse effect for the express purpose of feeling good about themselves? Are they not being unduly arrogant when they are portraying ordinary humans as groping in the dark, while in contrast they themselves are made to look so remarkably perspicacious?" and (c) has its appeal because it is grounded in the mythic notion of divine punishment for sin and in the Greek Hubris/Nemesis pattern.[33]

Methodologically, then, Hirschman identifies an argumentative pattern, traces its reasons for audience appeal, locates deeper cultural patterns that reinforce this appeal (including root metaphors and myths), and then compares it with the reality it is intended to map. His reason for doing this is to improve democratic discussion and debate. Shorthand arguments like these, however practically effective, have a way of closing off debate.[34] Hirschman thus provides a truly rational rhetoric, one that may be of use in strategic planning and one that enables its audience and advocates to make reasoned judgments.

A second argument, especially important for students of Marxism, is the *futility thesis*. The notion that social change simply does not work—*plus ça change plus c'est la même chose*—is a popular conservative argument (even if it contradicts the perversity thesis that usually accompanies it). Hirschman points out that conservatives usually make this point "with a certain worldly-wise wit as opposed to the alleged earnestness and humorlessness of the believers in progress."[35] The point is also usually made by invoking scientific laws (the elite domination theories of Mosca, Pareto, and Michels are good examples). The futility thesis has a remarkable parallel in the assumption by many leftists that the existing order is universally successful in reproducing itself. The "critical functionalism" of many contemporary students of the mass media is a good example.[36] Perhaps as a compensatory argumentative device to conservative use of the futility thesis in discussing the French Revolution, Marx and Engels developed an "inevitability thesis."[37]

The futility thesis depends on metaphors about masks and veils, promising a recognition scene in which all is revealed.[38] The problem, of course, is that such a promise again relies on the omnipotent wisdom of a class of experts over the presumed ignorance of the people. Not only is such an assumption arrogant, but it violates its own norms. In other words, it proclaims that people and social systems cannot *learn*, presumably even from learning the futility thesis.

There is, finally, the *jeopardy thesis*, the idea that a forward move will jeopardize previous accomplishments. For instance, the welfare state's move to equality will jeopardize hard-won civil liberties. The world, of course, is more complex than that. Hirschman makes the interesting point that the welfare state came earlier to Germany precisely because it had no strong liberal tradition, thus preventing the marshaling of liberal jeopardy arguments, as in the United States and Britain.[39]

Although Hirschman does not analyze conservative rhetoric in the context of a defense of socialism or Marxism, it is interesting to note the recurrence of his patterns in the "rhetoric of 1989." The attempt to liberate workers led to their oppression (perversity); radical change is impossible, because no "new man" will appear (futility); and socialism destroyed the advances of liberalism (jeopardy). Add to these arguments the stronger version of the futility argument that invokes "radical evil" as a cause of human action in a world that has renounced God, and you will have a complete rhetorical map of the conservative and liberal responses.[40]

What hardly anyone is now pointing out is the collapse of the conservative, neoconservative, and cold-war liberal arguments that communism will *never* democratize on its own (probably a more complex version of the jeopardy argument, with the argument from radical evil thrown in).[41] While it may be true that the words "socialism," "communism," and "Marxism" may be discredited for some years to come, it is not clear how long that will be. The rapid rate of social change in the West, and the volatility of mass response (I write as Los Angeles is burning), suggest that, now more than ever: "All fixed, fast-frozen relations, with their train of ancient and venerable prejudices and opinions, are swept away, all new-formed ones become antiquated before they can ossify. All that is solid melts into air."[42]

While this is not the time for the apocalyptic eloquence of the *Communist Manifesto,* it is also not the time to give into the rhetoric of futility, whether it is represented by George Will or Richard Rorty. To do so is to deny that human beings can learn. It is possible to learn something about human beings, rhetoric, and social hope from the history of Marxism, the labor movement, and communism. It is also possible to make a case for Marxism, both as an analytic method and as a guide to social change. Making that case requires understanding the rhetorical problems built into Marxism from its inception.

Marxism's Nuclear Contradiction

The picture of Marxism that emerges from Rorty's essay is a rather simplistic one. It seems to consist only of clanking jargon and the rejection of a market economy. Yet, as even most honest conservatives recognize, Marxism is a distinctive philosophical system and analytic method. It is difficult to summarize a system that seems to embrace, say, both Louis Althusser and Raymond Williams, but it nevertheless seems useful to start with the description of a set of assumptions. It is, of course, an assumption of this book that "ideas" do not exist independently of rhetorical action. That is, it is misleading to insist that there is a "pure" Marxist theory. Still, the rhetorical stance, or the prefiguring of argumentative ground, of Marxism is distinct from others such as conservatism or classical liberalism. In describing these assumptions, my purpose is to identify strategic problems these assumptions will generate for Marxist theory and politics, as well as to develop ways to respond to these problems. In the concluding chapter of this book, I will reflect further on what a "red rhetoric" might look like in response to the conservative and liberal challenge to Marxism.

First, Marxists share a fundamental "representative anecdote." Some Marxists defend the idea of human nature, while others reject the very idea of human nature as a mystification. What both camps share, however, is a conceptual vocabulary. As Kenneth Burke writes, a conceptual vocabulary—representative anecdote—must do two things: reduce human action and select a set of terms that justify such a reduction.[43] The reduction is necessary because any coherent statement about the world must emphasize certain aspects of the world, if only to make discourse manageable. This privileging of a certain aspect is usually in the form of a representative anecdote, a story about human action that is broad enough to account for all or most instances of that action, and yet is narrow enough to generate manageable and testable hypotheses. Neoclassical economics, for instance, depicts human beings as self-interested utility-maximizers. A literary critic might be more likely to talk about story-telling animals, just as a theologian might talk about children of God.

The various Marxisms share a common representative anecdote: Human beings are laboring animals. They must work in order to live and in order to fulfill themselves. The error of pre-Marx economists was their assumption that enjoyment of the fruits of material labor is sufficient for human beings. As Marx writes in the *Grundrisse*:

> It seems quite far from [Adam] Smith's mind that the individual, "in his normal state of health, strength, activity, skill, facility," also needs a normal portion of work and of the *suspension of tranquillity*. Certainly, labor obtains its measure from the outside, through the aim to be attained and the obstacles to be overcome in attaining it. But Smith has no inkling whatsoever that this overcoming of obstacles is in itself a liberating activity. . . . [Labor] becomes attractive work, the individual's self-realization, which in no way means that it becomes mere fun, mere amusement, as Fourier, with grisette-like naivete, conceives it. Really free working, e.g. composing, is at the same time precisely the most damned seriousness, the most intense exertion.[44]

Regardless of whether this is labeled an argument from "human nature" or not, it is a scientific observation about human needs that can serve as the basis for an ethical evaluation of modern labor-processes.

This first assumption can be productively contradictory, in Gouldner's sense of a "research-driven anomaly."[45] To assume that human beings are laboring animals can lead either to a privileging of economic analysis and economic activity or to a privileging of human self-expression and the critique of existing economic arrangements on spiritual grounds. Perhaps the most common indictment of Marxism has been that its "economic determinism" excludes other stories about human beings.

A second assumption seems to make a form of economic determinism central to historical analysis. The mode of production in a given social totality—that is, the level of development of productive forces in addition to the type of work relations that accompany those forces—is a determining factor in establishing that totality's social being. Exactly how and how much a mode of production determines social being is a subject of considerable debate. A minimal version of this assumption would mean that a capitalist economic system based chiefly on industrial production tends to have consequences for a host of seemingly independent things, such as individual psychology, artistic expression, religion, and politics.

Third, all hitherto existing societies have been characterized by a struggle between classes over the control or allocation of the surplus from production. Workers, at least under capitalism, produce more than is needed to sustain themselves. This surplus, under capitalism, is expropriated by capitalists. Marxists will differ about the notion of "surplus value." Because of formal problems in the theory of price, it seems to make more sense to talk of the *exploitation* of workers than of the extraction of surplus value.[46] A focus on exploitation and struggle *over* exploitation has important political consequences. For one thing, it provides a universalizing appeal. The workplace (or lack thereof) is something that virtually all people share as an experience. The tendency of radicals since the 1960s to substitute members of the "new social movements" (students, persons of color, women, sexual-bias minorities, environmentalists) for the "proletariat" runs the political risk of undermining the common ground necessary for both electoral and revolutionary politics. A comment by British literary critic Alan Sinfield is symptomatic: "'Man' is a powerful concept, but I cannot regret its loss to the left. A divided society should have a divided culture: an (apparently) unified culture can only reinforce power relations."[47] The problem here is that a reduction of political culture—rhetoric, if you will—to "identity politics" is to concede the process of coalition-forming and the building of national unity to the Right.

This is not to deny the importance of separate movements for lesbian and gay rights and for the rights of women. It is not only rhetorically important to have some universalizing strategies, but it is politically important to understand the difference between exploitation and oppression. As Erik Wright points out, it is possible to be oppressed without being exploited. Exploitation implies a mutual relationship between exploiter and exploited. The capitalist needs the worker, at least until the worker is replaced by a machine. The capitalist (and the worker) may oppress a gay man, but neither of them needs the gay man for anything. To them his fate is unimportant. The worker, however, has the chance to stop production, something that the capitalist cannot afford.

A focus on the language of oppression also has the tendency of emphasizing the victim status of particular groups and, thus, runs the risk both of patronizing them and of deemphasizing the role of human agency in social change.

Fourth, the level of development of the productive forces determines—in the sense of setting boundary conditions for—the sort of class structure and class struggle a given social system will have. A combination of increased exploitation of labor, for instance, with a centralization of economic power may make clashes between labor and capital inevitable over matters such as wages, work rules, and the length of the working day. A Marxist feminist might point to developments in reproductive technology (abortion, artificial contraception) as providing the material basis for the revolt of women against male domination. Marxists generally may be distinguished from other radicals by their conviction that a successful movement for social change must acknowledge material prerequisites for such change.

Fifth, because the productive forces tend to develop over time, "history" is generally predictable in terms of the succession of modes of production. Capitalism has outlived its usefulness as a mode of production. That is, it helped develop productive forces to their currently high level, but its chronic crises and its wastefulness of natural resources and human talent mean that it will (or at least can) pass away. The precise mode of its passing away will vary, both in terms of what sort of Marxist politics one subscribes to and in terms of what sort of resistance is offered by the contending classes. It would be fair to say that this proposition is no longer held by most Marxists. While feudalism may inevitably give way to capitalism, it is by no means clear what a postcapitalist economic system might look like or that its development is inevitable. As we shall see, the problem of transition between modes of production is the nuclear contradiction in Marxism. There are two ways to look at the mode of production problem. Albert Hirschman views the "inevitability" argument as a rhetorical strategy designed to combat the Right's "futility" argument. Believing that "God is on our side" never weakened anyone's fighting spirit.[48] So, too, with the transition to socialism. As Marx writes in the preface to *Capital,* active participation in revolutionary movements can help accelerate change as well as reduce the cost of change.[49] Still, Marx seems not to have recognized the extent to which capitalist crises can create revolutionary change to fascist or otherwise statist regimes and not necessarily to socialist ones.[50] The way to preserve an open-ended sense of history, a recognition of the importance of economic crises in social change, and a sense of social hope beyond the banalities of Rortyan politics lies in an argument by David Gordon and others. Capitalism appears to be patterned into "long swings" of growth and decline, culminating in a period of economic crisis in which instability requires major institutional reconstruction for renewed stability and growth. The previous crisis, that of 1929, resulted in the moderately statist solution of the New Deal and the social-democratic welfare state of almost all Western democracies. The current crisis, which has lasted since the 1970s, represents an opportunity for restructuring that has thus far been dominated exclusively by the Right. Gordon and others thus have found a way to retain the Marxist notion of capitalist crisis while retaining a sense of political open-endedness.[51]

Sixth, the class that controls the mode of production in a given society tends to repress, either through the threat of violence or through persuasion (or through a combination of both), radical alterations in the control of the productive forces. Marxists will differ in the extent to which they assess the relative power of such repression. Whether ideology is conceived in a narrow way as "false consciousness" or as a class-based "structure of feeling" or as "common sense" implicated in structures of power and domination, the critique of ideology as disseminated in communicative texts and in institutions is an important goal of Marxist practice.

A typical criticism of Marxism is that it undermines democracy by depicting audiences as passive idiots. Rorty, for instance, writes that this depiction masks the power hunger of intellectuals. Hirschman believes that it is the counterpart of the Right's futility and jeopardy theses. He writes, "Lenin, who for many years lived in Switzerland and elsewhere in Western Europe, may well have been influenced by the contemporary European intellectual atmosphere, with its virulent and visceral hostility to democracy. That atmosphere, exemplified by the writings of Pareto, Sorel, and many others, has often been held responsible for the rise of fascism. It probably deserves wider credit."[52] It is possible, however, to argue that people are mistaken and that there are social determinations of those mistaken beliefs, without believing in one's own infallibility. A complete acceptance of the New Class thesis, in either its neoconservative or Gouldnerian form, negates the possibility that human beings can learn from mistakes, or, indeed, that anyone should teach anyone else. It is possible (and easy) to criticize the pretensions of left-wing intellectuals without denigrating learning itself.

Another reason for accepting the notion that rulers repress change is that, like the theory of exploitation, it allows for a more realistic sense of politics. Marxists have made a fetish, perhaps, of the notion of revolution, and revolution has, perhaps, worked to fulfill what can only be called religious needs. On the other hand, the assumption that simple attention to the banalities of electoral politics, as Rorty proposes, will feed hungry children is far more utopian than Marxism itself, for it assumes that elites will always give up power and privilege without a struggle. Rorty, like the Sophists, appears to identify politics with speech, without recognizing that politics is not always about rational deliberation. Politics can be stern, harsh, and violent.[53] The vice of Marxism has been to assume that harsh rhetoric and violence are always necessary modes of engaging in politics, just as the vice of liberal reformism has been to assume too much goodwill on the part of the ruling class.

In summary form, then, distinctive Marxist assumptions are about (1) labor as a representative anecdote, (2) the influence of the mode of production on social being, (3) the inevitability of class struggle, (4) the limitations on political action set by the level of development of productive forces, (5) the tendency for modes of production to change into new ones, and the (6) tendency for ruling classes to preserve power repressively. Assumptions (2) through (6) deal with what could be called the dialectical (which seems to mean only murky and complex) relationship between *structure* and *struggle*. That is, these assumptions try to work through the relationship between the structures that determine and limit social action and the possibilities for human action and choice that exist within those structures.

The relationship between structure and struggle is the central, unresolved problem in Marxism. Gouldner calls this problem Marxism's "nuclear contradiction":

> The problem is that if capitalism is indeed governed by lawful regularities that doom it to be supplanted by a new socialist society (when the requisite infrastructures have matured), why then stress that "the point is to change it"? Why go to such great lengths to arrange capitalism's funeral if its demise is guaranteed by science? Why must persons be mobilized and exhorted to discipline themselves to behave in conformity with necessary laws by which, it would seem, they would in any event be bound?[54]

In other words, Marxism has two rhetorical problems. First, it must explain why audiences should accept its prescriptions, given the inevitability argument. Of course, as we have seen from Hirschman, inevitability can serve a vital rhetorical function. And, contrary to Gouldner, Marx's argument that change will accelerate and be more positive if one chooses to be a revolutionary seems to work somewhat effectively as a response. A second problem, however, is more significant. What sorts of communicative processes enable historical actors to see liberatory possibilities? The most persuasive recent case for socialism—Alec Nove's brilliant *The Economics*

of Feasible Socialism Revisited—ends on a note of aporia. He writes that
we all have learned the lesson that a total breakdown of the established
order is not desirable—it will more likely lead to fascism than to socialism.
On the other hand, it is impossible to specify how we bridge the gap between the present and even a moderate socialism. He confesses that he has
no way to theorize such a transition.[55]

As we shall see in Chapter 1, Nove's problem (and ours) stems from the
fact that classical Marxism tends to see the need for revolution as self-evi-
dent, without considering that people might need to be persuaded to that
belief.

"The Ruthless Criticism
of Everything Existing"

ON NOVEMBER 10, 1837, soon after becoming a student at the University of Berlin, Karl Marx wrote a letter to his father. The letter described the development of Marx's two great loves: for Hegel's philosophy and for his future wife, Jenny von Westphalen.

There are at least two items of interest in the letter for the student of rhetoric and communication. First, in the introduction, Marx deprecated the love poems he recently sent to Jenny: "All the poems of the first three volumes I sent to Jenny are marked by attacks on our times, diffuse and inchoate expressions of feeling, nothing natural, everything built out of moonshine, complete opposition between what is and what ought to be, rhetorical reflections instead of poetic thoughts."[1]

Second, he described the writing of a twenty-four page dialogue, "Cleanthus, or the Starting Point of Philosophy," where he attempted to unite art and science and was led to the acceptance of the Hegelian system. His philosophical endeavors left him in an agitated state. He sought relief by joining his landlord on a hunting expedition and, on his return, by immersing himself in what he called "positive studies." These "positive studies" included the reading of works on the law of property, criminal law, canonical law, and a work on the mechanical instincts of animals, as well as Francis Bacon's *Advancement of Science*. He then translated parts of Aristotle's *Rhetoric*.[2]

It is unclear from the letter or other writings of Marx what parts of the *Rhetoric* he translated or what affect they had on his work. Nonetheless, this letter serves as a kind of representative anecdote for the reception of rhetoric in the Marxist tradition: if mentioned at all, rhetoric is consigned to the margins of serious discourse, is rigidly separated from both art and philosophy, and is considered, at best, to be a branch of "positive studies."

The possibility that Marx knew something about the rhetorical tradition is at first sight an intriguing one, but the inevitable conclusion to be drawn from his writings is that the tradition had a negligible influence. To be sure, the historical writings, especially *The Eighteenth Brumaire of Louis*

Bonaparte, display a nearly Ciceronian style, full of antitheses and copia, but the absence of classical notions of invention and audience is rather obvious.

The response of the reader who is interested in mass communication or cultural studies may at this point be, "So what?" Why is the influence or lack of influence by the classical rhetorical tradition significant in understanding Marx?

In the first place, any study of communication is informed by a set of assumptions about the nature, function, and scope of communicative practice. Understanding a phenomenon such as conversation requires some sort of prefiguring of the data to be studied. Is communication simply an exchange of information, one in which faulty decoding by one or both partners may prevent full understanding? Does conversation occur within a web of tacit linguistic conventions or rules whose identification is the chief goal of scholarly research? Is it best understood as a dialogue that opens up its participants to the indwelling of Being? Or does using the term "communication" unconsciously commit the user to a set of Lockean liberal assumptions about politics, in which, as John Durham Peters puts it, the individual, not the community, is "lord of the signifier"?[3]

Similarly, it makes a great deal of difference in the study of mass communication whether one adopts a view of mass communication (in terms of the transmission of information across time and space) as a collective ritual that helps define self and community or as a branch of a larger "science of signs."[4] Since research into communication is always already guided by a particular philosophical stance toward communication, it at least remains an interesting question whether the dominant theory of communication in the premodern West has anything to say to contemporary critical scholars.

But there is a more important reason to confront rhetoric and Marxism. Marxism as a discourse community emerged from the breakup of the classical tradition. Marxism shared with liberalism an impatience with rhetoric and with political deliberation. There may be some use in distinguishing Marxism as an intellectual system by its failure or refusal to engage the rhetorical issues that preoccupied early political and social philosophers. Classical theorists such as Plato, Isocrates, Aristotle, and Cicero, as well as later figures such as Vico, Hobbes, Locke, Kant, Rousseau, and Edmund Burke, wrote about rhetoric or engaged in actual rhetorical practice. The father of capitalist political economy, Adam Smith, wrote a series of lectures on rhetoric. Two of the most important nineteenth-century rhetorical theorists, Thomas De Quincey and Richard Whately, wrote books defending free trade.[5] Marx and Engels, however, never seriously engaged the role of rhetoric in social systems.

The purpose of this chapter is to locate Marx and Engels within the tradition of antirhetoric characteristic of modernity. Marx and Engels's writings, despite shifts in vocabulary and political orientation, display a remarkable continuity in their view of human communication. This view is linked inextricably with Marxism's nuclear contradiction between structure and struggle. An analysis of Marx and Engels's political careers and key writings illustrates how the structure of their arguments creates moments of contradiction and ambiguity that lead to later strategic problems for Marxist theorists and advocates.

The Rise of the Self-Defining Subject

A major trend in contemporary rhetorical scholarship has sought to develop broad theoretical explanations of our modern *malaise* based on the decline of rhetoric as a pedagogical and political practice. Chaim Perelman and Wayne Booth trace modern scientism *and* irrationalism back to Descartes's emphasis on systematic doubt and self-evidence. Richard Weaver argues that the cultural cohesiveness of the West was dealt a fatal blow by the defeat of realism by nominalism in the fourteenth century. Richard McKeon blames the Church. Karl Wallace blames Peter Ramus and the logic of Port-Royal.[6]

The list could go on. All these writers share a sense that the modern era is characterized by a distinctive splitting of cultural visions: between a scientific and technological worldview reluctant to deal with problems of ethics and value and a romantic worldview in which the emphasis on individual self-expression seems to undercut the possibility of rational public speech. Political thinkers as diverse as Max Weber, Hannah Arendt, Leo Strauss, and Alasdair MacIntyre tell a similar story.[7] It is, as Terry Eagleton puts it, a story about a time when "the three great questions of philosophy—what can we know? what ought we to do? what do we find attractive?—were not as yet fully distinguishable from one another. A society, that is to say, where the three mighty regions of the cognitive, the ethico-political, and the libidinal-aesthetic were still to a large extent intermeshed."[8]

The genius of Marxism, of course, was to recognize that this society declined not because of faulty ideas alone but because of the imperatives of capitalist development. Marxism also recognized the real achievements of capitalism, although it tended to define these in technological terms rather than political ones. Marxism, in many ways the legitimate heir of classical republicanism, inherited a conception of discourse that was finally inimical to the practice of citizenship. The heritage of classical rhetoric, at its best, asked its audiences to move from being subjects to citizens.

Rhetorical analysis begins with the question of audience. What is the audience targeted or imagined or even brought into being by a text or performance?[9]

Classical rhetorical theory constructed a vision of its audience as participating in the crafting of civic virtue under the guidance of the citizen-orator. Rhetorical theory was not so much a distinct form of intellectual inquiry as it was the practical part of political education. Politics in turn was conceived not as a separate "sphere" from the social or familial but as the place where the human *telos* was to be achieved. Audiences are constituted by the orator as citizens capable of judgment. As S. M. Halloran puts it:

> The ideal orator was conceived as the person of such broad knowledge and general competency that he could apply the accumulated wisdom of the culture to any particular case in a sufficiently logical fashion to move his hearers' minds (*logos*), and with enough emotional force to engage their passions (*pathos*). The name given to the third of the traditional modes of rhetorical appeal, *ethos,* underlines the importance of the orator's mastery of the cultural heritage; through the power of his logical and emotional appeals, he became a kind of living embodiment of the cultural heritage, a voice of such apparent authority that the word spoken by this person was the word of communal wisdom, a word to be trusted for the weight of the person who spoke it and of the tradition he spoke for.[10]

The ideal orator stood in an ordered relationship with tradition and with the cosmos as a whole. The orator's use of language embodied the wisdom of the community as a whole. The orator was not self-defining but was motivated by a kind of self-interest. The "problem of incentives" that would return with such a vengeance in twentieth-century Marxist states was solved by the appeal of public glory. Albert Hirschman notes that the classical notion of public service possessed a sort of "invisible hand" explanation of the quest for public glory: the community as a whole benefits from having a class of spirited men who seek enduring fame for their contributions to public life.[11]

The classical vision of virtue-based politics, ethics, and rhetoric survived in uneven and contradictory ways down through the eighteenth century. Many of the political achievements of the eighteenth century were crafted through a republican political rhetoric. As Wood and Pocock note, "republicanism" is a political language or "paradigm" in which political debates are conducted, featuring such terms as "virtue," "the public" or "common good," and "corruption." These terms are anchored in a few core beliefs: "that human beings are essentially political animals, that they can fulfill their natures only by participating in self-government, and that the most important aims of the political community should be to promote virtue among the citizenry and to advance the common good."[12] Because republics require constant vigilance against the corruption of centralized power, republican orators frequently invoke memories of past republican glory and decay. Republican rhetoric is thus time-binding, insisting upon historical memory as the foundation for civic virtue. It is no accident, either, that rhetoric as a pedagogical practice and as a field of inquiry is essentially republican in its origins.

What displaced republicanism, largely because of capitalism itself, was the political language of liberalism. "Liberalism" insisted that individuals are the ultimate definers of moral value, that consensus on what would constitute civic virtue is not only impossible but dangerous, that politics is as much an arena for oppression of others as it is one of self-fulfillment, and that government must devise a system that recognizes and protects individual rights, especially, but not exclusively, property rights. Liberalism also had a characteristic stance toward communication. Eloquence, a veritable god-term in the language of classical republicanism, became suspect in liberalism, mainly because it seems to violate the sanctity of individual choice.[13]

In the realm of language and philosophy, especially the German philosophy that influenced Marx, the shift from the community to the individual was even more acute. Philosophers such as Johann Gottfried von Herder redefined the ancient view of human nature within the context of the self-defining subject inherited from the Enlightenment. As Charles Taylor writes, "Man comes to know himself by expressing and hence clarifying what he is and recognizing himself in this expression. The specific property of human life is to culminate in self-awareness through expression."[14]

If self-expression rather than clear communication or deliberation on public questions is the highest purpose of language, then rhetoric must yield to poetics as the chief focus of education: "the human center of gravity is on the point of shifting from logos to poiesis."[15] Art becomes a means of survival in an industrialized, disenchanted world. Literature becomes exclusively imaginative literature, which in turn is the expression of a "people's" soul.[16]

Liberalism, scientism, and romantic expressionism share a theory of public discourse. Truth consists of perfect transparency, whether of scientific results, poetic vision, or the general will. Rhetoric, like the republican politics and virtue ethics that nurtured it, had to disappear.

But, of course, rhetoric as a human practice did not disappear, even if the practice became suspect and traditional theory became ignored. As I argued in the Introduction, the result of rejecting the rhetorical notions of *Bildung, sensus communis, judgment,* and *taste* was a universalizing culture of critical discourse. It was this universalizing culture of critical discourse in which Marxism conducted its public argument. It relied on elimination of past prejudice, an audience alienated from its culture, and the dominant trope of irony to do its argumentative work. Its very persuasiveness was bound up with its rejection of the claims of ethos, practical judgment, and audience identification.

Reading Rhetorically

Before I analyze key texts in classical Marxism directly, it would be useful to summarize the understanding of rhetoric used in this work. The development of rhetorical theory in this century has helped us ask questions about audience, figuration, narrative, and strategy as they interact in practical discourse.

Edwin Black has taught us to examine what he calls the "second persona" in analyzing public discourse: the "model of what the rhetor would have his real auditor become."[17] This model is revealed particularly in the figural choices made by the orator. The "first persona" is what the classical theorists called "ethos," the embodiment of cultural values. The second persona, although present in classical accounts of audience, is now more easily seen as a rhetorical construction, given the seemingly infinite number of selves or "lifestyle choices" auditors possess with the rise of capitalism.

Despite this variety, it is possible to read rhetorical documents as constituting audiences in an essentially republican mode—as citizens capable of rational deliberation within a communal tradition—or in an essentially liberal mode—as individuals first. The latter sort of audience is not extended in time the way the republican audience is and is appealed to as a sort of universal audience able to transcend parochial concerns and traditions.[18] This liberal audience is particularly signaled by the presence of the figure of irony in rhetorical discourse. Irony is *the* figure of critical discourse. It parallels the self-reflexivity of CCD at a tropological level, because in it "figurative language folds back upon itself and brings its own potentialities for distorting perception under question." Hayden White explains how irony inevitably constructs two audiences. The proper audience for irony is "intrinsically sophisticated and realistic," compared with foolish and naive audiences who are not "radically self-critical" about the relationship between language and experience.[19] Irony can be both a tactical device and the basis of a worldview. In the latter case it tends "to dissolve belief in the possibility of positive political actions. In its apprehension of the essential folly or absurdity of the human condition, it tends to engender belief in the 'madness' of civilization itself and to inspire Mandarin-like disdain for those seeking to grasp the nature of social reality in either science or art."[20] What White fails to note here—probably because of his own defense of the ironic mode from within a generic cultural leftist position—is the way in which irony is by nature a *class*-based trope. It assumes a monopoly on knowledge by one group at the expense of another and, further, when extended into a worldview by habitual practice, is essentially *conservative* ideologically. Irony is the tropological version of Hirschman's conservative argument from futility.

In a figurative choice of irony we see the outlines of what Philip Wander, continuing Black's insight, calls the "third persona." Every discourse not only implies an ideal auditor but also an auditor who is somehow less than ideal or who is fit to be ignored completely:

> It may also be understood to imply other characteristics, roles, actions, or ways of seeing things to be avoided. What is negated through the Second

Persona forms the silhouette of a Third Persona—the "it" that is not present, that is objectified in a way that "you" and "I" are not. . . . The potentiality of language to commend being carries with it the potential to spell out being unacceptable, undesirable, insignificant.[21]

Such exclusions are evident not only in figural choices but in the choice of narrative point of view. All political argument rests on a fundamental narrative, whether of progressive enlightenment, class struggle, or divine redemption. What modern fiction, particularly the novel, has helped us to see is the way in which the choice of a point of view in narrative construction has ideological implications. How we see the social totality depends on the character or group of characters through whom we understand the flow of narrative.

It makes a difference in terms of social knowledge how point of view is configured. As John Gardner notes about Steinbeck's *The Grapes of Wrath,* its artistic failure is bound up with its failure to represent the social totality:

It should have been one of America's great books. But while Steinbeck knew all there is to know about Okies and the countless sorrows of their move to California to find work, he knew nothing about the California ranchers who employed and exploited them; he had no clue to, or interest in, their reasons for behaving as they did; and the result is that Steinbeck wrote not a great and firm novel but a disappointing melodrama in which complex good is pitted against unmitigated, unbelievable evil.[22]

This last point, about point of view, illustrates the way in which a story—by its very construction—lays itself open to charges by an opponent. It is the presence of an audience and of an *opponent* (whether in the form of a rival policy, person, or culture) that signals the rhetorical situation per se. The presence of opposition implies a link between rhetoric and dialectic in the Hegelian sense.

There are certain predictable points in any controversy at which argument will occur. The classical theorists called these *stases.* Any debater about public policy knows that certain fundamental questions about the existence of a harm, the question of who is to blame for the harm, how to resolve it, and how much it will cost will appear again and again. A lawyer knows that questions of fact, definition, quality, and jurisdiction will occur in any legal case.

Any persuasive case must learn to incorporate objections based on the stases inherent in the field of argument in which controversy occurs. Some objections, however, stem from the nature of controversy itself, and these objections are dialectical, in the Hegelian sense. A contradiction is best defined as an opposition that is both necessary for, and yet destructive of, a particular process.[23] Every social process has contradictory tendencies. Marx's understanding of capitalism was that its own need for growth contains self-negating tendencies. The two chief self-negating tendencies are inherent rivalry among capitalist firms and the drive to mechanize production.

What is not clear in Marxism is its awareness of its own dialectical character. If all social processes have contradictory tendencies, and if human beings are forced (whether by the Absolute Spirit, or, more likely, by the imperatives of maintaining psychological balance) to seek *unity* in contradiction, then Marxism itself must have contradictions and constructed unities as well. It was Alvin W. Gouldner's great contribution to Marxism to open up this question in terms of the contradiction between structure and struggle. Gouldner saw the promise of unity in the theory of the new class and its potential as an agent of liberation. There are other ways to talk about contradiction and synthesis in Marxism, notably a rhetorical method. I would argue that rhetoric itself is the art of synthesizing contradictory social reality.

Rhetorical practice itself is founded on the fundamental contradiction that the advocate must appear not to be engaged so much in an act of persuasion as in helping the audience discover what they already know. The advocate and audience may also become so self-conscious of rhetoric as a *performance* that rhetoric may become a substitute for action. There are other fundamental points in most controversies where self-negating tendencies appear in rhetorical practice.

First, in order to clarify an argument for an audience, an advocate inevitably must simplify it. This act of simplification opens the advocate up to charges of reductionism.

Second, another kind of overstatement occurs when an opposing person or group or system is necessarily depicted as powerful and evil. The advocate may be charged with being unfair or with promoting a sense of futility, as Hirschman argued about some forms of leftist political argument. Rhetorical judgment in this case involves finding a kind of mean between a charitable account of the opponent and a depiction of the opponent as all-powerful. (The failure to find this mean is perhaps evident in the Bush administration's depicting Saddam Hussein as Hitler but being unwilling to explain either its role in Hussein's acquiring military might or why he should not be completely vanquished.)

Third, in order to preempt charges of reductionism or oversimplification or overgeneralization, an advocate may have to qualify claims and their general applicability, thus leading to a motivation deficit on the part of the audience. In other words, audience hatred and willingness to act is more easily aroused by simplistic characterizations of the enemy, but the desire to be democratic, liberal, and self-reflexive instills habits of thought that limit the ability to motivate audiences. (Again, an advocate knows that it is not an either-or kind of thing but a question of finding the mean.) The need to present a case to an ideally rational universal audience may tend to limit adaptability to particular audiences.

All three of these inevitable contradictions are present in Marxism: the charge of "materialist" reductionism and the difficulty in choosing between reform and revolution caused by the motivational deficit of social democracy and the motivational surplus of communism.

To summarize, then, a rhetorical reading, in the fullest sense, of a body of texts requires an analysis of the complex and contradictory relationships among the rhetor's construction of ethos, implied audience, and marginalized audience. The raw materials of these constructions are narratives, figures, and those objects conventionally known as evidence. A text or body of texts thus forms a constellation of elements bound together by the rhetorical force inherent in the whole. At times a text is held together solely by the force of the style or the ethos of the rhetor, or by the accumulated weight of the historical evidence it thrusts on the audience. But texts, as it has been deconstruction's great achievement to teach us, are unstable entities. The presence of opponents will cause arguments to move forward, grow, or die. One reads rhetorically in order to accomplish two complementary purposes: moral evaluation, and predictive or explanatory understanding of the movement of texts as building blocks of ideologies—as those ideologies move in historical time.

Audiences and Alienation in Early Marxism

Let us return for a moment to the passage cited at the beginning of this chapter, the letter from the student Marx to his father:

> In accordance with my state of mind at the time, lyrical poetry was bound to be my first subject, at least the most pleasant and immediate one. But owing to my attitude and whole previous development it was purely idealistic. My heaven, my art, became a world beyond, as remote as my love. Everything real became hazy and what is hazy has no definite outlines. All the poems of the first three volumes I sent to Jenny are marked by attacks on our times, diffuse and inchoate expressions of feeling, nothing natural, everything built out of moonshine, complete opposition between what is and what ought to be, rhetorical reflections instead of poetic thoughts.[24]

A symptomatic reading of the letter indicates that Marx's opinions are already structured into a set of oppositions that prefigure the later, more crucial opposition of science/ideology: poetics/rhetoric, ought/is, reality/haziness, natural/artificial. Poetry, the letter implies, is closely connected with reality for Marx, while he is only able to attain the hazy realm of rhetoric. The "real presence" of poetry falls out into the artificiality of rhetoric. The negation of this negation—as evidenced by Marx's conversion to the Hegelian system—is philosophy, in which the poetic impulse is canceled but preserved. The lesson of deconstruction most useful for rhetorical scholarship is its indictment of philosophy for failing to recognize its own writtenness. Or, put in rhetorical terms, philosophy effaces its own rhetoricity in the name of full presence—an unmediated seeing. The goal of philosophy, if finally reached, is an end of conversation.[25]

One of Marx's first published writings repeats this logocentric assumption of Western metaphysics. Here is a cento of key comments from his letter to Arnold Ruge:

> Up to now the philosophers had the solution of all riddles lying in their lectern, and the stupid uninitiated world had only to open its jaws to let the roast partridges of absolute science fly into its mouth. . . . But if the designing of the future and the proclamation of ready-made solutions for all time is not our affair, then we realized all the more clearly what we have to accomplish in the present—I am speaking of the ruthless criticism of everything existing. . . . We only show the world what it is fighting for, and consciousness is something the world *must* acquire, like it or not. The reform of consciousness consists *only* in enabling the world to clarify its consciousness, in waking it from its dream about itself, in *explaining* to it the meaning of its own actions. . . . It is a matter of confession, no more. To have its sins forgiven, mankind has only to declare them to be what they really are.[26]

In the dialectical movement from poetry to rhetoric to philosophy, philosophy too gets canceled out and replaced by a new genre of discourse: critique. Marx's parodic impulse to link critique with religion perhaps says more than it intends. Marx (and whoever is included in the "we" he refers to) simply states the true condition of the world in a ruthless critique, much like the preaching of the law in Lutheran theology. The "world" is uninitiated, dreaming, and in a state of sin. Most important, the "world" need not be persuaded so much as simply shown the truth.

Whereas classical political philosophy had understood the necessity of myth (Plato) or at least oratory (Aristotle, Cicero) in the founding and maintenance of just regimes, Marxism simply does not find persuasion a problem. The audience *must* see the truth, like it or not. It is but a short leap from the letter to Ruge to the chillingly direct statement in the *Manifesto:* "Centralization of the means of communication and transport in the hands of the State."[27] Yet the term "audience" here is misleading, for Marx's own immediate audience is not the "world," but his fellow priests—emigré intellectuals and artisans—whose own credibility is never established and whose own interests are never clearly defined.

We see Marx, then, working with a severely limited notion of public discourse. But how does Marx understand his audience at this point in his career? The actual audience for the letter to Ruge as published in the *Deutsch-französische Jahrbücher* consisted of emigré German workers and the various sects of French socialists. Marx edited the short-lived journal to provide a bridge between the two. He had, of course, moved to Paris after completing his doctoral dissertation because a university career was closed to him, both because of his political beliefs and because of an oversupply of college graduates at the time.

Marx was not alone in being blocked from a university career. He was characteristic of a whole group of educated youths in Germany at the time, when absolute numbers of college-educated students increased threefold from 5,000 to 15,000. The effect was that in Prussia alone, in 1835, "there were 262 candidates for every 100 livings in the church, 265 candidates for every 100 judicial offices, and 194 candidates for every 100 medical appointments."[28]

As Gouldner argues, status anxiety resulting from blocked upward mobility was a major factor in the radicalism of Marx's circle. England, on the other hand, experienced fewer problems with a radicalized intelligentsia because of the safety valves made possible by the colonies and the expansion of the civil service. France was much like Germany in that it lacked such safety valves and, moreover, its educated population was disproportionately concentrated in Paris.

The workers, too, that Marx encountered in Paris were not the industrial laborers about whom Marx was to write so eloquently. Rather, they too were victims of status displacement, artisans whose skills were no longer needed in Germany.[29] It is the needs of this audience—blocked professionals and artisans—whose sense of meaninglessness becomes central in the first key term of Marxist thought, "alienation."

While in Paris, Marx became a convinced Communist and also formed his lifelong friendship with Engels. The *1844 Manuscripts*—evidently never intended for publication—have become a significant site of struggle among Marxists since their publication in 1930. The manuscripts articulate a philosophical anthropology as a justification for the abolition of private property. Pages and pages have been written either to prove that Marx was a true "humanist," and thus not responsible for actually existing communism, or to prove that Marx simply was engaging in a preliminary act of self-clarification before moving on to his epistemological break, the discovery of the science of history.[30] The burden of this chapter is to prove that despite other changes, Marx's conception of communication remained unchanged throughout his adult life.

The central category in the *1844 Manuscripts* is that of "alienation," which is used in a variety of different ways. It must have been painfully obvious to Marx in Paris that Hegel's drama of the Absolute Spirit, engaged in a cycle of alienation and de-alienation, was hopelessly detached from the drama of the Finite Mind in search of employment. Marx's strategy for encompassing his—and by extension, the human—situation is to invert the Hegelian drama of alienation, returning it to the human experience of and need for meaningful work. "Inversion" is common strategy for critics of the existing order—taking a needless abstract concept and setting it on its feet, the solid ground of "reality."[31] But Marx employs it here somewhat more sympathetically than in, say, the *German Ideology*. This form of inversion means to return a concept to its experiential roots.

Put simply, work has lost its meaning in capitalism. Work-relations prevent the worker from attaining self-actualization. In creating a world of objects by practical activity, human beings demonstrate the uniqueness of their species. Meaningful labor is the way in which human existence is fully realized. Alienation is a process in which what should be familiar becomes strange.[32] Workers cannot own what they have made. Their actions belong to the capitalist to whom their labor has been sold. They are unknown by the people who buy their products. In fact, all of social life becomes strange, no longer *heimlich*.

The narrative of alienation in the *1844 Manuscripts* is, like Hegel's narrative, strangely ahistorical. There is a crucial ambiguity in the idea that social life has become estranged. Read strictly in historical context, the manuscripts are referring to the life-experience of artisans and professionals who remember what the experience of liberty and of meaningful work was. What is not clear, however, is the status of the industrial worker who may have been displaced from the country. Was the fall into capitalism truly a fall from Edenic order, as conservatives from Disraeli to T. S. Eliot and Richard Weaver would argue?[33] Or was it part of a historically "necessary" process? Or something profoundly unstable and contradictory?

The concept of alienation thus contains two problematic points that would prove crucial to conservative and liberal refutations of Marxism, especially after the fall of communism. First, Marxism does not know itself as a rhetoric by and for intellectuals rather than workers. Second, Marxism sets itself up arrogantly as moral critic of the choices of generations of Western workers who chose some form of social-democratic reformism instead of "socialism." There is an answer to these indictments, but we need to see how they are authorized by Marx's texts.

The first problem with the notion of alienation lies in its two poles: subjective and objective alienation. At one point Marx explicitly refers to the worker as "unhappy," although the argument as a whole suggests that even a happy worker can still be objectively alienated. It is characteristic of Marx that he begins with the individual worker and not with the worker's *family*. Marx thus failed to depart from the basic assumptions of the political economists whom he criticized, for it is the individual who is the locus of alienation. He also, as later feminists would recognize, seemed to define the alienating experience of work in unconsciously male terms.[34]

Consider the following examples. Imagine a person who will endure miserable working conditions for a fixed period in order to guarantee a successful future for her children. That person will be subjectively alienated and objectively alienated for the fixed period. When the period ends, and if the goal is achieved, what is her state of subjective alienation?

Another worker, unable adequately to feed his family or provide for their future, endures miserable working conditions. Finally fed up, the worker joins other workers in order to bargain for higher wages. He goes out on strike in order to attain that right. His union wins. A succession of labor victories, both on the shop floor and in the legislature, ensures that his children will have an opportunity for an education. After his retirement, his daughter graduates from medical school. He looks back on his life. He is subjectively happy. Is he still objectively alienated?

Marxism's rhetorical problem thus comes to the fore. Only communism will free the worker from the slavery of wage labor. But it must first persuade the worker that he or she is unhappy. The worker may be unwilling to undertake the struggle required to go "all the way" to communism if the worker's material needs can be improved under capitalism. The worker, in the words of Lenin, will naturally acquire *only* trade-union consciousness.[35] Examining Marx's audience reveals that it is an audience of extremely literate men—artisans and professionals—not the workers themselves, who are presumably so degraded by their objective alienation that they cannot attend to his message. Marx's real rhetorical task is that of proving to alienated intellectuals that they have a stake in eliminating the objective alienation of the worker.

Alienation does not always lead to change. As Jon Elster points out, there are two different ways of looking at alienation in political terms. Alienation may make people increasingly prone to revolt. It need not, however, do so. The mechanism of "sour grapes," or "adaptive preferences," may set in. That is, one may re-adjust one's needs or wants to fit what appears to be the only feasible set of alternatives.[36] One searches in vain in Marx and Engels's work for an empirical investigation into the actual consciousness of workers (even *The Condition of the Working Class in England* does not do this). Elster's rational-choice Marxism is intended to refocus the discussion of ideology in Marxism in such a way as to respect the individual and individual psychological processes that have been neglected in the Marxist tradition. What is not quite clear, even if we now understand internal choices such as "sour grapes," is how actual *messages* shape such responses by audiences. The study of such shaping falls under the rubric of "ideology" in Marxist theory.

Some Versions of Ideology

Epistemological break or not, Marx and Engels's writings seem to unfold in logical order, each text attempting to solve a conceptual problem brought to the fore in the previous one. Capitalism alienates people. This alienation does not seem to lead to change, so there is a need to investigate blockages of correct consciousness, hence the problem of ideology. Objective conditions (1848) seem to make revolution possible, so an attractive program is proposed to entice people into the Communist movement. The revolution fails, leading to historical investigation into reasons for failure and for scientific investigation into the future course of the capitalist system.

The conceptual problem created by objective conditions of social change, by the experience of alienation, and by the concept of alienation itself is resolved by a turn toward the concept of ideology. "Ideology" is the single most unstable term in Marxism. Its instability makes it similar to the way "rhetoric" itself functions in Western culture. One could construct a narrative in which the rhetorical tradition somehow goes "underground" in the Marxist notion of ideology, or maybe even, in pidgin German, gets *"aufgehoben"* into it. A simpler argument would be to point out that the notion of ideology functions much like a notion of rhetoric would work in previous Western political philosophy—with the exception that Marx and Engels only construct an effective practical rhetoric/ideology and do not show us how it is to be made in future rhetorical situations.

Ideology is false or deluded speech about the world and the human beings who inhabit it. It is unclear, since Marx seems not to have retained the classical language of the virtues, whether ideological speech is also *wrong* in an ethical sense.[37] Marx's great contribution to the social sciences is that he is not content to show that mistaken speech is false logically or referentially. He also wishes to *explain how* that mistaken speech came about. There seem to be two conditions for the emergence of mistaken speech.

As Elster writes, false speech can be explained either in terms of a speaker's *position* or *interest*. A position-explanation locates false speech in terms of the cognitive errors a speaker makes because of an inability to see the whole of a phenomenon.[38] If I falsely state that the Sun moves around the Earth, it is because I have not been educated to move out of my limited position of observation. Similarly, if I believe that all women on welfare are black, have 10.5 children, and are living extremely well, I am mistaken because of where I live and how I have been educated. Marx and Engels's critique of Feuerbach rests on their argument that the leftist Hegelians' social position caused them to overemphasize the role of ideas in creating human misery. The first significant Marxist definition of ideology rests on this position-explanation and uses an optical metaphor to illustrate it: "If in all ideology men and their relations appear upside-down as in a *camera obscura,* this phenomenon arises just as much from their historical life-process as the inversion of objects on the retina does from their physical life-process."[39]

Ideology emerges generally from faulty seeing in historical time. It also occurs from faulty placement in social space: "Everyone believes his craft to be the true one. Illusions regarding the connection between their craft and reality are the more likely to be cherished by them because of the very nature of the craft."[40] In this case of false speech, the speaker's "occupational psychosis" is a cognitive failure caused by self-interest, wishful thinking, and one-sided training. According to Elster, it is a case of the *fallacy of composition,* assuming that what is characteristic of the part is also characteristic of the whole.

There is another form of position-explanation in which cognitive failure is traceable to needs to compensate for a miserable reality. Marx and Engels's indictment of religion as the "opium of the people" falls into this category. False religious speech occurs as the result of cognitive failure reinforced by the internal need for solace in a "heartless world."[41]

Read in this way, the letter to Ruge seems less unrealistic than it seemed earlier. Marxism becomes an educational program, directed toward all citizens, intended to correct flaws in social perception caused by the division of labor. If the first audience is alienated artisans and intellectuals, so what? Simply because they are predisposed to accept the message first they are not inherently better than other potential audiences. Prudence dictates that they must be addressed first. It also may be argued that Marxism thus arrogantly sets itself up above all social positions. Conservatives and poststructuralists (who have more in common than is typically realized) both would assault Marxist rationalism on the grounds of arrogance. A response is that even an argument about the class-positioning of Marxists assumes at least a mildly elevated position above one's own.

Unfortunately, Marx and Engels's real contribution to social theory—position-explanation—has been obscured and confused with interest-explanation. In an interest-explanation, ideology—and by extension, rhetorical action—becomes the transparent expression of a person's economic or occupational interests. The classic passage is this one:

> The ideas of the ruling class are in every epoch the ruling ideas, i.e., the class which is the ruling *material* force of society is at the same time its ruling *intellectual force.* The class which has the means of material production at its disposal, consequently also controls the means of mental production, so that the ideas of those who lack the means of mental production are on the whole subject to it. The ruling ideas are nothing more than the ideal expression of the dominant material relations, the dominant material relations grasped as ideas; hence of the relations which make the one class the ruling one, therefore, the ideas of its dominance.[42]

This passage is a major source of problems for Marxism. First, as Elster argues, it does not explain how the ideas of the ruling class get to be the ruling ideas. Second, it fails to explain how non-ruling-class or oppositional ideas get heard at all—a problem that opens up the usual conservative critique of leisured, armchair Marxist accounts into which this book

may be classified. Third, it makes "ideas" simply straightforward "communications" (almost in the sense of transportation) of interests, and not
themselves complex sites of struggle for meaning. Fourth, it contributes to
the vicious tendency of political groups and persons—now much in evidence in the press's discussion of "political correctness," even though the
neoconservatives who popularized the term are as vicious and vindictive as
the leftists they rightly criticize—to represent differing political beliefs produced solely by an intention to oppress another. This is not to deny that
interest-explanations are at times valid—the cynical use of religion by
Southern mill-owners comes to mind—but to universalize them is also a
form of cognitive failure. As we shall see later, much of the conceptual
confusion of contemporary "cultural studies" stems from its muddling of
the interest- and position-explanation aspects of the term ideology.

A solution to the tendency of position-explanations to slide into interest-
explanations is to focus on ideology as practical rhetoric, liable to all the
distortions and rationalizations that any political discourse possesses in
the heat of conflict. One can thus avoid name-calling and the scientifically
murky problem of intention by seeing how ideological choices are dictated
by practical rhetorical goals. This notion is implicit in the following passage, which makes it clear how some "ruling ideas" might emerge:

> [Each] new class which puts itself in the place of the one ruling before it is
> compelled, merely in order to carry through its aim, to present its interest as
> the common interest of all the members of society, that is, expressed in ideal
> form; it has to give its ideas the form of universality, and present them as the
> only rational, universally valid ones. The class making a revolution comes
> forward from the very start, if only because it is opposed to a *class,* not as a
> class but as the representative of the whole of society, as the whole mass of
> society confronting the one ruling class. It can do this because initially its
> interest really is as yet mostly connected with the interest of all other non-
> ruling classes.[43]

Thus an idea can be true at a particular point in history because it is in the
interests of everyone to accept it. Eventually, however, such ideas can be
indicted for cognitive failure, based on positions in shifting historical time.
The achievements of bourgeois liberalism are the best example. It is not
contradictory (in the strictly logical sense) to believe that religious and
communicative liberty were in everyone's best interest in, say, 1787 *and* to
object to the interests that motivated the constitution of those liberties.
(But, of course, having to make the latter argument suggests a point of ambiguity in the Marxist account.)

A final set of arguments about the Marxist notion of ideology require
careful examination, because they bear directly on the practice of cultural
critique as it emerged under the broad heading of "cultural studies" in the
1970s. The failure of the Marxist theory, according to Jon Elster, lies in its

use of functional explanation. Put simply, a functional explanation is one that explains behavior "by pointing to the fact that it has beneficial consequences for some agent or agents." It may be of some use to construct an ideal type of Marxist ideological analysis. If we take baseball (an American game) as an example of a social practice with economic, political, and cultural implications, what would an ideological analysis of it look like? There are several different strategies for analysis, depending on what side of the Marxist tradition one follows.[44]

First, one could note that the sport is organized as a profit-making commercial institution. Most of its revenues come from the sale of advertising during the broadcasts of its games. At one level, then, one might say that baseball exists only to deliver audiences to advertisers. The "content" of baseball is relatively insignificant.[45]

A second strategy would be to focus on baseball players as workers. The ballplayer is the consummate proletarian. Often from a working-class background, he lacks the requisite capital to own his own team and must sell his labor power to someone like George Steinbrenner (who at times acted like a Manchester factory owner sometime before the passage of the Ten Hours Act). The owner extracts surplus value from the ballplayer's labor. Although players' unions may humanize the conditions of play, long-term economic security exists only for a few players. The rest are prone to injuries, addiction, and exploitation by financial advisors. They persist in an activity where the chance of real success is small, because they have few other skills, and a large reserve of potential players both in the United States and the Third World is ready to take their place. The players have had instilled in them a sort of false consciousness about the joy of playing. All hitherto-existing history of baseball is the history of a struggle between players and owners. Player-owned teams would eliminate alienated baseball labor. After the revolution, everyone will have a chance at bat.

A third strategy would focus on the audience of baseball. Not only does baseball exist in order to deliver audiences to advertisers, but baseball itself functions as a prop for the status quo. Baseball serves to legitimate existing patterns of class and, perhaps, sexual oppression. It holds out the promise to the working class that anyone with sufficient talent may make it in capitalist society. It, along with other sections of the popular-culture industry, serves as a convenient distraction from reality. Baseball is a haven in a heartless world, the opium of the people. Corporate executives and unemployed steelworkers may play at being bleacher bums at Wrigley Field for an afternoon, but after the game the same unlovely capitalist world awaits all of them. It is no accident that mass spectator sports such as baseball reached their highest popularity during the Depression and especially after the historic postwar compromise between labor and capital.

A final strategy is, perhaps, authorized by some of Marx's writings on art, but is best represented by later traditions concerned with "structures of feeling," or even "the dialogic sign." Baseball enacts the utopia of popular emancipation. It provides a liberatory space, one that is certainly corrupted by the profit motive but that also reflects and responds to genuine human needs for play, release of tension, and communal solidarity. A comparison with football might reveal baseball as a projection of an earlier state of capitalism, in which a slower pace of work (much like factories before Taylorization) and a more individualistic craft spirit were possible. Baseball, in this reading, is not so much an instance of "false consciousness" as a "social text" capable of variant "decoding" by its audience. The goal of a critical reading of baseball is to reveal the emancipatory potential in the text.[46]

Readings one, two, and three rely directly on some form of functional explanation. Reading four recognizes the existence of economic interests and social-positional determination of cognition but seems to move beyond functional explanation. It is, as we shall see later, possible to reconstruct the Marxist notion of ideology in rhetorical terms, but for the moment we are focusing on those parts of classical Marxism that create problems for the credibility of the system.

If we recast Elster's arguments against functionalism in terms of these readings, we get the following six points.

1. The readings cannot explain why baseball (much less football) is the sport selected by the ruling class. In other words, there are accidents of history that cannot be accounted for by the theory.
2. There is no account of the motivations of both the ruling-class and non-ruling-class spectators for watching the sport.
3. Unlike functional explanations in the natural sciences (such as the working of natural selection in evolutionary biology), there is no specification of the mechanism by which the sport provides the desirable consequences.
4. The readings cannot account for change other than by change in specific productive forces.
5. If a specific conspiracy by a significant portion of the ruling class cannot be proven in establishing baseball as a mass spectator sport, then it is clear that the ruling class is as much susceptible to ideological deformation as are the spectators.
6. These readings cannot explain their own origins as an assertion, the privileged standpoint from which the critique is made. They fall victim to a version of the Epimenides paradox. In rhetorical terms, functional explanations tend to be blind to the ethos of the explainer. They also tend to construct an idealized audience of readers "in the know" and superior to those deluded by ideology. That such arguments "marginal-

ize" the audiences they intend to liberate is one of the least-attractive sides of radical cultural criticism.[47]

The Dream of Transparent Language

Elster explicitly chooses not to speculate on the sources of the appeal of functional definitions of ideology, other than to suggest that the explanation probably lies in individual psychology and the history of ideas.[48] A close look at discussion of language and communication by Marx and Engels reveals a link between a crudely reductionist theory of language and an erroneous view of ideology.

Marx and Engels never seem to have departed from the idea that language exists primarily to facilitate instrumental social relationships:

> From the start, the "mind" is from the outset afflicted with the curse of being "burdened" with matter, which here makes its appearance in the form of agitated layers of air, sounds, in short, of language. Language is as old as consciousness, language *is* practical, real consciousness that exists also for other men as well, and only therefore does it also exist for me; language, like consciousness, only arises from the need, the necessity, of intercourse with other men.[49]

There are two ways to interpret this passage. One is to think of language as the transparent expression of human needs and thus not significant in its own right. Another is to look for the social origins of language in the need for cooperation. Christopher Caudwell, the great and neglected Marxist literary critic, finds in the needs of the harvest the origins of poetry, song, and communication:

> In the collective festival, where poetry is born, the phantastic world of poetry anticipates the harvest and, by doing so, makes possible the real harvest. But the illusion of this collective phantasy is not a mere drab copy of the harvest yet to be: it is a reflection of the emotional complex involved in the fact that man must stand in a certain relation to others and to the harvest, that his instincts must be adapted in a certain way to Nature and other men, to make the harvest possible.[50]

If cooperation in the struggle against nature is at the root of the communicative impulse, that leads to a very different view of language. But the metaphors of "sublimates," "reflex," and "transparency" that recur in classical Marxist discussions of language undercut the more realistic and emancipatory view of language that Caudwell develops.

One could argue that the notion of transparency, while in part derived from the popular materialism of Marx and Engels's day, stems back to the dissociation of essence and appearance that lies at the heart of Western philosophy.[51] The establishment of communism promises to eliminate concealment of all kinds: "If we conceive society as being not capitalistic but communistic, there will be no money-capital at all . . . nor the disguises cloaking the transactions arising on account of it."[52] G. A. Cohen captures the fundamental metaphor of communism as that of transparency: "the yearning for transparent human relations can be satisfied in part, because we can specify removable social institutions, notably the market, which foster opacity."[53]

The metaphors of secrecy/openness and opacity/transparency recur in the *Communist Manifesto,* Marx and Engels's first real foray into political action. These metaphors organize arguments about political strategy—radicalism needs to come out into the open, to be "manifest"; about the reality of capitalism—it lays bare social reality; and about hope for the future—this time victory is inevitable.

Radicals must move away from the secret societies that had characterized earlier revolutionary politics—Freemasonry, the League of the Just—to an open declaration of aims. The *Manifesto* thus copies the movement of capitalism itself, which reveals both its aims fully and the reality of human relations. It is unclear whether the great Hymn to Capital at the heart of the *Manifesto* seeks to preserve elements of the social order displaced by capitalism or whether it simply wants to continue the restless destruction of traditional values:

> The bourgeoisie, wherever it has gotten the upper hand, has put an end to all feudal, patriarchal, idyllic relations. It has pitilessly torn asunder the motley feudal ties that bound man to his "natural superiors," and has left remaining no other nexus between man and man than naked self-interest, than callous "cash payment." It has drowned the most heavenly ecstasies of religious fervor, of chivalrous enthusiasm, of philistine sentimentalism, in the icy water of egotistical calculation. It has resolved personal worth into exchange value, and in place of the numberless indefeasible chartered freedoms, has set up that single, unconscionable freedom—Free Trade. In one word, for exploitation, veiled by religious and political illusions, it has substituted naked, shameless, direct, brutal exploitation.[54]

The two possible interpretations of this passage, marked "Raymond Williams" on one side and "Lenin" on the other, illustrate the way in which a rhetorical synthesis crafted for political action in a particular conjuncture—the uprisings of 1848—can have a very complicated afterlife.

The factor that normally unifies a rhetorical synthesis—the ethos of the advocate—is strangely veiled in the *Manifesto:*

> Finally, in times when the class struggle nears the decisive hour, the process of dissolution going on within the ruling class, in fact within the whole range of old society, assumes such a violent, glaring character, that a small section of the ruling class cuts itself adrift, and joins the revolutionary class, the class that holds the future in its hands.[55]

As in the letter to Ruge, things as they are become transparent—violently, glaringly so—and, in an odd metaphor, a section of the ruling class cuts itself adrift, although it is not so clear why, if everything is now obvious, the whole ruling class does not cut itself adrift. In any case, Marx and Engels's own ethos is not constructed here, but the potential problem is acknowledged, almost as a footnote. The problem, of course, was to become a staple of critiques of Marxism in the twentieth century.[56]

The fact that communication, debate, and deliberation are not a problem (at least at this point in the development of Marx's thought) is best illustrated by point six of the Communist program in the *Manifesto:* "Centralization of the means of communication and transport in the hands of the state." As James W. Carey has argued, there are two fundamental yet contradictory metaphors embodied in the term "communication": a "transmission" view that focuses on the transportation of information across distances, and a "ritual" view that stresses the role of communication as community-formation. Marx and Engels do not seem to have departed from a view of communication as essentially transportation.[57]

The Theory of Value

History, however, kept getting in the way of the naked transparency of class relations that 1848 seemed to promise. Marx increasingly devoted himself to analyzing the logic of capitalism as a system. A thorough analysis of *Capital* is beyond the scope of this book, but it is possible to demonstrate that the notions of audience and communication remain unanalyzed in supposedly "mature" Marxism.

Robert Paul Wolff has analyzed what he calls the "literary structure of *Capital*" in terms of the trope of irony. For Marx, all of capitalist society is seen as an illusory metaphor, in which reality is distorted into something monstrous by the equating of use value and exchange value. Wolff notes how the metaphor of stripping away the veil, organized by the classic philosophical opposition between appearance and reality, is linked with a consistent use of irony. The cure for capitalist mystification is an ironic understanding:

> Writing for an audience that had been reared on the mysteries and incantations of Christianity, he invoked its most powerful metaphors to force upon his readers a self-awareness of their complicity in the inversions and fetishism of capitalist market relations. By "coquetting with Hegel," as he himself described his discussion of the concepts of value and money, Marx clearly hoped to jolt the complacent apologists of capitalism into a realization of the opacity, mystery, and underlying irrationality of their putatively transparent explanations of prices, wages, and profits.[58]

What Wolff fails to note here—and his assumption that *Capital* has a literary rather than *rhetorical* structure is probably at the root of it—is that the metaphor of stripping away the veil and the use of irony open Marx up to the charge of having replaced the transparency of the capitalist economists with his own arrogant claim to transparency, and, further, that the consistent use of irony can serve as an elitist weapon against the lower orders in society. There is also an inherent problem in assuming that the relationship between use value and exchange value can ever become completely transparent.

Marx thought that his analysis of value was central to his whole system.[59] The dialectic of essence and appearance in the notion of value bears the same metaphoric pattern of hiddenness/revelation, inversion, and opacity/transparency that we have seen in previous writings. To use Marx's own example, making a table out of wood does not radically change its character as an "ordinary, sensuous thing." But as soon as the table becomes a commodity, "it changes into a thing which transcends sensuousness. It not only stands with its feet on the ground, but, in relation to all other commodities, it stands on its head, and evolves out of its wooden brain grotesque ideas, far more wonderful than if it were to begin dancing of its own free will."[60] The finished form of this world of commodities conceals two things: the social character of private labor and the social relations between the individual workers. These now appear to be relationships among things.[61] There is a distinct shift in the rhetorical conception of capitalism from the *Manifesto* to *Capital,* Vol. I. In the earlier work, capitalism makes everything *clear:* all is reduced to the cash nexus. In the latter work, capitalism reduces everything to commodities, but in so doing makes opaque both the notion of value and the relationships among people—between worker and worker, and between "consumer" and worker. The critique of this opacity is usually the starting point for making Marxist arguments plausible to uninitiated audiences.

The metaphor of opacity implies a corresponding transparency once socialism has been achieved. It should be possible for use values to be obvious. And yet, as the economic failures of centralized planning in the Soviet Union and elsewhere have demonstrated, it is not possible to do away with the valuable *information* that prices embody. Prices enable producers to predict what should be produced relative to other products. Alec Nove has demonstrated that the microeconomic role of price in providing information to producers can be retained in an otherwise socialist system that allows democratic control of macroeconomic decisions.[62]

Even more important for our purposes are the implications of the theory of value for problems of persuasion under socialism. As Nove writes, one of Marx's most misleading statements was the idea that "the government of men" could be replaced "by the administration of things": "One cannot administer *things!* One cannot address a cabbage or a ton of ball-bearings; one can instruct or persuade human beings to grow, make, or transport things."[63] The problem of incentives under socialism as well as the problem of inattention to consumption both stem from the assumption that the opacity-inducing character of exchange value can be eliminated. Actually existing socialism (or "socialism on earth," as Michael Burawoy calls it) has been characterized by inattention both to customer service and to consumer desire for variety and quality of products. The "drab grey world of socialism" that Margaret Thatcher loved to depict has its roots in the idea that social relationships can become transparent. Overthrowing capitalist exploitation requires that workers become *associated producers.* What is never discussed by Marx and Engels is the fact that the worker is simultaneously a consumer—under both capitalism and socialism. Based on his analysis of command economies, Nove concludes, "How can planning organs, on behalf of 'society,' determine *ex ante* the value (value-in-use, naturally) of what has been produced, unless and until the potential user is directly involved in the process, and in fact can say 'no'?"[64] A single-minded focus on workers' rights (understandable in the nineteenth century) becomes vulnerable to conservative rhetorical transformation when, say, public employees strike against the state. The transformation of labor, by Reagan and Thatcher, into a "special interest" is one of the more remarkable achievements of conservatism, but it did not occur without the complicity of radical theory.

The transaction between producer and consumer will require both some sense of consumer needs (hence the function of price as information) and that consumers be informed about products. Thus, some form of advertising will be necessary in order to ensure that actual communication between producers and consumers takes place.[65] Yet the possibility of advertising admits the possibility of distorted or manipulative communication. That possibility of course does not justify either a laissez-faire attitude toward advertising, as has occurred in recent years in the United States, or a wholesale restriction, as many sectors of the Left seem to desire. Advertising, like rhetoric itself, seems to be a necessary function of social systems and can be conducted under democratic auspices as much as any other aspect of social life. The problem with classical Marxism—and with the later systems, notably the Frankfurt School—is its inattention to the ethical relationship between producers and consumers under socialism. Once again, even in the "mature" *Capital,* not only is rhetoric (in the sense of persuasion) unnecessary but so is any *communication* whatsoever.

Attention to actual revolutionary struggles after 1848, however, appears to have altered Marx's views both of the need for centralized power and of the role of discourse in public life. The Marx of *Civil War in France* (1872) seems to envisage a polity of highly decentralized self-governing associations. One could argue that such a vision actually enlarges the scope for rhetorical action in public life, increasing the amount of bargaining and debate that would take place and reducing to a minimum the "scripted" aspects of politics. Roberto Unger's recent writings seem to develop such a vision in contemporary terms.[66] For now, it may be useful to consider Marx's actual analysis of a regime that came to power through a combination of coercion and manipulative rhetoric.

In Search of Louis Bonaparte's Audience

The Eighteenth Brumaire of Louis Bonaparte might be called the first work of a new genre of literature—one that explains why the Revolution failed to occur. Stated briefly, the thesis of Marx's book is that Louis Bonaparte came to power because of his ability to organize the lumpenproletariat into proto–storm troopers (the Society of December 10) and to satisfy the material interests of various social groups through the bureaucracy and the army. Marx also identifies the rhetorical power of the strategies and slogans of Bonaparte's movement and seeks to draw some conclusions about how the proletarian revolution can avoid the errors of the French republicans.

The work is one of the few writings of Marx to call forth some close postmodern readings. Jeffrey Mehlman, for instance, shows how Marx's own rhetorical practice subverts his attempt to represent history in lawlike terms.[67] Dominick LaCapra suggests that Marx's own remarkable rhetoricity in this text implies a somewhat different view of history than is implied by Engels's insistence in the preface that Marx has somehow found the master key to historical explanation. Marx seems to realize that performative speech acts play a larger role in politics than traditional historical materialism would suggest, but he fails to accept the consequences of such a realization for his whole project. The interesting contradiction between Marx's own rhetoricity and his theory of history is that his theory, as LaCapra writes, requires a world in which "rhetoric, would, so to speak, be rendered entirely superfluous, and the dream of transparency shared by idealists and positivists, by modern figures as seemingly diverse as Sartre, Habermas, the early Wittgenstein, and the early Althusser himself, would be realized."[68]

Bearing in mind the centrality of audience to any complete rhetorical reading, how would we characterize the audience of Marx's book? The argument of this section is that Marx's characterization of the audience of Louis Bonaparte obscures its similarities to later audiences who find political radicalism appealing.

It is true that Marx seems quite self-consciously rhetorical in this book. The prose is virtually Ciceronian in quality. The first chapter has an uncanny resemblance to Cicero's orations against Catiline, and it is possible that Marx may have drawn, consciously or unconsciously, on schoolboy

reminiscences of them. A wonderfully excessive bit of Ciceronian *copia* occurs, for example, in his description of the lumpenproletariat successfully
wooed by Bonaparte:

> Alongside decayed *roués* with dubious means of subsistence and of dubious
> origin, alongside ruined and adventurous offshoots of the bourgeoisie, were
> vagabonds, discharged soldiers, discharged jailbirds, escaped galley slaves,
> swindlers, mountebanks, *lazzaroni,* pickpockets, tricksters, gamblers, maque-
> reaux, brothel keepers, porters, *literati,* organ-grinders, ragpickers, knife-
> grinders, tinkers, beggars—in short, the whole indefinite, disintegrated mass,
> thrown hither and thither, which the French term *la bohème.*[69]

As LaCapra writes, Marx's description here is a sort of snobbish Victorian
fear of society's "Others."[70] It also sounds like an American image (circa
1952) of the sort of people to whom communism would appeal. One wonders, however, if Marx's rhetorical excess is not a sort of projective device:
a means of displacing Marx's own anxiety about his class-positioning and
his potential audience. I will further discuss this point in a moment.

Beyond Marx's own intriguing rhetorical practice, however, this book
makes direct observations about the role of discourse in history. First,
Marx notes the peculiarly repetitive qualities of revolutionary movements:
"they anxiously conjure up the spirits of the past to their service and borrow from them names, battle cries, and costumes in order to present the
new scene of world history in this time-honored disguise and this borrowed
language."[71]

This passage, of course, has oddly predictive force when applied to later
revolutions, from Stalin to the Weather Underground. It might be interesting
to pay some attention to the metaphor of the ghost in Marx's writings, as in
the "specter" haunting Europe or this revenant of past revolutions. The implication of the metaphor is that the role of the Marxist intellectual is to exorcise
those ghosts that will keep coming back to haunt future revolutions.

Second, although repetition seems parodic, it does have its heroic dimension. The bourgeois revolutions in France and England at least parodied
the past in a noble cause:

> But unheroic as bourgeois society is, it nevertheless took heroism, sacrifice, ter-
> ror, civil war and battles of peoples to bring it into being. And in the classically
> austere traditions of the Roman Republic its gladiators found the ideals and art
> forms, the self-deceptions that they needed in order to conceal from themselves
> the bourgeois limitations of the content of their struggles and to keep their en-
> thusiasm on the high plane of the great historical tragedy.[72]

So, too, Cromwell had borrowed his "speech, passions, and illusions" from
the Old Testament. What once was a heroic rhetorical strategy has degenerated into mere parody in Bonaparte's case.

This passage has two important features. First, it reveals Marx's continuing ambivalence toward rhetorical practice. He realizes that social change must be justified by arguments and images that stem from past experience, but those past arguments and images can get the revolution into trouble. How can any revolutionary movement based on historical experience successfully purge the bad effects of historical memory?

Second, it implies that "ideology" can function as a form of self-deception on the part of the revolutionary classes. Ideology does veil self-interest under the guise of universal interests, but in an unconscious way. This is a considerable advance over the view of ideology articulated in Marx's earlier works. It is also not surprising that actual rhetorical analysis of political texts makes this insight possible.

Third, Communist orators can and must break with a rhetorical logic of repetition and self-deception:

> The social revolution of the nineteenth century cannot draw its poetry from the past, but only from the future. It cannot begin with itself before it has stripped of all superstition in regard to the past. Earlier revolutions required recollections of past world history in order to drug themselves concerning their own content. In order to arrive at its own content, the revolution of the nineteenth century must let the dead bury their own dead. There the phrase went beyond the content; here the content goes beyond the phrase.[73]

Marx's remarks here clearly imply a self-reflexive, decontextualized culture of critical discourse. The passage is also very similar to the language in the letter to Ruge, even down to the similarity in the use of religious allusions. What real-life audience, other than criminals or disaffected intellectuals, would be willing to make such a leap into an undefined future? It is difficult to read this passage now without thinking of later attempts, from Stalin to Pol Pot, to eliminate "the poetry of the past." Still, without some break from the past, the inherited textuality of politics can be used to reactionary ends, as Louis Bonaparte's masterful use of slogans suggests:

> During the June days all classes and parties had united in the *Party of Order* against the proletarian class as the *Party of Anarchy,* of Socialism, of Communism. They had "saved" society from *"the enemies of society."* They had given out the watchwords of the old society: "Property, family, religion, and order," to their army as passwords and had proclaimed to the counterrevolutionary crusaders: In this sign thou shalt conquer.[74]

What one might call the political semiotics of these four slogans accounts for the peculiar stability of the bourgeois revolution. Marx argues that until they are destroyed completely, they will continue to infect the future. One wonders, of course, how one could ever argue for socialism without pointing out, as Eugene Debs did in the United States, that it is capitalism itself that is a threat to "property, family, religion, and order."

If we return, however, to Marx's characterization of the lumpenproletariat, we see an audience that might potentially share Marx's dream of transparency. Despite LaCapra's and others' argument that Marx uncannily predicts the rise of fascism, it makes equal sense to say that Marx's description prefigures the rise of "Marxism" itself. The seeds of the poetry of the future are in the present, but Marx's language has the effect of purposely not seeing them. One would think that the lumpenproletariat has the characteristics of Marx's desired audience, the people who would most readily break with the poetry and rhetoric of the past.

Hence the caricature of radical intellectuals and activists—by conservatives from Edmund Burke to Paul Johnson—as persons bereft of social ties and responsibilities. Richard Weaver makes the argument clearly:

> A prime object of militant communism is to produce a general social skepticism. . . . To this end, what it knows it must overcome is the binding element, or the cohesive force that holds a society together. For as long as this integrative power remains strong, the radical attack remains refuted and hopeless. This will explain the peculiar virulence with which Communists attack those transcendental unifiers like religion, patriotism, familial relationship, and the like.[75]

Much empirical historical data, of course, confirms the appeal of Marxism primarily to skeptical intellectuals or workers detached from primary-group institutions. Here, for instance, is Perry Anderson's list of the most significant Marxist theorists and their class origins: children of manufacturers, merchants, and bankers—Engels, Rosa Luxemburg, Georg Lukács, Theodor Adorno, Walter Benjamin, Herbert Marcuse, Paul Sweezy; large landowners—Plekhanov, Mehring, Labriola; senior lawyers or bureaucrats—Marx, Lenin.[76] Gouldner writes, "It appears that in every major class struggle that eventuated in the capturing of state power *and in a major property transfer in the twentieth century,* the victory was achieved by a political coalition dominated by intellectuals and the intelligentsia."[77]

The psychological prerequisites are explained by Aileen Kraditor, one of many conservative critics of Marxism who began life as a Communist. She analyzed the interaction of U.S. Socialist politicians and their audiences from 1890 to 1917 and finds that socialism was appealing in strictly ideological terms only to intellectuals and to those workers who had lost their ties with private-sphere institutions. Those in the middle class or working class who voted with Debs or for the municipal Socialists in Milwaukee or elsewhere did so entirely on the basis of short-term economic gain, not because of a broader commitment to "socialism." Kraditor, in a passage that must be directed as much to a younger version of herself as to anyone else, tries to prove that self-deception is as much a feature of the Socialist revolution as previous bourgeois ones:

> The radical evangel is attractive en masse only to the extent that . . . [private-sphere] institutions have decayed, or to those individuals who (for whatever reasons) have cut their bonds with those communities. The radical allegiance

then becomes an antidote to anomie. What makes it attractive to the deracinated person is not the liberation hoped for but the hope for liberation—its function in the present, not the future realization of its program.[78]

The point of cataloguing these arguments is to locate those points in the Marxist system that seem to generate the most persuasive counterarguments. Not surprisingly, a rhetorical focus seems to be an efficient way to locate these counterarguments.

The best case against Marxism—and Socialist institutions generally—can be made by critiques that focus on the Marxist view of language, ideology, and value in audience-centered terms. Put most strongly, in a way that would appeal equally to traditional liberals and conservatives, the critique could be summarized as follows.

Marx, the perceptive analyst of the self-deceptions of the bourgeois economists, sought in the transparency of his antirhetoric a permanent antidote to self-deception. The classical, biblical, and republican traditions that he sought to displace acknowledged, in varying ways, the permanent character of the human need for self-deception and sought to develop institutions that might help limit the consequences of human passions and interests and the self-deception resulting from them. They also understood, again in varying ways, the importance of symbols, rituals, and traditional authority—rhetoric, if you will—in nurturing human institutions.

The problem, of course, with this argument is that it can equally be lodged against liberal individualism and what passes for conservatism in the twentieth century. Liberal individualism can no more account for the role of rhetoric in public life than can the Marx and Engels of the *Manifesto*. Those conservatives (like Weaver) who want to restore rhetoric in the name of a unifying tradition ignore traditions like the Anglo-American one—or even the Western tradition in general—that are constituted, as Alasdair MacIntyre writes, by *continuities of conflict* rather than mystical unity. The spirit of civic republicanism that animated the American Revolution—as well as its appeal to broad sectors of the public—is curiously ignored by conservatives who want to attack the role of intellectuals in public life.

Conclusion

My purpose in this chapter has been to subject some classical Marxist texts to a reading informed by rhetorical methods. Marx's attention to the role of class struggle in history, his ethical critique of exploitation and alienation, and his scientific anatomy of the logic of capitalism remain as valid now as in the nineteenth century (perhaps more valid, since the real world of capitalism now more closely approximates his theoretical model). On the other hand, language, audience, ideology, the formation of class consciousness, even the production of commodities—all are products of rhetorical action in situations of contingency. Marx could not see that, which is why Marxists after Marx have had to import concepts such as the vanguard party, Freudianism, cultural studies, and, finally, poststructuralist discourse itself, in order to account for the relationship between structural possibilities and popular struggle. Rhetorical analysis of rules for the creation of discourse in particular modes of production, as well as the analysis of how languages of class are created and repressed in particular social formations, would be useful contributions to the still-developing project of historical materialism. Such a project, however, will tend toward parodic repetition until we have isolated the sources of Marxism's own persuasiveness and its rejection of persuasion in the name of transparency. Even a "Marxism without guarantees," to use Stuart Hall's phrase, must learn to abandon Marxism's founding myth of a world without rhetoric.[79]

❧ 2 ❧

Marxism After Marx:
The Problem of Mediation

THE ABSENCE OF A CONCEPT of audience in classical Marxism neatly parallels another absence: a thorough definition of the concept of "class." As is well known, the final chapter of *Capital,* Volume III, stops after a page. It begins, "The first question to be answered is this: What constitutes a class?" After just two paragraphs comes the note from Engels: "Here the manuscript breaks off."[1]

Marxism's claim to validity, whether in moral, political, or scientific terms, rises or falls with the concept of class. It is clear that much, if not all, of human misery is connected to the economic order. What is not clear is how human beings can (and if they should) be moved to change that order. In classical terms, how does a class move from being a class in itself to a class for itself?

One of the most important recent contributions to Marxist theory is Erik Olin Wright's *Classes,* a rigorous reformulation of class theory and a persuasive empirical test of Marxism. He argues that methodological debates in Marxism tend to respond to the fact that Marx and Engels were up to two very different things: providing an abstract structural map of class relations in *Capital* and providing concrete conjunctural maps of classes-as-actors in the political and historical writings.[2] Although Marx predicted that over time there would be greater and greater convergence between the abstract and concrete class analysis, significantly different conceptual and practical problems remain for Marxist analysis, depending on the level of abstraction at which a theorist is working.

At the highest level of abstraction is the mode of production itself, which consists of a *class structure* that determines class interests, and *class formation,* which refers to class consciousness and action. The capitalist mode of production consists of two primary contending classes whose struggle defines a particular epoch. At a middle-range level of abstraction—that of a given social formation—however, Marxist theory recognizes the existence of more than the two primary classes and the fact that classes and actors may be based in different modes of production and stages of development simultaneously. Class struggle, at the level of the social formation, will exist in the form of class alliances. Finally, at the lowest level of abstraction is the particular conjuncture, which includes contingent historical factors.

According to Wright, Marx dealt extensively with structural aspects of the capitalist mode of production and with class formation in particular historical conjunctures, but he did relatively little to theorize structural aspects of class in particular social formations and the actual process of epochal struggle at a mode-of-production level. The whole subsequent history of Marxism is an attempt to cope with these differing levels of abstraction in the classic texts.

What is missing from Wright's account is a theory of *mediation* between class structure and class formation. In other words, how do institutions, practices, and messages shape class formation? What alternative institutions, practices, and messages are available to those who wish to reshape class formations within the framework of structural possibilities?[3] In the rest of this book I attempt to provide one part—or at least alternative versions of that one part—of a larger theory of mediation. My purpose in this chapter is to analyze the concept of mediation and to focus on the specific political alternatives that have been proposed to mediate structural possibilities and popular struggle. The two key alternatives for party organization as a means of mediation are Leninism and the Social-Democratic Revisionism of Bernstein. The two key alternatives for discussing the formation of popular consciousness are Lukács's theory of reification and Gramsci's theory of hegemony. Each of these alternatives seizes on a particular aspect of classical Marxism as a legitimating force, and each constitutes its audiences differently.

The Concept of Mediation

Any investigation of the problem of "consciousness" in Marxist theory must begin with Hegel and with Hegel's theory of mediation. It appears that the concept first emerges in Hegel's thought in his early reflections on Christology. The problem of alienation, which appears as the gulf between the finite and the infinite, is mediated by identification with the figure of Jesus, who discovers God within himself and overcomes alienation by a life of love. The ordinary-language usage of mediation is as an attempt at reconciliation. The theme of reconciliation appears on a cosmic scale in the concept of Absolute Knowledge. For Hegel, all things are mediated—that is, they are related to everything else and to the Whole. The Absolute is, finally, the process of reality coming to know itself. Reality comes to know itself in and through the human spirit. The determinate shape assumed by the Absolute in history is the national spirit.

It is a commonplace argument against Marxism that Marx and Engels took up—uncritically from Hegel—the idea of a forward movement of history, even as they demythologized both the human and national spirit into labor and class, respectively. (A response to this argument is that there are weak and strong versions of forward movement. If one does not accept at least the weak notion that human beings could learn from their mistakes and thus progress, there is no reason to engage in controversy in the first place.) Whatever the metaphysical roots and limitations of the concept of mediation, it does serve a useful function in classical Marxism. At the most abstract level, labor mediates between human beings and nature. The productive activity of the "self-mediating natural being" is the primary condition for human self-constitution. This self-mediation, however, is blocked by historically specific forms of second-order mediation, such as money, exchange, and private property. The "secret of the fetishism of the commodity" is explained by the fact that—under capitalism—the production of use value is mediated by and subordinated to the production of exchange value. (In response, then, to criticism of the use-value/exchange-value distinction in the previous chapter, it is one thing to accept the necessity of the mediation of one thing by another, and another to accept that mediation is identical to subordination.) Finally, mediation is also mediation between theory and practice, accomplished by practical activity.[4] It can be a kind of negation, as Lenin puts it: "negation as a moment of connection, as a moment of developing, of retaining the positive," simultaneously canceling and preserving elements of that which is negated.[5]

The concept of mediation thus appears when division exists, whether between theory and practice or between the ideal and the actual.[6] Although Kenneth Burke never deals with the concept of mediation in Hegel or Marx, his discussion of identification in *A Rhetoric of Motives* provides some interesting possibilities for "mediating" the concepts of rhetoric and mediation.

Just as Hegel proclaims that Division is the starting point of philosophy, Burke writes:

> Identification is affirmed with earnestness precisely because there is division. Identification is compensatory to division. If men were not apart from one another, there would be no need for the rhetorician to proclaim their unity. If men were wholly and truly of one substance, absolute communication would be of man's very essence. It would not be an ideal, as it now is, partly embodied in material conditions and partly frustrated by these same conditions; rather, it would be as natural, spontaneous, and total as with those ideal prototypes of communication, the theologian's angels, or "messengers."[7]

The study of rhetoric, then, is the study of the realm of division. The practice of rhetoric involves the construction of identifications, themselves rooted in the properties (and property) of persons, groups, and objects. Identification, according to Burke, may work through stylistic identification, through identification of the audience's interests with the speaker's interests (an identification subject to mystifications of the term "property"), or through metaphoric extension of the parent-child relationship described by the Freudian notions of identification and transference.[8]

In more classical terms, the division between speaker and audience is mediated by strategies that unite a proposed action with the accepted values, beliefs, and goals of the audience and its culture (*logos*); strategies that unite action and the mood of the audience (*pathos*); and, finally—and perhaps most important of all—strategies that make the speaker a credible representative of the audience's aspirations (*ethos*). The Aristotelian *pisteis,* seemingly banal after a century of use in public-speaking classrooms, looks much fresher when considered under the heading of mediation. Any account of persuasion or rational decisionmaking that neglects the role of communal values, emotions, and the need for identification will develop problems with practical effectiveness. As I argued in Chapter 1, the self-negating aspects of social practices make the mediating and synthesizing function of rhetoric essential to human life and growth.

There are, then, some useful parallels between the rhetorical notion of identification and the Marxist-Hegelian notion of mediation. There is no necessary opposition—despite recent attempts to turn Burke into a post-structuralist—between a view of human beings as laboring animals and one of human beings as symbol-using animals. Symbols are not mere symbols, but are part of human praxis, the mediation of human beings and nature. Symbol-use—in the sense of rhetoric generally, and more specialized forms such as advertising—mediate the relationship between use value and exchange value. Symbol-use also is part of the practical political activity that mediates historical structures and popular struggle. Symbol-use, finally, is deeply involved in the familial and social processes involved in mediating—both for good and for ill—a sense of subjectivity in the first place. (Neither Burke nor Marx and Engels theorized the role of masculine and feminine identifications—both familial and social-symbolic—in the larger order of mediations of self and nature, use and exchange value, and theory and practice. As I will argue in the final chapter, analyzing the centrality of male identifications in the discourse of both socialism and capitalism is perhaps the most urgent task for politically committed rhetorical critics.)

The concept of mediation, then, despite its murky Hegelian roots, is extremely useful in creating linkages between Marxism and rhetoric. To return to the conceptual scheme devised by Wright, we could locate the function of rhetoric as a mediating space between class structure and class formation. The theoretical object denoted by this space is "class represen-tation." At the mode-of-production level, rhetoric as rules for the produc-tion of discourse mediates class structure and class formation. The historic shift from the dominance of the rhetorical tradition as a stance toward dis-course to a culture of critical discourse can be theorized at this level. At the level of the social formation and the conjuncture, the *primary rhetoric*— that is, the dominant communal values, moods, and identifications as ex-pressed in cultural narratives, figures, and arguments—will serve as a me-diation that either blocks or challenges class formation. When the authors of *Habits of the Heart* find that Americans speak a primary language of individualism tempered by vestiges of secondary languages of republican-ism and biblical justice, they are theorizing this level of rhetoric.[9] That sense of judgment and taste, which is promoted by rhetorical education and experience, serves as a guide at the strictly conjunctural level.

Rhetorical action, then, as Celeste Condit puts it, "mediates the relation-ship between language and external material conditions." Emphasizing the role of rhetoric in social and political action does not lead to a poststructur-alist descent into discourse at the expense of the material, as long as we recognize that "rhetoric is constrained by objective realities, and in turn, rhetoric structures both objective truths and objective realities, as persua-sion results in and from social change."[10]

Revisionism as Rhetorical Strategy: Bernstein's Search for an Audience

The preceding discussion of mediation was intended to demonstrate that a rhetorical perspective is not inherently incompatible with Marxism. There remains the question of whether any set of institutional and rhetorical po-litical strategies whatsoever can facilitate the transition to socialism or communism.

One of the less-attractive features of the Socialist tradition has been its tendency to develop rigid labels for positions that somehow violate the can-ons of orthodoxy. "Revisionism" is the oldest of those labels. Before World War I, it was applied, as Leszek Kolakowski writes, to "those writers and political figures who, while starting from Marxist premises, came by de-grees to call in question various elements of the doctrine, especially Marx's predictions as to the development of capitalism and the inevitability of the Socialist revolution."[11] By the post–World War II period, of course, "revi-sionism" had become an all-purpose label applied by Communist parties to other Communists who disagreed with them. The creator of revisionism in the first sense was Eduard Bernstein.

Like the other three strategic stances discussed in this chapter, Bernstein's "revisionism" remains a viable option for Socialists. One could argue, in fact, that Rorty's position on the "end of socialism" replicates Bernstein's evolutionary socialism now at the time of another "crisis of Marxism." If one actually reads *Evolutionary Socialism,* however, it appears a bit more radical than the left wing of the Democratic party. Bernstein defends class-based politics and a workers' party (even as he wishes to open Socialist politics up to the middle class and the peasantry). He defends municipal ownership of monopolistic industries. He encourages the development of alternatives to capitalism, such as producers' and consumers' cooperatives. If these are all banal—Bernstein uses the better word *Gegenwartarbeit,* the "everyday work" of the party—compared to the cataclysmic Revolution, they are still significant structural changes in the United States, at least.

My purpose here is not so much to defend Bernstein as to describe how his stance works as a rhetorical stance toward political action. Using the term "rhetoric" here involves some potential ambiguity. "Rhetoric" is a relatively unique term in that it functions simultaneously as a term of abuse in ordinary language ("mere rhetoric"), as a conceptual system ("Aristotle's *Rhetoric*"), as a distinct stance toward discourse production ("the rhetorical tradition"), and as a characteristic set of arguments ("Reagan's rhetoric"). To add some precision (if not necessarily greater clarity) to my analysis, I want to use a term developed by Thomas B. Farrell. A "communicative praxis" is a rule-governed system guiding rhetoric and action in a social formation. It possesses the following five features: (1) a conception of the "public"; (2) a preferred medium for communication; (3) a concrete set of political goals; (4) a preferred means of legitimation; and (5) a fundamental source of contradiction.[12] For example, Farrell identified the concept of a communicative praxis in the American pragmatic tradition. This tradition, represented by the Democratic party at its best, believed in an inclusive conception of the public, with fair distribution of access to positions of authority. It tried to define the public interest in the broadest possible way, attempting to transcend sectional, racial, and class interests. Its preferred media of communication were the citizen-discussion group and the natural extensions of those discussions: petitions, lobbying, voting—but even strikes and boycotts in extreme cases. These preferred media implied that political communication itself was best when framed in terms of practical policy questions or programs. The Democratic party's goal was a political system in which justice was defined as fairness and in which an activist government steered the economic and political systems in ways responsive to the citizenry. Its legitimation required both a collective sense of patriotism—something like Myrdal's "American Creed"—but, perhaps most important, a conviction that government could distribute resources efficiently and fairly. Its fundamental contradiction—not so much in the negative sense of contradiction as in the Hegelian sense of the principle of movement—was that its preference for framing political issues as matters of technical policy tended to privilege technical expertise. One cannot privilege technical expertise without undercutting an inclusive notion of the public. The increased nationalization of politics with the New Deal and with the extension of the mass media of communication also created barriers to media access. Nationalization, while necessary to fulfill the universalizing claims of the praxis, helped limit the formation of informed publics.

A political rhetoric, as opposed to a communicative praxis, consists of characterizations, narratives, and ideographs that serve as unifying devices for legitimation strategies.[13] A characterization—for instance, "Northeastern liberal"—provides "the first step in the move from the material experience of daily life to collective valuation through the simple process of providing concrete but motivationally loaded names to politically salient entities."[14] Narratives structure "the particular relationships between and among various characterizations. They thus provide an understanding for how material reality holds together and functions."[15] Ideal cultural values or ideographs are incorporated into narratives as primary purpose terms.[16] The Bush administration, for instance, has told a story in the aftermath of the Los Angeles riots in which "liberals" created the underclass through 1960s antipoverty programs, which undermined "self-reliance." The communicative praxis underlying this story is that of "liberalism" (in the nineteenth-century sense). A critic can reconstruct a "communicative praxis" from analysis of a political rhetoric as it interacts with other political rhetorics over time in a social system.

Bernstein forged his communicative praxis of "revisionism" in the context of a debate within German social democracy. A "crisis of Marxism" occurred when the long depression of 1873 to 1896 ended. Even before that time, both the standard of living of German workers and the electoral following of the Social Democrats increased. The fact that "peasants do not sink; middle class does not disappear; crises do not grow ever larger; misery and serfdom do not increase" means that socialism should build a radical coalition on the realistic premise that "there is increase in insecurity, dependence, social distance, social character of production, functional superfluity of property owners."[17] Revisionism thus emerged as a *crisis in historical narrative.*

Bernstein's arguments caused much debate in the German party and elsewhere. Rosa Luxemburg wrote an important book—*Reform or Revolution*—in response to Bernstein. Although the German party formally rejected revisionism in 1903, the actual practice of the party seemed to follow Bernstein's suggestions. The moral collapse of German social democracy, when it voted the war credits during World War I, has often been used as an argument against revisionism, even though Bernstein himself actively opposed the war.

The term "evolutionary" in the title of Bernstein's central work, *Evolutionary Socialism,* is somewhat misleading.[18] The German title is *Die Voraussetzungen des Sozialismus und die Aufgaben der Sozialdemokratie*— better translated as "The Premises of Socialism and the Tasks of Social Democracy." Making too much of the title difference is also misleading, since Bernstein did not veto the translation. Still, the idea that socialism is somehow "evolutionary" has both Darwinian echoes and the implication that it is a natural, perhaps inevitable, process.

In fact, the first rhetorical task Bernstein faces is to recast the sense of temporality in socialism. He rejects both the catastrophic future of the *Communist Manifesto* and the notion of inevitability. One version of revisionism accepts the notion of inevitability but rejects revolution. It is clear that Bernstein does not take that position. He writes, in the 1909 Preface to the English edition, that his principal aim is "the strong accentuation of what in Germany is called the GEGENWARTARBEIT—the every-day work of the socialist party. . . . Unable to believe in finalities at all, I cannot believe in a final aim of socialism."[19]

The reason for a focus on the present is that Marxist predictions about the future cataclysm have simply not come true and, indeed, will not come true. The *Communist Manifesto,* even though it was right about the "evolutionary tendencies" of capitalism, was wrong about at least three things: (1) the amount of time required for capitalism to collapse; (2) the increased polarization of classes; and (3) the increased centralization of capital. Most important, the classic writings were not just scientific descriptions, they were acts of persuasion. They helped bring about a "social reaction" against "the exploiting tendencies of capital."[20]

Throughout *Evolutionary Socialism,* Bernstein is anxious to invoke the authority of both Marx and Engels for his conclusions. He cites example after example of places where both of them—but especially Engels—talk about the possibility of peaceful change. He is, nonetheless, perfectly willing to criticize Marx and Engels directly, both for their faulty predictions and for their tendency to emphasize the economic over the political. After citing the famous passage from the 1859 Introduction where Marx discusses the ideological forms in which people become conscious of class struggle, Bernstein writes, "On the whole the consciousness and will of men appear to be a very subordinate factor of the material movement."[21]

Bernstein also displays a remarkable sensitivity toward rhetorical factors. He notes that Marx and Engels overstated things because it is useful to do so at the beginning of an enterprise. He also recognizes the paradoxically traditionalist quality of Socialist argument, but says that

> tradition usually forms the most powerful means of linking those together
> whom no strong, constant, effective interest or external pressures knit to-
> gether. Hence the intuitive preference of all men of action, however revolu-
> tionary they may be in their aims, for tradition.[22]

Additionally, by using the term "cant" to refer to the constant invocation of tradition by his opponents, Bernstein accuses them of having an unwittingly religious motivation. (He says that the term came from the repetitious singing of psalms—"canting," like "chanting"—by English Puritans.)

This final move by Bernstein represents a useful rhetorical strategy against more orthodox opponents. Bernstein's argumentation generally is much more temperate and generous to his opponents than is the norm in Marxist writing. He mentions his chief opponents Kautsky and Luxemburg by name but does not impugn their motives. Luxemburg, however, uses an ideological *interest-explanation* (in Elster's sense) to refute Bernstein. Bernstein, it seems, advances his theses in order to strengthen the "petty bourgeois" elements in the party. The irony, of course, is that Bernstein grew up in a working-class family, while Luxemburg and Kautsky did not.

Whatever other problems Bernstein's position has, his ethics of controversy needs to be retained by Socialists. The insistence on labeling opponents' positions on the basis of class interest (part of a general trend in modernity that Wayne Booth calls "motivism") is not only ineffective in building coalitions, but it undermines the possibility of reasoned argument.[23] Any socialism that places the economic realm above the political (and, I would add, the rhetorical) realm cannot work. Bernstein writes, "Democracy is a condition of socialism to a much greater degree than is usually assumed, i.e., it is not only the means but also the substance."[24] Yet this is not so much an error on the part of previous Socialists as it is an unintended positive consequence of Socialist agitation. To say, as the *Communist Manifesto* did, that "the proletarian has no fatherland," fails to recognize that now, thanks to socialism, that proletarian has become a citizen.[25]

To emphasize the importance of the political does not, contrary to writers like Ernesto Laclau and Chantal Mouffe, mean an abandonment of class or economic analysis.[26] For Bernstein, it is possible to affirm an economic interpretation of history without denying the existence of many noneconomic forces and motives. Economics is simply "the cardinal point" of the major moments of historical change.[27]

Bernstein thus rejects neither class analysis nor even the possibility of revolution. He only wishes to increase an element of flexibility in Socialist politics. First, a recognition of differences among national parties is needed. Level of education and economic development, as well as "subjective" matters of national culture, will make for differences of political strategy.

Second, he intends to preserve the right of revolution, viewing it as compatible with reform: "This imperceptible and inalienable right is as little touched if we place ourselves on the path of reform as the right of self-defence is done away with when we make laws to regulate our personal property disputes."[28]

Third, the practical activity of Socialists must be the strengthening of the

trade unions, the cooperative movement, municipal ownership, and universal suffrage. This practical activity "is directed towards creating circumstances and conditions which shall render possible and secure a transition
(free from convulsive outbursts) of the modern social order into a higher
one."[29]

It is this last argument that makes Bernsteinian revisionism appear to
have been falsified by history. Although it is simply unfair to say that Bernstein was overly optimistic (he did, after all, have to live in exile for some
time), some of his criticisms of Marx seemed quite wrong after World War
I and the Crash of 1929. One could also make a good case that the centralization of capital and concentration of power did occur along more orthodox Marxian lines in this century.

A final argument deals with Bernstein's view of liberalism. Bernstein
views liberalism rather unproblematically as a direct precursor of socialism, at least in its "spiritual qualities." He has no problem even with the
insistence on individual economic responsibility that was essential to
Manchester liberalism: "The recognition of individual responsibility is the
return of the individual to society for services rendered or offered him by
society."[30]

Bernstein's stress on individual responsibility also involves a recognition
of the need for what more bohemian Socialists might regard as "bourgeois" morality: "With the roving proletarian without a family and home,
no lasting, firm trade union movement would be possible."[31]

This passage parallels Marx's discussion of the *lumpenproletariat* in the
Eighteenth Brumaire in some interesting ways. In the previous chapter, I
argued that total revolution tends to be most appealing to those without
family, religion, and property. This fact opens Marxism up to the charge by
Aileen Kraditor and other conservatives that Marxism can never be an authentic representative of the working class as a whole, but only of *lumpen*
elements and of deracinated intellectuals. Bernstein seems to recognize that
Marxism is now presented with a brutal bargain: The total immiseration of
the proletariat might bring on revolution, but there is every chance that
such immiseration will breed habits fatal to democracy.[32]

The last section of Bernstein's book points forward to his own later work
but also to what might be viewed as the fundamental contradiction in evolutionary socialism. He writes that we need to move from cant to Kant.
Not only should we view socialism as an ethical ideal in a Kantian sense,
but we must use the Kantian stance of critique to address received Socialist
opinion, to "warn it that the contempt of the ideal, the magnifying of material factors until they become omnipotent forces of evolution, is a self-
deception."[33]

Having worked through Bernstein's arguments, it is now possible to recast them as rules about the five features of communicative praxis: the pub-

lic; communicative forms; goals; principles of legitimacy; and fundamental contradiction.

First, his conception of the public. On the one hand, Bernstein retains an emphasis on class-based politics. On the other hand, he wishes to reach out to other groups whose interests may coincide with the working class—specifically, the peasantry and the middle class. In principle, however, since socialism is an ethical, regulative ideal along the lines of Kant's categorical imperative, Socialist arguments may be addressed to and accepted by anyone. As we shall see later, a universalizing conception of the public runs the risk of losing the audience-centeredness needed for sustaining activist cadres and promoting social change.

Second, his preferred forms of communication are the standard ones of liberal democracy: the newspaper, popular agitation, and party and parliamentary debate. The defense of the freedoms of speech and press are crucial.

Third, his political goal is a strengthening of Socialist institutions such as unions, cooperatives, and workers' parties, both within and across nation-states, without necessarily prescribing what the future of those institutions may look like.

Fourth, Bernstein contends that the legitimacy of socialism is guaranteed primarily by its conformity with ethical principles (although socialism's consistency with generally accepted notions of evolution and scientific progress underlies those principles).

Fifth, although there were external events (World War I, the dismal behavior of the Socialist parties during the war, the seeming success of the Soviet Revolution, and the Crash of 1929) that seemed to falsify revisionism, there was also an internal contradiction that laid it open to attack and further development. What revisionism cannot account for is the problem of mediation. Although it does a better job than previous Marxism of recognizing the importance of communal values (even religion) in crafting political strategy, at the same time it does not examine how the ruling class may block those strategies in *rhetorical*, rather than strictly coercive, ways.

The Kantian roots of revisionism are also clear when Bernstein rejects any claim to know or care about the future. Kantian ethics, as is well known, is nonconsequentialist—that is, one should do the right thing regardless of its effects on anyone or anything. (It is probably no accident that Kant was far more hostile to rhetoric than any previous philosopher, including Plato.)[34] As numerous critics have argued, Kantian ethics ultimately has to bring in consequences in order to make it persuasive: adherence to rules makes everyone better off in the long run. Still, unlike either the virtue ethics of Aristotle or Mill's utilitarianism, Kant (and Bernstein) cannot retain their ethical principles and try to persuade another to adopt them. Bernstein appears to imply that sober, virtuous workers will simply do the right thing if given their civil rights.

A final source of contradiction has to do with the brutal bargain I mentioned earlier. Both the inevitability thesis of classical Marxism and class hatred were powerful motivational tools for recruiting disaffected workers and intellectuals. Bernstein's calm, rational, generous tone was bound to irritate someone like Rosa Luxemburg or Lenin who (if one reads their biographies) seemed to be using socialism to fill a deep spiritual hunger. One may interpret this observation in two ways, of course: Either the revolutionaries were "canting" or else revisionists missed an important datum about political change. As many sociologists of religion have noted, strong churches seem to require completely committed members. Absent of external rewards (such as social prestige) for church membership, liberalization of religious organizations inevitably leads to membership loss. So, too, the organizing of unions, the fight for protective legislation, and the development of vital Socialist institutions required both a more vivid sense of the future and a greater sense of exclusivity than "tame" social democracy was able to provide. If Richard Rorty is right about the "end of socialism," then Bernstein's stance may become persuasive only in light of the universal recognition that any attempt to attain more than Bernstein's *Gegenwartarbeit* runs the risk of totalitarianism.

One can, however, retain a sense of the importance of mediation that a rhetorical analysis provides and still take a position far to the left of Bernstein. The fundamental difference between reformist and revolutionary strategies is that the first addresses or tries to constitute a more or less unified audience in the social formation, while a revolutionary strategy necessarily addresses a partial and partisan audience and refuses dialogue with others. Marxist political judgment is finally a sense of prudence about the choice between the two strategies. In some ways, however, Lenin provides us with the most rhetorically sensitive Marxism of all, because it is most conscious (of all the various Marxisms) of the need to develop strong institutions and messages to promote class consciousness.

Lenin: From Rhetoric to Propaganda

The "Spirit of 1989" has all but liquidated Leninism as a Socialist option. Even those who do not view the collapse of the Soviet Union as a lesson about the futility of *any* attempt to change the world seem united in their conclusion that Lenin's theories of the party and revolution had much to do with the horrors perpetrated in Marx's name in this century.

There is a curious double standard operating here, of course. Moral analysis after 1989 has become a sort of perverse utilitarian calculus, counting up the greatest ill for the greatest number. Add up the number killed under Lenin, Stalin, Mao, Ho Chi Minh, and Pol Pot, and you will get an irrefutable demonstration of the evils of communism.

The numbers bespeak great evil, of course (although some exceptions could be made for Lenin and Ho Chi Minh), but no one ever tries to add up equivalent numbers for deaths from famine, starvation, industrial accidents, civil unrest, and colonial wars caused by the policies of the Western capitalist countries since 1917. Would they equal the death toll from communism? Exceed it? Does it matter?

There have been a few attempts to make a balanced assessment of the Leninist tradition. The most extreme of these, perhaps, has been Alexander Cockburn's, who has argued for a need to revise the Stalin death toll downward by several million and who has developed a sort of checks-and-balances view of the Soviet Union's role in world history:

> The Soviet Union defeated Hitler and fascism. Without it, the Cuban Revolution would never have survived, nor the Vietnamese. In the postwar years it was the counterweight to U.S. imperialism and the terminal savageries of the old European colonial powers. It gave support to any country trying to follow an independent line. Without it, just such a relatively independent country as India could instead have taken a far more rightward course. Despite Stalin's suggestion to Mao that he and his comrades settle for only half a country, the Chinese Revolution probably would not have survived either. It was Communists who spearheaded the fight for civil rights for black people in the United States in the 1930s; and without the threat of the Soviet model in the competition for the loyalties of the Third World, Truman probably would not have felt the pressure to desegregate the Army when he did.[35]

On the one hand, a conservative reader could not be blamed for reading these arguments as a version of the Christian notion of *felix culpa*: that happy fault of Eve that made the incarnation of Jesus Christ possible. On the other hand, Cockburn gives us a more complex version of political reality than has emerged from most of the discussions of 1989.

Robin Blackburn interprets the ruthlessness of the Leninist tradition against the backdrop of the ruthlessness of World War I itself:

> The industrial carnage of the First World War, and its devastating impact on the lives of some hundreds of millions of people, could appear to justify not only the Bolshevik seizure of power but also the ruthlessness with which they defended this seizure. The Bolsheviks were scarcely disposed to take lessons in humanitarianism from those who bore responsibility for the hecatombs of Ypres and the Somme, or used starvation to cow central Europe in 1918–9, or from statesmen who savagely repressed the aspiration to colonial independence.[36]

Blackburn also makes the even more valuable point about Western cooperation with Stalinism. In the early 1930s half of U.K. and U.S. machine exports went to the Soviet Union. Imports of Western technology in the 1930s and 1940s laid the basis for Soviet growth through the end of the 1950s. Although some have defended Stalin's forced collectivization and the Gulags as forms of Soviet "primitive accumulation," it seems clear that Soviet growth occurred in spite of Stalin's policies rather than because of them. No one in the West seems ready to point out that it was precisely at the point of Stalin's death and the possibility of liberalization in the Soviet Union that the West imposed an economic and military blockade that forced the Soviet Union to waste tremendous resources on the military.[37] It is not entirely certain, either, that the Soviet economic collapse of the 1980s stemmed from irrationalities connected with central economic planning, as Nove argues.[38] How much of the crash occurred because of massive military investments caused by Western policies? The only way, perhaps, to answer these arguments will be from interpreting internal Soviet government documents from the 1950s.

Discussions about the achievements of the Soviet Union are a useful counterweight to the simplistic conclusions drawn by Western—even Socialist—commentators. For our purposes, however, they represent a strain of *realism* in Marxist rhetoric that is a useful way of interpreting Leninism as a rhetorical stance or as a communicative praxis. As I argued in the previous section, Bernstein's revisionism, then and now, is vulnerable to the charge of being overly optimistic, both in his lack of a theory of capitalist mediations and in his underestimating the violence of capitalist resistance to socialism. Bernstein's Kantian socialist ethic, however attractive in peacetime in the capitalist West, seems hopelessly irrelevant in, say, colonial Vietnam or in a battle at Verdun. The Leninist response to Bernstein is succinctly captured in Bertolt Brecht's great poem, "An die Nachgeborenen": "You who will emerge from the flood in which we drowned remember when you speak of our weaknesses the dark time from which you escaped. . . . Alas, we who wanted to prepare the ground for kindness could not be kind."[39]

Lenin's realism is fundamental to his conception of the first element of a communicative praxis, his view of the *public*. Principles of Marxist science and a realistic assessment of politics require a vanguard party in order to ensure the victory of socialism. This party's rhetoric and political action provides a kind of Aristotelian mean between workers' emphasis on economic power and intellectuals' utopianism. Lenin's theory of imperialism requires that the vanguard party direct its energies to the weakest link of capitalism first: the semi-colonial rather than advanced countries. Lenin thus reintroduces the element of Marxist internationalism present in the *Manifesto*.

Under the pressure of external conditions, Lenin moved between the almost anarchist, council-based politics of *State and Revolution* and the rigid "democratic centralism" of the period of War Communism both as privileged forums for communication and as visions of Socialist goals.

The principle of legitimation of Leninist praxis consists of a rhetoric blending the prestige of science, appeal to class hatred as reinforced by the behavior of the Czarist regime and its equivalents, and a discourse of realism. It is the discourse of realism that emerges as the source of the fundamental contradiction in Leninism: a realist rhetorical stance is essential to revolution, but realism by its nature is best suited to authoritarian statism rather than democracy. A realist view of the public becomes a self-fulfilling prophecy that justifies blocking their access to power.

The key text in which the Leninist stance and its contradictions are apparent is *What Is to Be Done?*[40]

Lenin developed the terms "economism" and "opportunism" to criticize those social democrats who argued for a concentration on economic as opposed to political struggles. This shift of emphasis supposedly occurred through Bernstein's influence and could be seen among British Fabians and French Ministerialists as well.[41] The emphasis is linked to a call for greater "freedom of criticism," but this freedom, Lenin writes, means "freedom to introduce bourgeois ideas and bourgeois elements into socialism."[42] The popularity of Bernstein's ideas is caused by "the extensive participation of an 'academic' stratum in the socialist movement."[43] This characterization, of course, ignores the class background of opponents of Bernstein such as Lenin and Luxemburg themselves. Luxemburg actually had a Ph.D.

Alvin Gouldner makes an interesting point about the Leninist critique of Bernsteinism. Lenin is right: "Revisionism represents in part the growing influence of intellectuals in the German social democratic movement, especially after the repeal of Germany's anti-socialist laws."[44] Intellectuals had a greater class interest in a *political* over an economic view of socialism, because their "social origins, educational background, and communication skills allowed them to profit from the institutional changes implicit in the new politics." They could become deputies or ministers or experts or lawyers in the new bureaucracies.[45] In an interesting twist of the Leninist argument, Gouldner then applies a similar interest-explanation to Leninism itself:

> The limited public apparatus of Leninism, however, dwarfed by Czarist repression, allowed intellectuals many fewer opportunities for career fulfillment as politicians or state bureaucrats. Leninism, then, represents the ideology of intellectuals whose political ambitions in the public life are more sharply thwarted; who are thus more severely alienated from the status quo; and who had relinquished hope for normal political influence in society.[46]

Now there are some problems with this argument, both because it conflates interest-explanation and position-explanation (to use Elster's distinction) and because it makes political choice a direct expression of class interest rather than a product of persuasion. Audience rationalization and speaker appeal to self-interest are effective elements but are not the *only* elements of persuasion. Nonetheless, Gouldner continues the Leninist emphasis on realistic assessment of politics and political motives.

Not only does Lenin impugn the motives of his opponents, but he provides a scientific justification for silencing them: "Those who are really convinced that they have made progress in science would not demand freedom for the new views to continue side by side with the old, but the substitution of the new views for the old."[47] A rejection of science in the name of "freedom of criticism" leads to "eclecticism and lack of principle." Lenin then writes the famous line: "Without revolutionary theory there can be no revolutionary movement."[48]

Correct theory, developed by the vanguard party, is needed to lead the masses to revolutionary consciousness:

> There could not have been Social-Democratic consciousness among the workers. It would have to be brought to them from without. The history of countries shows that the working class, exclusively by its own effort, is able to develop only trade-union consciousness, i.e. the conviction that it is necessary to combine in unions, fight the employers, and strive to compel the government to pass necessary labour legislation, etc.[49]

It is only by a productive uniting of the workers and intellectuals in the party that change takes place:

> The theory of socialism, however, grew out of the philosophic, historical, and economic theories elaborated by educated representatives of the propertied classes, by intellectuals.[50]

It is possible, as Gouldner does, to erect a whole theory of Marxism—as the false consciousness of the new class of technical intelligentsia and humanistic intellectuals—out of passages like these. To make this move, however, is to give interest-explanation too much power in social analysis and political action. It is rather the fundamental realism of the Leninist view that is most important.

Robert Hariman has developed a theory of realism as a "generally available discursive practice—a familiar, pervasive, and often pre-eminent way of speaking in order to discipline comprehension and conduct."[51] The discursive practice of realism, according to Hariman, asserts simultaneously an epistemology, a political theory, and a rhetoric. It "claims to be seeing the world clearly and so presumes that objective knowledge is available to anyone who knows how to acquire it." It assumes that politics is a competition among states (to which I would add classes or interest groups) who pursue power through rational calculation "and so presumes that attention to other practices or values is a distraction inevitably leading to failure to achieve or understand the consequences of political acts." It, finally, asserts a rhetoric that is appealing "by explicitly and implicitly defining itself over

other discourses that are identified as inferior vehicles for knowing the political world because they are too discursive, too caught up in their textuality to serve rational calculation."[52]

Realist rhetoric thus works within the master trope of metonymy:

> The complexities of political life are reduced to a calculus of power, justice
> (defined as a discourse, the fodder of human illusion) is reduced to self-inter-
> est (by implication, a material condition), appearances are reduced to the
> reality they conceal, and, ultimately, discourse itself is reduced to the world
> it would represent.

Realism also has a communicative style that is rational because unadorned.
It is also based on symbols of security and danger that work to reinforce
both the authority of the realist speaker over other social groups and the
authority of the state itself.[53]

While Hariman applies his theory of discursive realism to the rhetoric of
Henry Kissinger, it works equally well to interpret that of Lenin (whose
work it is presumably the main task of Kissinger to undo). Realism is a
rhetoric that must deny its own rhetoricity in order to function. When external conditions reveal its status as rhetoric, its actual claims to validity
disappear. Some elements of realism are vital to any effective politics whatsoever, but when reified into a worldview they harden habits of communication that are detrimental to the democratic practice. A low view of the
public may be prudent in designing propaganda, but it may lead to the
public's dehumanization as well. The number of comments in Lenin's writings after 1917 about building socialism with people damaged by capitalism is remarkable:

> Things would not be so bad if we did not have to build socialism with people
> inherited from capitalism. But that is the whole trouble with socialist con-
> struction—we have to build socialism with people who have been thoroughly
> spoiled by capitalism.[54] We want to build socialism with the aid of those men
> and women who grew up under capitalism, were depraved and corrupted by
> capitalism, but steeled for the struggle by capitalism.[55]

This "realistic" assessment of the Soviet public is justified by an appeal to a
homely construction metaphor:

> We are placing people of the old type under proper control, under the vigilant
> supervision of the proletariat, and making them do the work we need. This is
> the only way we can build. If you are unable to erect the edifice with the mate-
> rials bequeathed to us by the bourgeois world, you will not be able to build it at
> all, and you will not be Communists, but mere phrase-mongers.[56]

This last statement contains all the features of realist discourse in one paragraph: a claim to objective seeing, an obsession with security, and an assertion that opponents are caught in the web of textuality. It also, however,

returns us to the problem raised by Marx in the *Eighteenth Brumaire* about the vulnerability of lumpen audiences to any appeal for radical change. Bernstein's emphasis on instilling bourgeois liberal habits of character in the working class is perhaps his most significant difference from Lenin.

Lenin's insistence that capitalism had ruined people took a more positive turn in his discussion of the new capitalist method of management, Taylorism. It was

> a combination of the refined brutality of bourgeois exploitation and a number of the greatest scientific achievements in the field of analyzing mechanical motions during work, the elimination of superfluous and awkward motions, the elaboration of correct methods of work, the introduction of the best system of accounting and control, etc.[57]

Thus, as François George has written, "the construction of socialism presupposes alienation in its most profound sense: submission to authority and repression of individual possibilities of imagination, autonomy, liberty, creativity, i.e., of organization."[58] Later theorists, notably those of the Frankfurt School, would react against the Leninist celebration of capitalist management but, as we shall see in Chapter 3, retained his sense that capitalism had ruined the masses.

As I suggested earlier, it is unfair to blame Leninism—using a rhetorical appeal to a concept of radical evil—for the millions killed in the name of Marxism-Leninism. Nor, as Roy Medvedev has argued, is it fair to assume that greater democracy could have prevented total anarchy and starvation in 1917.[59] The Roman meaning of the term "dictatorship of the proletariat," so often invoked as the source of fundamental evil in Marxism and in Leninism, is often overlooked: Marx and Engels

> were at pains to stress not only the exceptional nature of this form of authority, its assumption of extraordinary powers and its violent character, but also its necessary limitation in time and therefore the fact that it was transitional in character.[60]

The worst features of realism as a discourse could only be reinforced by the Cold War. Stalinism, the fight against Hitler, and the Cold War only contributed to the stagnation of Leninism as a communicative praxis. Its low opinion of its public did not help, either, however effective Leninist rhetoric was to be in mobilizing millions worldwide.

It is, finally, the brutality of the problem of rhetorical and political mobilization that is magnified in the time after the fall of communism. Liberalism and Social Democracy "won" the Cold War, but at a price whose total cost we may never be able to calculate. The appeal of Social Democracy depended both on its ability to distribute resources more or less equally and on the moral appeal of its difference from communism. Communism in turn appealed to audiences who needed greater motivation than the increasingly technical discourse of Social Democracy. Medvedev's hope for a union of Social Democracy and communism in a higher political synthesis seems much more improbable even than in 1981, but if the events of 1989 have taught us anything, it is that history holds more surprises than either Marx or Adam Smith predicted.[61]

Lukács and the Theory of Reification

Bernstein and Lenin present us with two different versions of what might be called the positive moment of mediation: an identification of the structures that will actively promote socialism. Bernstein emphasizes the *gegenwartige* (everyday) work of the Social Democratic party as motivated by a Kantian ethical ideal, in principle accessible to all persons of goodwill. Lenin promotes the revolutionary activity of the vanguard party as mediator both of theory and practice and between intellectuals and the working class. Neither systematically discusses the negative moment of mediation: how capitalist institutions reproduce themselves and block positive change.[62] It is never quite clear for Bernstein what blocks positive change other than a sort of ignorance and lack of ethics on the part of rulers. For Lenin, blockage is reducible simply to class interests and a state monopoly on violence.

The work of Lukács and Gramsci, for our purposes at least, can best be understood as an attempt to theorize negative mediation. Subsequent Marxist theorists of culture and communication can be read as choosing either Lukács's account of negative mediation as reification or Gramsci's account of it as hegemony.

It is impossible to make sense of Lukács's notion of reification without considering the element of positive mediation in his own career. It would be an interesting study to collect the discourses in which Marxists describe their conversion to Marxism. Lukács's account in the autobiographical sketch and interviews in *Record of a Life* is quite revealing. Lukács approached Marxism from an ethical and religious standpoint. It is significant that Lukács was probably the first significant thinker to revive interest in the work of the Danish existentialist Søren Kierkegaard, who was equally preoccupied with the need for a "leap of faith."

The Kierkegaardian archetype of Abraham and Isaac seems to resonate throughout Lukács's career. He describes his preoccupation with what is perhaps the foundational issue of politics: "How is it possible to act unethically and yet rightly?" He cites Hebbel's play about Judith where Judith—before she goes out to murder the oppressor of her people—says to God: "If you place a sin between me and my deed, who am I to quarrel with You about it, and to escape what you impose?"[63] Lukács's own life was enacted in the narrative form of Abraham and Isaac: Ordered by God (in this case,

History or Totality) to murder his son, Abraham obeyed only to have Isaac
saved at the last minute through divine intervention. Brecht, as Hannah
Arendt writes, raised this ethical issue to the level of an aesthetic ideal:
"The dramatic conflict . . . is always the same: Those who, compelled by
compassion, set out to change the world cannot afford to be good."[64] This
sort of narrative reaches its greatest extreme in the attempt to come to
terms with the legacy of Stalin and Mao. What is the maximum amount of
murder that is justifiable in developing the productive forces for Socialist
"primitive accumulation" (Stalin) or to root out the last vestiges of traditional ideology (Mao)?

Such thought-processes—an "inner balancing of accounts," as Lukács
puts it—made it possible for Lukács to join the party. The analogy to religious conversion appears in another statement:

> For the point about communism is that it is a little like the saying, *qui mange
> du pape en meurt.* You cannot just sample Marxism. Either you must be con-
> verted to it—and I know that is no easy matter, since it cost me 12 years
> before I took the decisive step—or else it is perfectly possible to view the
> world from a left-wing bourgeois perspective.[65]

This statement makes evident the nuclear contradiction we have observed
in Marxism all along: How can a perception of the truths of structure lead
to an acceptance of the need for struggle? What sort of *rhetoric* makes it
possible to make the "decisive step"? Does the process of rhetorical mediation work differently for intellectuals and for the masses?

Paradoxically (perhaps), the process of mediation seems to work in a
more mythic and religious fashion for intellectuals than for the masses. The
perception of social and psychological fragmentation and the promise of
wholeness serve as powerful enticements for commitment to Marxism.
(One could say that the current assault by Rorty and others on the possibility
of wholeness serves as a defense mechanism against the moral excesses a
vision of wholeness often leads to. The inability to talk about a middle ground
is equally symptomatic of the disease of twentieth-century intellectuals.)

Intellectuals of a certain type respond instinctively to fragmentation.
Lukács, like the young Hegel and the young Marx, seems to have begun his
career with a negative comparison between his lifeworld and that of ancient Greece. Ancient Greece was an integrated and organic civilization
that produced the great epic poems of Homer. Increasing fragmentation—
the tragic fissure between ought and is, subject and object, individual and
community—is the story of Western culture since Greece. Capitalism has
only accelerated the process.

Lukács sought to enlarge Marx's account of commodity fetishism as an
explanation of social fragmentation: "How far is commodity exchange to-

gether with its structural consequences able to influence the *total* outer and inner life of society?"[66] This process of influence is summarized under the heading of "reification":

> The act (or result of the act) of transforming human properties, relations and actions into properties, relations and actions of man-produced things which have become independent (and which are imagined as originally independent) of man and guide his life. Also transformation of human beings into thing-like beings which do not behave in a human way but according to the laws of the thing-world.[67]

Commodity exchange influences human life in several ways: The drive for capitalist accumulation leads to increasing fragmentation of the work-process itself; rational-legal rules of conduct displace older personal loyalties; both the private and public spheres are rationalized and bureaucratized; rationality itself becomes instrumental rationality, the logic of efficient adaptation of means to ends.

One does not, of course, need to be a Marxist to make these observations about capitalist society. They were made before Lukács by figures as different politically as Disraeli and Weber. What makes Lukács's indictment explicitly Marxist is that he does not see the "thingification" of human relations as an inevitable product of human nature or history. Nor does he see it possible that religious faith or unifying public rhetoric could limit the effects of reification.

Lukács would find such arguments infected themselves by the process of commodity production, for commodity production has influenced even (and perhaps, especially) the highest philosophical products of the capitalist era. Lukács later characterized his early work on ideology as an attempt "to demonstrate that the most subtle intellectuals' reactions of philosophy to the world arise in the last analysis from the appropriate generalization of the primary life-reactions to the realm of economics."[68] The classic instance of such work is his reading of Kantian philosophy. Kant's argument that the "thing in itself" is never fully knowable is a projection of the experience of the middle classes under capitalism. Kant's critical philosophy finds its ultimate limit in the universal rationality to which middle-class rationality aspired, but it cannot escape those limits. Kant's theory of knowledge projects

> the tendency of the middle classes to understand our relationship to external objects (and consequently our *knowledge* of those objects) in static and contemplative fashion. It is as though our primary relationship to the things of the outside world were not one of making or use, but rather that of a motionless gaze, in a moment of time suspended, across a gap which is subsequently impossible for thought to bridge.[69]

The middle classes are simply unaware of their own historical conditions of existence in capitalism as a system. Kant's own quest for autonomy of the will ironically is imposed heteronomously by capitalism.

The concept of reification was to prove profoundly useful for a variety of reasons. First, it provided an advance over the simple notion of ideology as a product of conspiracy or of false consciousness. False speech now becomes explainable as a failure of vision or a lack of wholeness. One's position within the social and temporal totality accounts for irrationality. The reason why this is an advance is that it allows arguments to be made without impugning the goodwill of one's opponents and that it provides a closer theoretical fit with the actual behavior of people under capitalism. Capitalists do not always know exactly what they are doing. Workers are not always deeply in false consciousness.

Second, the concept explains why the position of the proletariat is uniquely privileged epistemologically. Only the proletariat approaches the world from the standpoint of production; it makes things directly and is in a better position to understand the malleable quality of cultural and political systems. Although Lukács never says this directly, he seems to restore a craftlike element to the production of philosophy. It appears as if philosophers do not so much discover the world as make it—under conditions not of their own choosing. An intellectual thus has some characteristics of the worker. When the proletariat and intellectuals are brought together under the auspices of the vanguard party, they are able to create a world in which thought and action are unified. The party anticipates a world in which reification will disappear. Human relationship to the world becomes one of self-conscious activity.

Third, the concept of reification provides a justification for the vanguard party itself. The party exists to *anticipate* a fully realized class consciousness.[70] The guilty Marxist conscience is relieved by understanding that workers and intellectuals need each other to compensate for each others' "occupational psychoses." The worker intuits the importance of work in constructing the human world but does not have the leisure to develop that insight. The intellectual, educated by philosophy and by the development of the productive forces to understand the role of the human mind in constructing reality, tends to underestimate practical activity. The party, besides being the most useful way to promote revolution, also provides a communicative space where the blindspots of workers and intellectuals are mutually corrected.

Finally, the concept of reification restores the heritage of German philosophy to Marxism, which had been in danger of being reduced to vulgar materialism. Lukács makes it possible for Marxist philosophy to speak to the rest of the intellectual community—illustrated, perhaps, by Lukács's significance to figures as diverse as Thomas Mann (in the character of

Naphta in *The Magic Mountain*) and Martin Heidegger (who may have written *Being and Time* in part as a response to *History and Class Consciousness*).[71]

By enhancing the credibility of Marxist philosophy, Lukács also provided more *work* for committed intellectuals. His literary studies did the same thing. He persuaded several generations of critics that narrative is a way for cultures to work out key problems in the social and economic order. Perhaps the most influential example is Lucien Goldmann's profound reading of Jansenism's "tragic vision" as a coping mechanism for a particular class that had missed its chance at power and was caught between the nobility and the crown.[72] A more recent use is Fred Pfeil's reading of postmodernism. Performers such as Laurie Anderson, the Talking Heads, and even David Letterman appeal to the life situation of a particular class, the professional-managerial class whose ascendancy may be blocked and that feels itself superior to—yet constrained by—the ruling class.[73]

Lukács's defense of the great tradition of European realism continues the ethical thrust of his vision of wholeness in a way that seems not to have been retained in contemporary uses of Lukács. The reason for the greatness of a Balzac or Tolstoy is that he is able to help us know the social totality. Proletarian fiction, of the sort advocated by the guardians of Socialist realism, fails to give us knowledge because it cannot represent adequately the actions and aspirations of the ruling class.[74] Modernist fiction fails to give us any knowledge at all, because it gives up the possibility of knowing the reality of social life—an abdication of responsibility fully explainable, of course, by the problematic status of artists under late capitalism. The later Lukács, for whom one is tempted to coin the term "Marxist neoconservative," defines one major role for the party as preserving the precious heritage of Western culture, a heritage capitalism is bent on destroying.[75]

Whatever its other achievements, Lukács's work is an effective rhetoric for restoring the privileged status of intellectual and artistic expression—even under conditions of Leninist discipline. It makes possible a vision of the Communist utopia in artistic, creative terms rather than mere material abundance. It justifies the narrative quality of Marxism as an epic poem about cultural reconciliation and the end of a fragmented, reified world. Finally, and perhaps most important, it justifies critical cultural work as a way of solving the problem of negative mediation.

The fundamental contradiction of Lukács's cultural theory lies, not surprisingly, in his sense of rhetoric and audience. The working class cannot speak for itself. Intellectuals cannot become members of the party without a religious conversion. Becoming a Marxist requires a total break with the past, but, as Lenin realized, Marxists are damaged goods just like everyone else who has lived through capitalism. A complete acceptance of the dominance of reification can lead to cultural elitism, a Marxism that appeals only to those few artists and intellectuals who can speak from the standpoint of totality. Lukács's focus on negative mediation left him with the party alone as the guarantor of the hope of positive mediation. "Western Marxism," unable to achieve Lukács's Kierkegaardian leap of faith, would need to look elsewhere for strategic thinking about revolution.

Gramsci, Hegemony, and the Promise of Democracy

No term from the Marxist tradition retains as much currency among academic leftists as "hegemony." Here is a characteristic, recent use of the term: "Gramsci's theory of hegemony is helpful here because it considers power relations not only within such 'coercive' state apparatuses as government, law, and judiciary, but also within such 'consensual' civil institutions as the family, the church, cultural and political associations, and institutions of popular entertainment."[76] This article, an otherwise interesting analysis of American television and the youth rebellion of the 1960s, concludes that subversive forces were contained and defused by liberal pluralism: "The face of hegemonic power and authority was rendered invisible by the reconstruction of American society as a plurality of different perspectives and points of view. The face of hegemonic authority was further rendered invisible by the shifting and retooling of institutions associated with coercive state apparatuses to incorporate dissident social formations."[77]

The problem with this use of Gramsci is that it focuses on a moment of negative mediation in Gramsci rather than on a positive one. As M. S. Piccirillo has argued so persuasively, most "radical" criticism of popular culture rests on denying the validity of experience and thus emphasizes only the negative moment of hegemony.[78] What Gramsci intended as a political solution to the "crisis of Marxism" posed by the failure of revolution in the West has instead become an all-purpose term that celebrates the "discursive power" of elites. I explore the reasons for the degeneration of Gramsci's concept further in Chapter 4. My purpose here—and the concern of this chapter—is to describe the concept of hegemony as a solution to the problem of mediation.

The most significant recent account of Gramsci's theory of hegemony is that of Laclau and Mouffe. Using a different vocabulary than the one I have proposed in this chapter, they nonetheless locate the crisis of fin-de-siècle Marxism within the structure-struggle opposition I have described:

> Marxism finally lost its innocence at that time. Insofar as the paradigmatic sequence of its categories was subjected to the "structural pressure" of increasingly atypical situations, it became ever more difficult to reduce social relations to structural moments internal to those categories.[79]

Laclau and Mouffe go on to analyze how various theorists—Kautsky, Luxemburg, Bernstein, Sorel, Lenin, and, finally, Gramsci—solve this problem. The construction of Orthodox Marxism is based on an appeal to an *argument from appearance* and an *argument from contingency*. In the first argument, "everything presenting itself as different can be reduced to identity" as an artifice of concealment ("Nationalism is a screen which hides the interests of the bourgeoisie") or as a necessary form of the manifestation of an underlying essence ("The Liberal State is a necessary political form of capitalism"). In the argument from contingency, those social categories or sectors (women, for instance) not reducible to class forces are branded contingent in relationship to the real movement of History.[80]

Leninism appears to have retained the arguments from appearance and contingency as part of its broader social analysis while developing the theory of the party as a way of breaking the tyranny of History. "Revisionists" such as Adler and Bernstein use an emphasis on politics and Kantian ethics to construct a "transcendental subject" of history who is now an ethical subject rather than a class subject. Laclau and Mouffe write:

> In Bernstein's analysis of political mediation as constitutive of class unity, a barely perceptible ambiguity has slipped through to vitiate his entire theoretical construction. The ambiguity is this: if the working class appears increasingly divided in the economic sphere, and if its unity is autonomously constructed at the political level, in what sense is this political unity a *class* unity? ... The class character of the unification between the political and economic is not produced in either of the two spheres, and the arguments remain suspended in a void.[81]

Another revisionist response, Sorel's appeal to myth, has the same problem. Why does a mythically reconstituted subject have to be a class subject? Sorelian influence on fascism appears to confirm this point.[82]

One does not have to reject class-based analysis and politics entirely in order to accept elements of Laclau and Mouffe's analysis. Their argument rests finally on a disappointed quest for absolute certainty that leads to a radical cleavage between Discourse and Reality. Still, their analysis of Gramsci's politics is perfectly congenial with the line of reasoning I have presented thus far in this chapter.

I believe, on the one hand, it is essential to present the notion of hegemony as a form of political strategy. Russian Social Democrats initially used the term to refer to the leadership role that the working class (and its party) would take in promoting revolution. The party leads the forces of change (including non-working-class elements such as the peasantry). In Russia, and in other "backward" nations, it takes on the hegemonic role normally assigned to the bourgeois class. This notion of hegemony as leadership solves the crisis of Marxism by retaining some element of historical inevitability while allowing for elements of contingency (the party fills the vacuum resulting from a weak bourgeoisie).

Gramsci, on the other hand, develops a completely different view of hegemony. It rests, first, on a redefinition of the concept of "ideology" in more holistic terms than those of classical Marxism or Leninism. Gramsci emphasizes institutional and cultural aspects of ideology. Laclau and Mouffe rewrite the Gramscian view of ideology in contemporary terms as "an organic or relational whole, embodied in institutions and apparatuses, which welds together a historical bloc around a number of basic articulatory principles."[83] For Laclau and Mouffe's "articulatory principles" we might substitute a "rhetoric," or "communicative praxis."

Gramsci's first insight was to recognize that the Revolution in the West would not occur through a war of movement, or frontal attack, as in Czarist Russia. Rather, it would occur through a war of position, or trench warfare, in which intellectuals would play a different role than in Lenin's vanguard party.[84] Gramsci's *Prison Notebooks* center on the problem of the political function of intellectuals. All people have a philosophic instinct, but this instinct is better developed among intellectuals than others. The problem with intellectuals, however, as Gramsci writes, is that they know but do not always understand and, in particular, do not always feel.[85] In contrast, "the popular element 'feels' but does not always know or understand." Intellectuals are defined rather broadly as all those who have "an organizational function in the wide sense."[86] (One wonders here, of course, if the constraints of prison censorship may not have conferred greater significance to Gramsci's choice of the term "intellectuals" than was intended.)

Intellectuals may be divided into two groups: organic intellectuals, who are needed by any new class seeking to develop a new social order; and traditional intellectuals, who are tied to an earlier historical period. Both groups of intellectuals help construct a cultural-social unity ("hegemony") that forms the basis of a "historic bloc." This last term represents Gramsci's other major contribution to Marxism. History, for Gramsci, is a succession of historic blocs created by political praxis and not merely a succession of modes of production. Gramsci's celebration of 1917 as the "revolt against *Capital*" captures the voluntaristic aspects of his Marxism very well.[87] A historic bloc represents a unification of various groups with differing interests who have nonetheless come to social-cultural unity under the leadership of the party. The party thus has a cultural-communicative function, an organizational principle (democratic pluralism), and thus an anticipatory function, though not in the sense of Lukács's anticipated class consciousness. For Gramsci, hegemony is the theory of overcoming alienation, while for Lenin it is merely a theory of domination.[88]

The process of creating a new social-cultural unity is mediated by the party as the "Modern Prince." It takes the place of "the divinity or the categorical imperative."[89] The actual living of democracy within the party serves as a starting point for the extension of democracy outward into the whole society.

In recent cultural theory that invokes Gramsci, the role of the "Modern Prince" has atrophied. In keeping with Romantic definitions of culture and literature, advanced cultural critics focus almost exclusively on popular and "high" culture texts, with a view to deciphering the power relations and emancipatory potential encoded in them. Anything that deals with power is "political"—a definition that seems to rule out the "real" types of politics Gramsci was interested in.

Even those who use hegemony to discuss actual political institutions and texts tend to focus on the hegemonic role of traditional intellectuals. They focus on the way in which dominant classes "maintain their place not only through acts of coercion, but also through symbolic action which renews and recreates the social order."[90] This focus, even though it was intended to eliminate the mechanistic aspect of the classical Marxist view of ideology, may tend to make hegemony seem, as Todd Gitlin (whose followers seem not to have read closely) writes, like "a sort of immutable fog that has settled over the whole public life of capitalist societies."[91]

To better use Gramsci's notion of hegemony, it is helpful to establish a continuum of domination. Let's assume for a moment that a particular group holds power. It may be "big" businessmen, or men in general, or the white race. They do not hold power for any "legitimate" reason; in fact, they probably hold power because of past injustices. Life would be better if they did not hold power, at least for the oppressed. How do they retain power, even when an objective observer can see both the injustice of the situation and substantial opportunities for the oppressed group (workers, women, blacks) to revolt?

First, the ruling group may employ coercion or the threat of coercion to exact compliance. This strategy has short-term benefits but long-term problems, because it requires constant vigilance and because the ruled group may not produce what the ruling group needs from it as effectively under conditions of constant monitoring.

Second, the ruling group may exert rigid control over the information possessed by the ruled group or may even actively promote a "false consciousness" among the ruled group through institutions that it actively controls. The situation of a Southern textile-mill worker, circa 1920, would fit this strategy. The worker is entirely dependent on the mill-owner for his or her food and shelter and even for educational and religious needs. Any attempts to bring in outside information are rigorously suppressed. This strategy, of course, has limited value in a society with diverse interest groups (and social-democratic checks on capitalist power) and increased geographical mobility.

Third, the ruling group may exert more subtle control over the "common sense" of a whole people by employing intellectuals to represent the status quo in terms that make it seem inevitable and necessary. Dominant sources of information and of motivational appeals will "naturalize" the social order, sometimes even within remarkably broad limits, but the net result is that the ruled accept the necessity of things as they are. The mobilization of ruling-class funds behind magazines like *The American Spectator,* think tanks like the American Enterprise Institute, and organizations like the National Association of Scholars illustrates one way in which the ideas of the ruling class get to be the "ruling ideas." The policy successes of the Reagan and Bush administrations might lead an observer to think that it has actually been only the *Right* that reads Gramsci. However, because of increased mobility and pluralism, the ruling group cannot control things completely and is as vulnerable to cognitive error and wishful thinking as are other groups. Traditional hegemony may be a web of sorts, but it is still a web, not a wall.

A Gramscian explanation of Reaganism, for instance, is that it helped promote a commonsense view of the "market" as more efficient and moral than "government." Such, even for the Left, has become the key lesson to extract from the fall of communism. The Reaganite defense of the Market, however, occurred through the mobilization of nationalist appeals to military glory. The hegemony of the Right is contradictory precisely at two points: Its delegitimation of "government" can lead to a distrust of even Republican politicians (hence the political failure of George Bush and the rise to popularity of H. Ross Perot); and its rhetoric becomes unstable when the Market leads to the exportation of jobs overseas (hence the appeal of Patrick Buchanan).

The theorizing of the positive moment of hegemony remains limited, probably because of a seemingly congenital negativism among Western leftists since World War II. Gramsci does provide an inspiring defense of the importance of education and of the role of the party as the place where new democratic modes of consciousness can be developed. Gramsci, too, has clarified the sort of things the party must say in building social-cultural unity. The party must build on the moral unity of a social order, expressed in popular forms by representative symbols, myths, and folkloric wisdom, and must guide that moral unity to a new, more sophisticated level. Gramsci, himself of unusually humble origins for a Marxist intellectual, clearly did not believe that capitalism had ruined the wisdom of the people.[92]

Nor had capitalism ruined the heritage of Western culture. Gramsci regarded Marxism as the most recent synthesis of Western tradition, presupposing "the Renaissance and the Reformation, German idealism and the

French Revolution, Calvinism and English classical economics, secular liberalism and this historicism which is at the root of the whole modern conception of life."[93] As Paul Piccone writes, Gramsci saw Marxism as a way to work out "the practical means to destroy the last and most advanced forms of internal social divisions and thus achieve mankind's emancipation."[94] Thus, the principle of legitimacy for Gramscian communicative praxis is the same as that of liberalism: the narrative of human evolution through learning to cooperate. There is, then, more continuity, perhaps, between the hegemony of traditional and organic intellectuals than recent accounts might suggest.

It is unfortunate, however, that the actual moment when hegemony becomes counter-hegemonic is undertheorized in Gramsci. Gramsci seems to realize, contrary to Marx, that the revolution cannot simply draw its "poetry from the future," but it is unclear what specifically will "spark" a decisive change in popular consciousness. Gramsci uses the intriguing term "catharsis" to describe such a decisive change in popular consciousness. The transformation that occurs, "catharsis," occurs when the perception of "structure" changes from "an external force which crushes man, assimilates him to itself and makes him passive" to a perception of "freedom."[95]

Paradoxically, then, Marxism's emphasis on the way in which economic structures limit the possibility for exercising moral virtues seems to give way to the rhetorical need to personalize impersonal structure in a hated group or person. It is not at all clear how central the notion of catharsis is to Gramsci's work or if his notion bears some similarity, say, to Frantz Fanon's ideas about the therapeutic quality of violence by oppressed groups.[96] What is important for our purposes is that Gramsci, mainly because he was removed from opportunities for popular struggle, was unable to theorize systematically (either in an abstract or a concrete way) how moments of counter-hegemony are made. This problem is the moment of nuclear contradiction in Gramscian theory, at least as it has been appropriated in recent years. How can an authentic democratic pluralism be founded other than on an initial moment of *exclusion:* hatred for the ruling group(s)? How can pluralism itself be built without a temporary dictatorship of the proletariat? Laclau and Mouffe's program for a post-Marxist radical democratic politics rejects the idea of a fundamental antagonism based on class and instead substitutes "a polyphony of voices, each of which constructs its own irreducible discursive identity."[97] Not only is this position easily caricatured by the Right (consider the "political correctness" campaign); it also authorizes a fragmentation that jeopardizes the achievements of social democracy. It is ironic that Gramsci, who was deeply optimistic about the possibility of transforming popular consciousness and who was also committed to the concept of the vanguard party, should have found his greatest influence among cultural critics who are fixated on the most tawdry products of the capitalist culture industry and among political theorists who reject any form of party organization.

Gramsci's Marxism solves the problem of mediation created by classical Marxism with an emphasis on praxis and creative activity. "Knowing is never a passive reflection of the given but an act creating the mediations necessary to direct life."[98] One of those necessary mediations is the art of rhetoric, an art whose traditions are most compatible with Gramsci's version of Marxism.[99]

Conclusion

My purpose in this chapter has been to analyze the problem of mediation in twentieth-century Marxism. The gap between structure and struggle presents a moment for theorizing both negative and positive mediation. Key contradictions in a theory of mediation are usually revealed when the theory's account of audience/public is examined closely.

Bernstein theorized mediation positively through the agency of the Social-Democratic party and the ethical subject. The latter mediation seems to undercut the possibility of theorizing adequately the process of negative mediation, the way in which the ruling class blocks change. Lenin theorized mediation positively through the concept of the vanguard party, but emphasized the negative effects of capitalism on the public capacity for political deliberation. This emphasis had destructive political consequences from which it is difficult to imagine Marxism ever recovering. Lukács's theory of reification provided a thorough account of mediation in negative terms but reinforced the destructive Leninist view of human agency. Gramsci seems to have provided a more complete account of mediation, including both positive and negative poles, but was unable to develop the theory completely.

In the next three chapters, I examine in more detail the subsequent fate of Lukács's theory of reification and of Gramsci's theory of hegemony, as the successes and failures of both communism and social democracy influenced Marxist analysis of communication and culture. Marcuse and Habermas take the moment of negative mediation represented by Lukács and develop philosophical strategies for preserving liberatory possibilities. Marcuse will find his moment of positive mediation in art, while Habermas will find it in a theory of communication free from domination. Williams will take up the Gramscian celebration of popular consciousness and develop a theory of culture as mediation.

✻ 3 ✻

Marcuse's Disappearing Audience

ONE OF THE STRANGER MOMENTS in the political career of Jimmy Carter was his famous "malaise" speech of the summer of 1979. In that speech, Carter condemned the electorate for their self-centeredness and un-willingness to rally around the Carter administration's plan to solve the energy crisis. Carter's argument was influenced by his media guru Patrick Caddell's reading of Christopher Lasch's best-selling *The Culture of Narcissism: American Life in an Age of Diminishing Expectations.*

Lasch, a Socialist intellectual historian at the University of Rochester, argued that "late capitalism" has actually changed the personality structure of its subjects. Since late capitalism is characterized less by the need to instill an ethic of hard work in its subjects than a need to promote mass consumerism and an accompanying emphasis on "impression management," the result is a new character disorder, "the narcissistic personality." Lasch proceeded to illustrate his argument with diatribes against popular psychology, television, and even feminism and ended it with a somewhat halfhearted hope for a Socialist revolution to help matters.[1]

Although it is unclear if Carter ever read Lasch's book, Lasch himself was invited to Camp David to participate in discussions of the American malaise.[2] If the 1980 election returns were any indication, the American public seems not to have taken the pessimism of Carter, Caddell, and Lasch terribly seriously, much less the indictment that the American public, rather than the Carter administration, was responsible for the lack of direction in American politics.

That moment of "malaise" is interesting for our purposes because it represented a brief entry into conventional politics of the somewhat arcane cultural theory of the Frankfurt School—the major influence on Lasch's book.[3] The political figure who replaced Jimmy Carter, Ronald Reagan, seemed to the American intelligentsia almost a fulfillment of Lasch's and the Frankfurt School's predictions about the course of politics under late capitalism. For here was a president, woefully ignorant about details, who raised the use of the mass media, especially television, to new heights of "manipulation."

As I argued in Chapter 2, the heritage of Marxist theorizing about culture and communication is divided among four key moments: Bernsteinian revisionism, Leninism, the Lukácsian notion of reification, and the Gramscian notion of hegemony. The Frankfurt School represents what might be called the reification of reification, an indictment of capitalism so extreme that it eliminates any hope for large-scale social change. From a rhetorical standpoint, the Frankfurt School also represents an exaltation of the dialectic at the expense of any rhetorical possibilities. In this chapter, I focus on Herbert Marcuse as a representative of the Frankfurt School's position.[4] In an interesting coincidence, Herbert Marcuse, the last surviving member of the Frankfurt School, died during the summer of malaise. It is not difficult to imagine his response to the presidency of Ronald Reagan, the man who as governor of California had proclaimed Marcuse unfit to teach.

Given the reduction of philosophy to an essentially private occupation, the appearance of Herbert Marcuse's name in the mass media and in the discourse of the student Left in the 1960s came as a dramatic reversal of traditional role expectations for philosophers. Labeled by *Time* magazine as the "guru of the New Left," dismissed by American Maoists as a "CIA stooge," condemned by guardians of orthodoxy such as Pope Paul VI and *Pravda,* and, more seriously, threatened with death by the Minutemen, Marcuse's career became a confirmation of his thesis that our one-dimensional society turns all liberating speech into a commodity.[5]

Although the influence of Marcuse upon the New Left has been greatly exaggerated, and although his powerful articulation of the Frankfurt School's theories of culture and communication is less in vogue now, after the remarkable explosion of Marxist theoretical practice since the 1960s, his works remain an important resource for constructing a critical theory of rhetoric. For Marcuse, the historical memory of audiences under state socialism and under advanced capitalism was in danger of being erased by the functional language of technology, positivist philosophy, and bureaucracy. It has been insufficiently acknowledged that Marcuse is preeminently a philosopher of *communication,* a philosopher whose dissenting vision of the truth centers on an ideal form of human speech. In this chapter, I analyze Marcuse's philosophy of communication as it emerges through his discussion of dialectic, his criticism of contemporary positivist notions of language, and his analysis of contemporary rhetoric. In the final part of this chapter, I examine his theory of aesthetics and discuss its limitations from a rhetorical standpoint. Marcuse resolves the mediation problem in Marxism by emphasizing the importance of philosophy and art in preserving the memory of happiness—a memory that serves as a basis for radical political action.

Marcuse's Dialectic

Contemporary rhetorical theory may simply be gloss on Aristotle's observation that rhetoric is a counterpart *(antistrophos)* of dialectic. Before I outline Marcuse's specific contributions to the theory of dialectic, it is necessary to review the history of the term.

According to Aristotle, dialectic was invented by Zeno of Elea as a means of refuting an opponent's position by elaborating the contradictions in which that position is involved.[6] For Socrates, dialectic was a means of evaluating definitions through a process of questions and answers. Thus, the activity of defining *(dialegein)* was dependent upon the activity of discussing *(dialegesthai)*. In addition to being a means of unmasking sophistic self-deception, dialectic was used by Plato as a means of classifying relationships between general and specific concepts, for example, the connection of all things with the Forms and with the Form of the Good. Aristotle distinguished between the realm of the dialectical and the realm of the apodictic. In dialectic, the premises of arguments were those of the experts in the relevant fields (just as in rhetoric the premises were those of the popular audience of the time). In apodictic speech, knowledge was based on true or primary premises. The Stoics emphasized apodictic speech, thus turning dialectic into formal logic that remained divorced from ethics and rhetoric for centuries.

In the modern era, Kant developed a transcendental dialectic that sought to expose the illusion of using categories and principles of understanding that lie beyond the bounds of possible experience. Hegel changed the concept of dialectic to the logic of the Whole of reality. He understood dialectic as the tendency of a notion to pass over into its own negation as the result of conflict between its inherent contradictory aspects. Although Hegel described the dialectic of history as the embodiment of Spirit (Geist), Marx turned that dialectic "on its head" by applying its logic to the relationship between the development of productive forces and class struggle.[7]

Although the relationship of dialectic to rhetoric has seldom been discussed by writers in the tradition of Plato, Kant, Hegel, and Marx, both notions of communication came under attack with the rise of modern science. As W. S. Howell writes, the theory of communication which emerges in the eighteenth century is characterized by a rejection of reasoning on the basis of abstract value premises and by a new emphasis upon factual data.[8] As I argued in Chapter 1, Marx himself, in many ways the great inheritor of the tradition of classical political philosophy and its quest for the best regime, was the victim of a fascination with modern science and its emphasis on perfectly transparent communication. The reductionist form of dialectic that survived in orthodox Marxism-Leninism stemmed from this aspect of Marx and Engels's work.

However, in a curious sort of return of the repressed, contemporary work in the human sciences seems to be characterized by a conflict between a sophisticated neo-Marxism seeking to return to classical notions of dialectic, and a new rhetoric (whether symbolic interactionist or poststructuralist) seeking to return to a pre-Platonic notion of communication. The new rhetoricians, at least in their most extreme poststructuralist moments, seem willing to reject the possibility of truth or the possibility of the best regime in the name of an anarchic freeplay of the imagination. This split between the Marxist dialectic and the new rhetoric is part of the larger alienation of Western culture that occurs with the rise of capitalism. A few recent writers, such as MacIntyre and Beiner, reject this dichotomy and propose a rejuvenation of the Aristotelian notions of political judgment and virtue. Neither the poststructuralists nor the neo-neo-Aristotelians, however, seem willing to identify specific institutional barriers to the enactment of good speech and the creation of the best regime. If Marcuse can be faulted, as we shall see, for slighting the rhetorical implications of his notion of dialectic, his work does provide a clear sense of what liberatory rhetorical practice must fight against in our current historical conjuncture.

For Marcuse, dialectic, in the Platonic sense, is the true method of philosophy. Knowledge is to be found not by observation of natural phenomena, but by communicating with others: "The truth of being is discovered and preserved by human speech *(logos, legein)*. Human speech is essentially talking with another about something; only in discussion *(durchreden)* with one another can it fulfill its discovery and preservation function."[9] Dialectic is thus a method rather than a set of substantive, unchanging philosophic positions. Marcuse's own commentaries on Plato, Hegel, and Freud work to separate those philosophers' particular contributions to dialectical method from the inadequacies of their metaphysical commitments. Thus, one may retain the truth of Plato's or Hegel's dialectic without committing oneself to the theory of Forms or of the Absolute Spirit. Despite the fact that the inherent historical limitations of their times led Plato and Hegel to endorse repressive political systems, it is possible to recover liberating implications from their works. At a time when many feminists and other people on the Left seem willing to reject the heritage of Western culture in the name of a revolutionary leap into the void, Marcuse's example is even more meaningful than it was in the 1960s.

As Marcuse notes, his aim is not to revive Hegelian thought but rather to revive those aspects of human freedom that are manifest in the Hegelian dialectic.[10] Much like Heidegger's discussion of Sophocles, Marcuse's aim is to find the center of a philosophical work, to judge what humanity is according to the work, and to relate that meaning of "humanity" to the exigencies of the contemporary historical situation. Plato, Hegel, Marx, and Freud are therefore important to Marcuse not so much for their particular philosophical systems as for their common use of dialectic to attack the prevailing conceptions of their times, whether in rhetoric, epistemology, economics, or psychology. All true dialectic has the function

> to break down the self-assurance and self-containment of common sense, to
> undermine the sinister confidence in the power and language of facts, to

demonstrate that unfreedom is so much at the core of things that the development of their internal contradictions leads necessarily to qualitative change: the explosion or catastrophe of the established state of affairs.[11]

Marcuse develops his defense of dialectical logic in Chapter Five of *One-Dimensional Man,* "Negative Thinking: The Defeated Logic of Protest." Like McKeon, Marcuse traces modern philosophical methods back to their classical sources, yet with a different focus. In Marcuse's interpretation of Plato, for instance, dialectic is the ability to distinguish the true from the false. *Logos* (reason) comes from *legein* (to speak). An understanding of the truth comes from discussion rather than through empirical observation, because the material things of this world are merely transitory phenomena. As Ernst Bloch writes, "That which is cannot be true."[12] Socrates appears destructive from the standpoint of the polis because he refuses to accept the truth of established reality: "The search for the correct definition, for the 'concept' of virtue, justice, piety, and knowledge becomes a subversive understanding, for the concept intends a new *polis.*"[13] Once one attains an erotic, philosophical understanding of the Good, as Socrates did, one will never view the world of immediate experience in quite the same way. What I discussed in Chapter 2 as the problem of mediation in Marxism gets worked through in Marcuse's work as a sort of erotic, aesthetic intuition of the Good—a Platonic view of philosophy that seems, in principle, to devalue the contingent world of rhetoric.

Marcuse, however, is unable to accept Plato's linking of dialectic to the theory of Forms. Plato was incapable of thinking beyond the horizon of the Greek world and grasping the historical character of being.[14] Only in Hegel's work did a historical view of the dialectic become possible.[15] Hegel articulated fully the implications of Plato's later dialogues *(Philebus, Sophist, Theaetetus):* "Every being is in a state of division, ambiguity, and movement, while it is in existential relation with other beings, in order to build a new unity of being with some other being."[16] Hegel added to the Platonic dialectic by grounding it in considerations of consciousness and labor. For Hegel and for Marx after him, "the objects of labor are not dead things but living embodiments of the subject's essence, so that in dealing with these objects, man is actually dealing with man."[17]

Marcuse's comparison of the modern operationalist philosophy of grammar with previous philosophy illustrates the rhetorical significance of the notion of embodiment of the subject's essence. For the operationalist, a thing is what it does, or, rather, a substance is defined by the operations that must be performed for that substance to exist. In fact, concepts that cannot be defined in terms of operations are to be discarded. Marcuse describes how the "science" of human relations dealt with the statement of a worker, "Wages are too low," as cited in the well-known Hawthorne

Works management study. This statement was "operationalized" as "B's present earnings, due to his wife's illness, are insufficient to meet his current obligations." To retain the original statement would imply that B's complaint cannot be relieved on a purely individual basis. Such an implication would require admitting the existence of a universal or group interest that "wage-earners" have (that is, B is a member of a class).[18]

In the Hawthorne Works example, operational sociology and psychology at least appear to be attempting to better subhuman conditions. Marcuse describes another case in which "empirical" social scientists decided to "judge the extent to which an election is an effective expression of the democratic process." The objective criteria by which these social scientists made this judgment included: "a democratic election requires both parties to engage in a balance of efforts to maintain established voting blocs, to recruit independent voters, and to gain converts from the opposition parties."[19] Such an operationalizing of democracy is a model of undialectical thought. History is purged from the definition (the question, "Why are there only two parties?" may not be asked), leaving a mere acceptance of the status quo of American democracy.

A dialectical view of language and philosophic method leads to the conclusion that logic cannot be a purely formal concept. Categories and forms of thought cannot be separated from the substance of thought. Language and being are not separable, either. True language, like true being, can only be understood within the context of historical change and spiritual development. The reification of language and behavior into operationalized abstractions by analytic philosophy and by contemporary social science are the results of a denial of history and spirit.

A truly dialectical paradigm for analysis of language would demand "its development in a multi-dimensional universe, where any expressed meaning partakes of several interrelated, overlapping, and antagonistic 'systems.'" There are three primary levels of experience to which a given meaning may stand in relation:

(a) to an individual project, i.e., the specific communication (a newspaper article, a speech) made at a specific occasion for a specific purpose; (b) to an established supra-individual system of ideas, values, and objectives of which the individual project partakes; (c) to a particular society which itself integrates different and even conflicting individual and supra-individual projects.[20]

For Marcuse, "real" communication (dialectic as end, rather than method) occurs only through whole areas of misunderstanding and contradiction. Even the best communicative intentions can be negated by historical and natural forces beyond the control or understanding of a person or group.[21]

It is this view of the contradictory elements of communication that led Marcuse to defend (up to a point) extremist tactics by the student Left during the 1960s. An early version of such a defense occurs in a commentary on Hegel in Marcuse's 1938 essay, "On Hedonism":

> Hegel pointed out that general progress comes about in history only through particular interests, for only particular interest can stir the individual to the passion of historical struggle. "The particular interest of passion is therefore inseparable from the activity of the universal; for it is from the particular and determinate and from its negation, that the universal results." . . . The struggle for the higher generality, or form of society, of the future becomes in the present the cause of particular individuals and groups, and this constitutes the tragic situation of world-historical persons. They attack social conditions in which—even if badly—the life of the whole reproduces itself. They fight against a concrete form of reason without empirical proof of the practicability of the future form which they represent. They offend against that which, within limits at least, has proven true. Their rationality necessarily operates within a particular, irrational, explosive form.[22]

This defense of the irrational moment of the spiritual movement toward rationality is accompanied by a discussion of happiness. As I wrote earlier, Marcuse's concept of dialectic requires an erotic/aesthetic intuition of the Good as a foundation. This intuition of the Good can be defined in terms of *happiness:*

> General happiness presupposes knowledge of the true interest: that the social life-process be administered in a manner which brings into harmony the freedom of individuals and the preservation of the whole on the basis of given objective historical and natural conditions. With the development of social antagonisms the connection of happiness with knowledge was obscured.[23]

What Marcuse does (and this is too little recognized still) is found simultaneously a historical materialist epistemology and ethics. The role of philosophy is to serve as the mediator between existing social antagonisms and concrete possibilities for change. Marcuse redefines dialectic in terms of a method that describes the possibilities for a more rational society; he defines existing society in relation to the negation of that society and then describes what tendencies in the given society may lead to its negation. The task of critical, dialectical philosophy is to define a "transcendent project," in which "transcendent" is defined not in relation to the Forms or the Absolute Spirit but in relation to historical possibilities for freedom from economic and political repression. This redefinition of "transcendent" is what makes Marcuse a historical materialist. His linking of the Good and Happiness places him squarely within the classical tradition of Plato and Aristotle. The role of philosophy in the transcendent project is similar to that of Plato. Philosophy must free "thought from its enslavement by the established universe of thought and behavior, [elucidate] the negativity of the

Establishment (its positive aspects are abundantly publicized anyway), and [project] its alternatives."[24]

The Rhetoric of Advanced Industrial Society

The role of the dialectical thinker is to use the power of negative thinking to break through the established universe of discourse. Marcuse's two central works of the 1960s—*One-Dimensional Man* and "Repressive Tolerance"—can be read as a late twentieth-century counterpart to Plato's *Gorgias*. It starts with accepted assumptions about language and communication in philosophy, the social sciences, politics, and the mass media and assaults them in the name of a higher vision of justice.

Marcuse defines the limits of dialectical vision and rational rhetoric clearly in *One-Dimensional Man*. Advanced industrial society has systematically absorbed public protest through a variety of sophisticated rhetorical techniques. His theory may be summarized in the following four observations:

1. Technological development has rendered freedom from repression possible (that is, labor can be reduced, sufficient goods are available to sustain the entire population at an adequate living standard).

2. However, various social factors prevent political activity from eliminating repression. (In classical terms, the relations of production fetter the productive forces. Marcuse, for all his antirhetorical character, was a masterful translator of Marxist concepts into contemporary language.) Marcuse includes among these social factors the following:

> concentration of the national economy on the needs of big corporations, with the government as a stimulating, supporting, and sometimes even controlling force; hitching of this economy to a world-wide system of military alliances, monetary arrangements, technical assistance and development schemes; gradual assimilation of blue-collar and white-collar populations, of leadership types in business and labor, of leisure activities and aspirations in different social classes; fostering of a pre-established harmony between scholarship and the national purpose; invasion of the private household by the togetherness of public opinion; opening of the bedroom to the media of mass communication.

These factors lead to the decline of the public sphere and to a corresponding absence of critical thought. A chief mechanism of the public's decline is the strategy of repressive desublimation, in which selected aspects of sexual behavior—for example, tolerance of premarital sexual intercourse, legalized abortion, and relaxed obscenity laws—are permitted by the state in order to enhance its image as a guarantor of freedom or to displace energies that might be sublimated into political activity.[25]

3. Political activity generates only a simplistic, mimetic form of communication.[26] Besides manipulating sexual fantasies, contemporary mass com-

munication has worked to collapse the public and private spheres. Social-ization of children no longer occurs through the authority of the family but through the mass media and, secondarily, the schools. The individual as such has been replaced by a set of ritual responses manipulated by politi-cians and advertisers. The language of one-dimensional society repeats nouns or adjectives such as "free world," "socialism," and "private enter-prise" with no reflection upon the history or varied meanings of the terms.

4. The tendency to substitute signal responses to language for critical thought is part of a broader tendency toward the "functionalization" of language. There are several rules that Marcuse describes as part of the "language of total administration." As a kind of rhetoric, these rules aim to produce a "happy consciousness—the belief that the real is rational and that the system delivers the goods."[27]

Rule A: *Replace thought with operations.* For example, replace philosophi-cal reflection about democracy with empirical studies of "democracy" opera-tionalized as voter satisfaction with the two-party system.

Rule B: *Eliminate real political tensions by bureaucratic abridgment.* For example, consider what abbreviations such as NATO, USSR, and AFL-CIO leave out: difficult questions (such as why Greece and Turkey are in a *North Atlantic* organization), uncomfortable political realities (abridging "Soviet" and "Socialist" in USSR, and the significance of the merger of the AFL and the CIO as the result of cold-war pressures on the labor movement).[28]

Rule C: *Unite contradictions through paradox.* Expressions such as "clean bomb" and "harmless fallout" are realistic caricatures of a dialectic in which opposites are reconciled in an illusory unity. The fact that it is possible to advertise a "Luxury Fall-Out Shelter" (with TV and a Scrabble board) is but a logical expression of a pluralistic society that can find a place for all opposing views (even the American Nazi party).[29]

Rule D: *Replace persons with functions, while leaving language highly "personalized."* "It is 'your' congressman, 'your' highway, 'your' favorite drugstore, 'your' newspaper," even though all of these are highly standard-ized things or functions.[30] *Time* magazine repeatedly used the inflectional genitive to make individuals appear to be mere appendages of an institu-tion: Virginia's Byrd, U.S. Steel's Blough, Egypt's Nasser.[31] Edward Teller, the "father of the H-bomb," is described as "brush-browed," while von Braun is "bull-shouldered."[32] (*Time* had its revenge on Marcuse in 1968 when it described the philosopher as looking like "Kris Kringle" and printed a photograph of him amiably stroking his cat Freddy. And *Time's* obituary of Marcuse in 1979 rather neatly summed up his life in these words: "Tolerance never repressed him."[33]

Rule E: *Replace concepts with images.* In the world of *Time* the ideas of Herbert Marcuse are less important than his "Kris Kringle" appearance or his love of animals. Images allow the placement of a thing in its proper position in the whole; concepts threaten contradiction and thinking apart from the system. *Time*'s language is a journalistic counterpart of the quest of positivist philosophy and social science to eliminate concepts from rational thought.[34]

Rule F: *Permit radical dissent, but co-opt it through strategic framing.* The *Time* story about Marcuse illustrates how the system incorporates dissent by, in effect, patting it on the head, and then using its existence to confirm how good and tolerant the status quo is. This process was labeled "repressive tolerance" by Marcuse in an essay that was to prove to be his most controversial. It would be useful to review his arguments, because they summarize the key methods and insights of his dialectic.

Marcuse begins his essay by calling tolerance a *practice*—not an abstract political ideal. A dialectical understanding of tolerance locates its historical origins and its contradictory relationship to different levels of social practice. Tolerance has a concrete historical origin in the bourgeois revolution of the seventeenth and eighteenth centuries. Tolerance for the bourgeoisie was not simply an all-encompassing moral ideal—part of the natural rights of all human beings. It also served as an agency for the bourgeoisie to gain power. Tolerance served the cause of political liberty as long as "Men were (potential) individuals who could learn to hear and to see and feel by themselves, to develop their own thoughts, to grasp their own true interests and rights and capabilities, also against established authority and opinion."[35]

If the concept of tolerance originally served to liberate the individual, Marcuse contends that contemporary society has destroyed the individual through "systematic moronization by publicity and propaganda."[36] Tolerance now serves the purpose of providing the illusion that freedom exists in society, while political power remains in the hands of elites.

Both liberation and repression are moments of the "tolerance" concept. Any practice, as we saw earlier, can be absorbed into the purposes of the form of life in which the practice is embedded. The contradictions of radical political practice in one-dimensional society are most evident when thinking about tolerance:

> According to a dialectical proposition it is the whole which determines the truth—not in the sense that the whole is prior or superior to its parts, but in the sense that its structure and function determine every particular condition and relation. Thus, within a repressive society, even progressive movements threaten to turn into their opposite to the degree to which they accept the rules of the game. To take a most controversial case: the exercise of political rights (such as voting, letter-writing to the press, to Senators, etc., protest-demonstrations with an a priori renunciation of counterviolence) in a society of total administration serves to strengthen this administration by testifying to the existence of democratic liberties which, in reality, have changed their content and lost their effectiveness. In such a case, freedom (of opinion, of

assembly, of speech) becomes an instrument for absolving servitude, and yet (and only here the dialectical proposition shows its full intent) the existence and practice of these liberties remain a precondition for the restoration of their original oppositional function, provided that the effort to transcend their (often self-imposed) limitations is intensified.[37]

As I have argued before, it is in the concept of the implied audience and the characterization of the mass audience that the contradictions of Marxist theory are usually found. Marcuse is no exception. Marcuse makes his dialectical argument about tolerance in the company of other academic thinkers—Robert Paul Wolff and Barrington Moore, Jr.—and to a highly educated audience. His most obvious goal is to persuade genteel hand-wringing liberals that tolerance has its limitations. He does not advocate violence himself, but tells his intellectual audience that they have no right to "preach abstention" to those radical minorities who are breaking the tyranny of the established order. He argues that the emergence of a "free and sovereign majority" can come only through the action of "minorities intolerant, militantly intolerant, and disobedient to the rules of behavior which tolerate destruction and oppression."[38] It is unclear, then, what role Marcuse's own discourse has other than that of preaching restraint to liberals. How will Marcuse's own vision of liberation reach the militant, intolerant minorities? How will bourgeois liberties be restored when the time of their necessary suspension is over? A possible avenue of mediation exists insofar as students and leftist intellectuals (in addition to racial minorities and the Third World) displace the proletariat as the agents of historical change, but this leaves, as with Lenin, the vast majority of the public in advanced industrial societies completely ruined by capitalism.

To summarize, then, Marcuse's analysis of the rhetoric (in the Platonic sense) of advanced industrial society yields a powerful vision of an all-powerful system ready to absorb all liberatory possibilities. Marcuse completes the program for analyzing the negative mediation between structure and struggle that was begun by Lukács on reification and Gramsci on the hegemonic role of traditional intellectuals. Before moving on to discuss the moment of positive mediation in Marcuse (already prefigured in our earlier discussion of the erotic and aesthetic aspects of Marcuse's vision of the Good), we need to examine the contradictions of Marcuse's indictment of advanced industrial society in more detail. Recall that I am using "contradiction" here in a simultaneously dialectical and rhetorical sense as key points of ambiguity in an unfolding argument that open the advocate up to strong refutation by an ideological opponent and that help an argument move forward in historical time by providing opportunities for work by other advocates within the same tradition.

A standard argument against Marcuse and other radical social critics is that they lack a sense of judgment and proportion in their criticism. Thus,

Marcuse tends to see "system" where others see "society" and unreasonably and immorally blurs clear distinctions between, say, Brezhnev's Soviet Union and Nixon's United States, or between Virginia and Minnesota. Marcuse also never really understood the liberatory elements of American pragmatism or the anarchist strain in indigenous American radicalism. He simply saw system. As Albert O. Hirschman writes, the Left sometimes unwittingly replicates the Right's futility and perversity arguments by proclaiming that no reform is possible within the existing system.[39] Marcuse's role, then, as media-appointed "guru" of the New Left, was to encourage neglect by radicals of opportunities for real change within the system and, in effect, helped elect Nixon and de Gaulle.

A harsher argument stems from Marcuse's view of students and intellectuals as agents of historical change. Hans-Martin Sass's critique of the "Repressive Tolerance" essay calls Marcuse and the Frankfurt School "the elite circle of egg-heads who feel called upon to revolt our cruel world."[40] Alasdair MacIntyre, no doubt thinking about the passages in Marx's *Eighteenth Brumaire* that I discussed in Chapter 1, condemns Marcuse for believing that "petty-bourgeois bohemia closely allied to the Lumpenproletariat" can become "the potential catalyst of change."[41] MacIntyre argues that traditional Marxism rightly condemned bohemia because its sensibility "effectively cuts it off from the vast mass of mankind, on whom the bohemians are in economic fact parasitic." But Marcuse exalts them because of his inherent elitism and, as MacIntyre puts it later, his desire to invite us to reexperience Stalinism:

> This isolation in values of bohemia is just what Marcuse values, and the problem of communication with, of joint action with the majority does not arise, because the majority are to be objects of benevolent revolutionary concern, not subjects with an autonomous voice of their own.[42]

The proper Marcusean response here is to point out that his analyses are dialectical in that they emphasize the contradictory character of all political analysis and practice, including his own. He condemned the excesses of the student Left forcefully as time went on, and he continued to speak for reasoned political action at great personal risk and cost (something MacIntyre simply does not mention at all).

MacIntyre is right, however, in arguing that Marcuse's assault on the values of the majority creates substantial problems for political communication and joint action. That problem—how to reconcile the need for a rhetorically powerful indictment of the status quo to motivate radical change with the need to reach the majority "damaged" by the status quo—is a problem we have seen in Marx, Engels, Bernstein, Lukács, and Gramsci. It does not necessarily lead to Stalinism—that is a cheap argument—but it does diminish respect for actually existing democratic systems.

Perhaps the fairest (but still harsh) critique of Marcuse comes from Alain Touraine. Touraine lumps together Marcuse, Althusser, Bourdieu, and Foucault under the heading of *critical functionalism*. They see society as "dominated by ideological apparatuses of the State or by omnipresent powers symbolized by Bentham's Panopticon or identified with its mechanisms of reproduction."[43] The result is highly destructive:

> The necessary critique of a declining or corrupted type of social movement ended up arbitrarily in the image of a society without actors. The image of our societies as entirely dominated by systems of control and manipulation is so far from observable fact that it lured many sociologists to replace field studies by doctrinaire interpretations. It transformed itself in some countries into the dominant ideology of a self-destroying intelligentsia.[44]

Earlier dialecticians such as Plato saw the need for bridging the gap between the philosophical vision of the Good and the public. However one interprets the ultimate political meaning of the *Phaedrus* or the *Republic,* it is clear that rhetoric and myth serve such a mediatory function for Plato. Marcuse, however, could only discuss positive mediation in the form of aesthetics. Rhetoric is quite literally the "un-thought" of the tradition with which Marcuse and the Frankfurt School were working.[45]

Marcuse's Aesthetics

By the end of *One-Dimensional Man,* Marcuse allowed Critical Theory to remain in the Weberian "iron cage" that Lukács had built for Western Marxism some years before: "The critical theory of society possesses no concepts which could bridge the gap between the present and its future; holding no promise and showing no success, it remains negative."[46] In defense of Marcuse, one could argue that the functions of philosophical/critical discourse must remain separate from those of political ideology and action. The rejection of "bridging the gap" could serve (oddly enough) as a sort of Straussian binding of intellectual discourse. What critics like MacIntyre have indicted as elitism and exalting of "bohemia" might actually be a humble willingness to let radical groups or "the people" work out the future for themselves.

On the one hand, Marcuse's discussion of art should be considered in the light of the unique function of philosophical discourse to preserve memory and to think about alternative futures. On the other hand, it is probably no accident that the only positive form of mediation Marcuse can find is the faculty of aesthetic judgment. The key points in Marcuse's work on positive mediation and aesthetic judgment are in *Eros and Civilization* and *The Aesthetic Dimension.*

Marcuse's purpose in *Eros and Civilization* is to explore the possibility of a nonrepressive civilization. He argues that a logic of gratification—a way of uniting sensuousness and ideas under the law of form—must be created to combat the logic of technological domination. Marcuse contends that a logic of gratification can be derived from Kant's work on aesthetics, provided that Kant's ahistorical and private notion of practical reason can be replaced with the Marxian-Hegelian dialectic.

Kant's philosophy was based on the antagonism between the subject and the object. This antagonism is reflected in the dichotomies between sensuousness and intellect, desire and cognition, and practical and theoretical reason. Given this antagonism, some way of mediating between the realm of practical reason ("freedom under self-given moral laws for moral ends") and the realm of theoretical reason ("Nature under the laws of causality") must be found.

How does freedom act in nature? Marcuse writes,

> A third "faculty" must mediate between theoretical and practical reason—a faculty that brings about a "transition" from the realm of nature to the realm of freedom and links together the lower and higher faculties, those of desire and knowledge. This third faculty is that of judgment. ... While theoretical reason (understanding) provides the *a priori* principles of cognition, and practical reason those of desire (will), the faculty of judgment mediates between the two by virtue of the feeling of pain and pleasure. Combined with the feeling of pleasure, judgment is aesthetic, and its field of application is art.[47]

Through the imagination the artist is able to generate universally valid principles in sensuous, objective form. Kant calls the two main categories defining art "purposiveness without purpose" and "lawfulness without law." These categories, for Marcuse, embody the essence of a nonrepressive civilization: "The first defines the structure of beauty, the second that of freedom; their common character is gratification in the free play of the released potentialities of man and nature."[48]

Despite Friedrich Schiller's alternative description of Kant's two categories as only processes of the mind, Schiller (the second important influence on Marcuse's aesthetics) develops them into the concept of a new type of civilization. Schiller believes that industrial society destroys the cognitive function of sensuousness. The aesthetic function, however, if developed properly, would work through the basic human play impulse and abolish domination, leaving human beings free both morally and physically. Schiller speaks of the "wound" that civilization has inflicted upon modern man.[49] Schiller argues that art can preserve the possibility or memory of psychic and social wholeness as a means of preparing the populace for liberation. The road to politics must pass through the aesthetic—in this case, historical/political drama.[50] Kant himself had already relegated rhetoric to the status of mere ornament, and Marcuse follows both Kant and Schiller in making artistic expression rather than rhetorical deliberation the most liberating form of human speech. It is but a short step from this assumption to some of the most easily caricatured passages in Marcuse's writings—for example, the encomium to the French student revolt for its insistence that radicals must "pass from realism to surrealism, from Marx to Fourier," and Marcuse's remark that "a socialist society can and ought to be light, pretty, and playful."[51]

There are, of course, problems in appropriating Kant for Marcuse's project. On one hand, Kant's emphasis on an ethics of duty rather than on happiness hardly seems consistent with Marcuse's more classical view. On the other hand, Kant's rejection of rhetoric in the name of democracy and free individual choice (as embodied in the following passage) seems quite consistent with Marcuse's rejection of "the rigged game of patience and persuasion":

> Rhetoric is the art of carrying on a serious business of the understanding as if it were a mere play with ideas. . . . I must admit that a beautiful poem has always given me a pure gratification, while the reading of the best discourse, whether of a Roman orator or of a modern parliamentary speaker or of a preacher, has always been mingled with an unpleasant feeling of disapprobation of a treacherous art which means to move men in important matters like machines to a judgment that must lose all weight for them on quiet reflection. Readiness and accuracy in speaking (which taken together constitute rhetoric) belong to beautiful art, but the art of the orator (ars oratoria), the art of availing oneself of the weaknesses of men for one's own designs (whether these be well meant or even actually good does not matter), is worthy of no respect.[52]

Ronald Beiner has made much of the influence of Kant upon later political philosophy and argues for the replacement of Kant's theory of taste and aesthetic judgment by an Aristotelian theory of rhetoric and political judgment. Beiner links the recovery of rhetoric to the recovery of the public sphere and the republicanism that made that sphere the noblest one for human action. I will return to these themes in Chapter 5, but for now I want to emphasize that Beiner's argument lacks a dialectical sense of the decline of rhetoric. That is, he locates the decline of rhetoric in the arguments of Kant rather than seeing the decline as a complex interrelationship between intellectual argument and social processes of capitalist rationalization. Marcuse, at least, is sensitive to the limitations that the latter impose on liberating speech of all kinds.

Marcuse's last work, *The Aesthetic Dimension*, both expanded his earlier discussions of art and served as a response to revivals of "socialist realism" in radical circles. Marcuse continues to stress the revolutionary potential of art, but "literature can be called revolutionary in a meaningful sense only with reference to itself, as content having become form." There may be more subversive potential in the poetry of Baudelaire or Rimbaud than in Brecht's most radical plays.[53]

The more utopian aspects of *An Essay on Liberation,* however, are gone. The pessimism of the later Freud is invoked against the "'happy conscious-ness' of radical praxis: as if all of that which art invokes could be settled through the class struggle."[54] Marcuse realized that much of the radicalism of the 1960s was not so much a determinate or even indeterminate nega-tion of one-dimensional society but simply another version of the techno-cratic "happy consciousness" that the system will deliver the goods.[55] There are inexorable forces that work against all human achievements:

> Eros and Thanatos assert their own power in and against the class struggle. Clearly, the class struggle is not always "responsible" for the fact that the "lovers do not always remain together." The convergence of fulfillment and death preserves its real power despite all romantic glorification and sociolog-ical explanation. The inexorable human entanglement in nature sustains its own dynamic in the given social relations and creates its own metasocial dimension.[56]

Marcuse thus asserts even more strongly the Freudian-Marxist revisionism of *Eros and Civilization.* Beneath the superstructure of ideology and cul-ture exists a material base of the forces and relations of economic produc-tion, but beneath both base and superstructure lies *nature.*[57] Marcuse thus combines a Freudian idea of memory and sexuality, a Platonic idea of beauty, and a Kantian idea of aesthetic judgment into a mediatory space that somehow stands above both historically determining structures and possibilities for political struggle. This mediation—that rejects mediation in the traditional sense—is finally about remembrance:

> In the aesthetic form ... the terror is called up, called by its name, and made to testify, to denounce itself. It is only a moment of triumph, a moment in the stream of consciousness. But the form has captured it and given it permanence.[58]

Marcuse's aesthetic contains that paradox of the interaction between speaker *expression* and audience *impression* that Susanne K. Langer has explored in *Feeling and Form.* Marcuse's aesthetics reveals an inability to link expression with impression in a way that leaves the community, rather than the self, dominant in discourse. Marcuse separates aesthetic quality both from the world of the work of art and from the world of the viewer—and from the traditions in which both stand.[59] It appears that the only ex-planation of the way in which a work acts upon an audience is the rather mechanistic notion of drives. A good work of art appeals to the human "drive to form" and to the pleasurable and happy memories of the mimetic play of childhood. A bad work of "art," such as a Hitler speech, appeals to the baser needs for imitation and ritual that hearken one back to unpleasant childhood experiences.

It could be argued, as Christopher Lasch and Gerald Graff have, that Marcuse's view of art contradicts his social analysis. Marcuse, like the self-reflexive writers Barth, Barthelme, and Coover and like the followers of Derrida, allows art to be relegated to a marginal, elite sphere of one-dimensional society. Lasch writes,

> The divorce between art and experience, the exaltation of Eros as a separate sphere, are precisely the conditions that underlie repressive desublimation, which frees erotic expression from censorship only when it has banished Eros to the margin of existence and deprived it of its transforming power. Defense of the "autonomy of art" no longer serves any critical purpose. . . . It is not the "aesthetic dimension" we need to recover but the sense of reality itself.[60]

Marcuse's concept of repressive desublimation should thus have enabled him to criticize cultural radicalism more effectively.

Although Lasch and Graff are persuasive in their attacks on antirealism, they perpetuate the existence of the problematic that gave us antirealism in the first place: the assumption that *literature* can serve as a significant mediation between structure and struggle. Perhaps a revival of realism would be a good thing for the arts, but it is by no means clear what it would do for politics. Lasch and Graff are as romantic as Marcuse.

Romantic conceptions of the social function of art inevitably accompany condemnations of the mass media as manipulative and propagandistic. There is no role for rhetoric as a dialogue in which speaker and audience cooperate in the creation of argumentative forms. On one hand, the concept of *rhetorical* form, as Thomas B. Farrell has written, views the participation of the audience as central.[61] On the other hand, the tradition of rhetoric recognizes that *leadership* is a necessary thing in political life and thus allows "common sense" (Gadamer's *sensus communis*) to be *attributed* to audiences.

The somewhat Lukácsian idea of attributed consciousness preserves the Hegelian insight that historical progress often occurs through the action of radical minorities who seek to make their partial vision universal. Attributed consciousness sets up an implicit requirement that revolutionary vision of a radical minority will be judged later in terms of the *sensus communis* and the opportunities for audience participation it creates. Such was the original meaning of the "dictatorship of the proletariat"—the original Roman term clearly denoted "dictatorship" as a temporary thing.

Conclusion

The view of rhetoric I have offered in this chapter begins by seizing and reframing those dialectical moments, or knots, identified throughout the history of Marxism. Rhetorical form provides unity between theory and practice *and* structure and struggle. The audience is *delighted* by the prospect of synthesis, by the identification of speaker and hearer and of fact and value—to the extent that the rhetor presents an explanation of the rhetorical situation he or she *teaches*. Through emotional proof, the rhetor *moves* the will of the audience. Rhetorical form thus bridges thought and action through the application of the three traditional offices of rhetoric: *delectare, docere,* and *movere.*[62]

These terms from Ciceronian rhetoric indicate a conception of the human psyche as a dialectical unity of will, intellect, and a capacity for delight and wonder. This unity, however, can only be created by skilled rhetors committed to a vision of a rational society. Marcuse's critique of the manipulative quality of mass communication (like Plato's critique of rhetoric) might be read more charitably as a critique of the media's lack of reflexivity. A rhetoric that reflects upon its own contradictions and yet embraces them, seeking to be clear, to delight, and to move, may help to solve that modern disorder of the will that the history of Marcuse's "radical minorities" in the New Left so painfully illustrates. True rhetoric would allow human beings to escape the numbing experience of their own powerlessness without lapsing into senseless violence. Democracy as *responsiveness,* the provision of opportunities for communication, is the literal opposite of violence.[63] This more optimistic, Gramscian view of democracy and of popular audiences is at the root of another major contributor to Marxist work on communication, Raymond Williams—whose legacy is the focus of my next chapter.

❧ 4 ❧

Time, Place, and Cultural Studies:
The Legacy of Raymond Williams

BEGINNING IN THE EARLY 1980S, the American study of communication began to be influenced by radical perspectives from abroad. Mass communication as an academic practice in the United States prior to the 1980s had been conducted largely as "administrative research." Its priorities were set by government and industry, even as it masqueraded as value-free social science, and it focused narrowly on questions of media effects. Its institutional location was in schools of journalism and in traditional behavioral science departments.

There were alternative, "critical" researchers such as Herbert Schiller and Dallas Smythe, but they had relatively little influence. Their research was largely classical Marxist, even Leninist, in spirit, centering on the institutional analysis of multinational media corporations.[1] Their work was vulnerable to the charge of having a simplistic notion of mediation. Audiences were simply commodities to be bought and sold. The actual *meaning* of messages these audiences consumed was neglected. Since this charge was equally applicable to the administrative tradition, and since a new generation of media researchers had grown up deriving many of their cultural "meanings" from popular music and television, there was both a scientific and experiential basis for the shift to something called "British cultural studies."[2]

In an introductory essay about British cultural studies, John Fiske defines it as "concerned with the generation and circulation of meanings in industrial societies." The term "cultural" is "neither aesthetic nor humanist in emphasis, but political."[3] In a move characteristic of British cultural studies, politics means the study of a society divided along various lines: race, sex, class, age. Class is "no longer the primary axis of division. . . . Gender may now have replaced it as the most significant producer of social difference."[4] Social relations among the complex network of groups must be understood

> in terms of social power, in terms of a structure of domination and subordination that is never static but is always the site of contestation and struggle.

> Social power is the power to get one's class or group interest served by the social structure as a whole, and social struggle—or in traditional Marxist terms, the class struggle—is the contestation of this power by the subordinate. In the domain of culture, this contestation takes the form of the struggle for meaning, in which the dominant classes attempt to "naturalize" the meanings that serve their interests into the "common sense" of the society as a whole, whereas subordinate classes resist this process in various ways, and to varying degrees, and try to make meanings that serve their interests.[5]

The study of discourse is central to British cultural studies, because it demonstrates how subjects are constructed through cultural processes. Although the focus on the construction of the subject may seem to continue the Western Marxist theme of reification, the intention of British cultural studies is quite the opposite. As Fiske concludes:

> Despite the cultural pessimism of the Frankfurt School, despite the power of ideology to reproduce itself in its subjects, despite the hegemonic force of the dominant classes, the people still manage to make their own meanings and to construct their own culture within, and often against, that which the industry provides for them. Cultural studies aims to understand and encourage this cultural democracy at work.[6]

The optimism of cultural studies and its emphasis on cultural democracy strike a Gramscian note against the pessimism of Marcuse and the Frankfurt School. Cultural studies' semiotic vocabulary, its contention that class has disappeared as the central social cleavage in advanced industrial society, and its celebration of the popular represent significant departures from the Marxist tradition.

My purpose in this chapter is to interrogate the problematic of cultural studies from a rhetorical standpoint. My argument is that cultural studies as an academic practice has developed into a perversely postmodern version of the Marcusean "happy consciousness": "The System will always deliver you pleasure if you decode strenuously enough." Further, it operates within a conception of discourse that is utterly useless for political practice.

What was, paradoxically, the most valuable aspect of the cultural studies tradition, the work of Raymond Williams, seems to have not traveled across the Atlantic at all. The term *British* cultural studies would no doubt have sounded strange to Raymond Williams, who had good reason for doubting the legitimacy of something called "Britain." He also would have recognized a familiar move in the assumption that rude provincials—many of them midwestern, many of them holding on to the quaint idea that students might need to learn public speaking—needed to be enlightened by more cosmopolitan folk.

It is this last ideological move that highlights the contradictions of contemporary cultural studies. Cultural studies is not so much British as Euro-international. It no longer has any continuity with place or with *authentic* subcultures whose lifeworld has been invaded with increasing ferocity since the 1960s. It jettisons the concept of class in favor either of a celebration of postmodernist jouissance or a pseudo-Gramscian notion of hegemony. Unlike the Frankfurt School, which was never able to understand American culture, British cultural studies borrows its European pedigree (one should never underestimate the willingness of an American academic to swoon in the presence of an English accent) to celebrate the anarchic proliferation of "lifestyle choices" in the United States.

Raymond Williams's cultural materialism, which never departed from the Marxist tradition, is partially responsible for the drift of cultural studies away from class analysis. His insistence on rejecting the notion of base and superstructure and his optimistic assessment of popular consciousness represent points of contradiction that later theorists would try to resolve. I will proceed by explicating some key aspects of Williams's work, discuss the significance of the "second wave" importation of French theory into cultural studies, and conclude by identifying ways in which Williams's legacy might be appropriated in the United States.

Williams's work is at first so deceptively simple and personal that it is easy to miss the fact that he has resolved a number of the problems with the Marxist theory of mediation.[7] His own communicative practice, as a worker in adult education and as a novelist, addressed at least a broader implied audience than any other Western Marxist except, perhaps, E. P. Thompson. He saw more clearly than any other Marxist the way Marxism itself was deeply implicated in the space-binding ideology of capitalism. His own rootedness in place enabled him to understand both "ordinary" working people and the contradictory rhetorical appeal of conservatism to them. He helped preserve and expand the moral dimension of the Marxist critique of capitalism. And he did all this from within a theory of communication and culture.

Perhaps the best summary of Williams's life and of his distinctive intellectual contribution to Marxism was made by Terry Eagleton in his obituary essay. Williams had an unusual "inner balance and resilience" that "came essentially from his class background—indeed . . . the whole of his lifelong political project was secretly nurtured by a formative early experience of working-class solidarity and mutual support which had left him unusually trusting and fearless."[8] Williams "had known what community could be, and would not rest until it was re-created on an international scale."[9] His contribution to the creation of community was the study of words—words not as a flight from an unbearable reality into a pristine realm of the imagination—but words as "condensed social practice, sites of historical struggle, repositories of political wisdom or domination."[10]

I will focus on three moments of Williams's work: his critique of Marx, his use of the concept of "structure of feeling, the method of keywords," and his final great theme of the country and the city.

The Metaphors of Marxism

Williams, more than any other Marxist theorist, has a sense of the contradictory legacy of Marx. Williams's early work, for instance, finds more to praise in Edmund Burke than in Marx.[11] He criticizes Marxism in *The Country and the City* for uncritically celebrating industrialization and urbanization when its main target should have been the division of labor.[12] Yet Williams recognizes that dialectical (though a word he seldom uses) thought cannot be exempted from contradiction. He rarely analyzes the work of Marx and Engels directly, but when he does the results are extremely useful.

Williams notes the pervasiveness of contradiction in the language of *The German Ideology*. This discussion of ideology can be read in a strong, reductionist version or in a weaker version more congenial to Williams's concerns. Marx and Engels's "language of 'reflexes,' 'echoes,' 'phantoms,' and 'sublimates' carries the inescapable implication of a secondary activity, and the implication, it would seem, of 'consciousness' as a secondary activity."[13] If, however, we read this solely against the background of mechanistic materialism, we will lose the rhetorical context of the argument: "This was part of a polemic against the assumption that the whole of human history was determined by ideas, whether human or extra-human in origin: an assumption which complacently and cruelly ignored the long history and present facts of human labour, through which the necessary physical existence and survival of human beings were gained and assured."[14] According to Williams, Marx and Engels's use of a materialist argument against a cruel and complacent idealism was liable to be misread by partisans of that idealism and by later Marxists themselves:

> The counter-emphasis, that human labour is central, necessary, and thus genuinely originating, remains as Marx's major contribution to modern thought. But what can then be seen as happening is a way of formulating this emphasis which, ironically, is in danger of converting human labour—its "material preconditions," "material production," and "material intercourse"—to, in its turn, a specialized and even reified element of human totality.[15]

Another important insight into the contradictions of classical Marxism comes when Williams analyzes "base and superstructure" as metaphor. This metaphor, intended to do the rhetorical work of refuting idealism and the historical division of labor on which it rested, ends up installing a categorical division of labor:

> As a polemical point against the general assumption that all human history was directed by autonomous ideas the metaphor retains its relevance and

force. But as a method, or as a set of tools for analysis, it leads us in wholly wrong directions.[16]

Metaphors have consequences, Williams tells us, but his characteristically close attention to figurative structures has more to do with the classical rhetorical tradition's interest in how figures enhance or impede the success of argument than with the poststructuralist assumption that we can never escape figurative language.

Williams, too, traces a middle course in the evaluation of art. He of course rejects the Stalinist view that art is a weapon of the class struggle, but he does not leap either to the Frankfurt School's elevation of art above history or to the more recent rejection of aesthetic judgment under the guise of the democratization of the canon.

> It is not necessary to deny the effectively permanent value, within traceable historical and cultural continuities, of certain works of art from many historical periods, to be able to argue that *judgment* also, in its real terms of accessibility, recognition, understanding of theme and form, comparison, is itself an historical process.[17]

The problem with the Stalinist view was that its reflection theory was not materialist enough. It suppressed the equally material social processes involved in the making of artworks. The replacement of reflection with the more Hegelian "mediation" does not necessarily help, either. The metaphor is that of reconciliation between enemies or strangers—extended in idealism to reconciliation between opposites in a totality. The contradictions implied by use of the metaphor are that it does not advance on the reflection theory if it is used simply to indicate how cultural forms—such as "the media"—distort reality in ideological ways. As a positive term—for instance, when the Frankfurt School uses it to discuss the role of consciousness as "a positive process in social reality"—it may, however, tend to reinforce the division of labor between base and superstructure. The only solution is to "see language and signification as indissoluble elements of the material social process itself, involved all the time both in production and reproduction."[18]

Finally, a truly historical analysis of culture must reject the static quality of Marx and Engels's assertion that any society's dominant ideas are no more than ideal expressions of dominant material relationships. In a passage that uses one of Williams's most important contributions to cultural theory, he writes,

> In any developed social order, we can expect to find not only interaction but also actual conflict between residual, dominant, and emergent forms of thought, in general as well as in special areas. Moreover there is often conflict, related to this complexity, between different versions of the dominant, which is by no means always a ready translation of a singular material class interest.[19]

Williams thus resolves the transparency problem in Marxism I identified in Chapter 1. He does so by retaining Marx's insistence that history is patterned and that this pattern is bound up with human labor and struggles over the surplus produced by human labor. Williams analyzes culture with the same methods the later Marx applied only to political economy. He completes Marx by insisting that culture itself is a product of human labor.

Structures of Feeling

Raymond Williams's death in 1988 called forth a number of moving obituaries, many of them from former students. The obituary written by Terry Eagleton captures an important theme in the reception of Williams's work in the United Kingdom and in the United States: "He refused to be distracted by the wilder flights of Althusserian or post-structuralist theory and was still there, ready and waiting for us, when some of us younger theorists, sadder and wiser, finally reemerged from one or two cul-de-sacs to rejoin him where we had left off."[20] Eagleton had—what seems now like long ago—assaulted Williams's focus on lived experience as rooted in a "Romantic populism" that went hand in hand with "political gradualism": "a deep-seated trust in the capacity of individuals to create 'new meanings and values' *now.*"[21]

  If Williams was dismissed by the second wave of cultural studies as hopelessly old hat, a theoretical equivalent of Hugh Gaitskell, his residual identification with working-class traditions—and the concept of class itself—led to his dismissal by the American importers of cultural studies. Lawrence Grossberg, for instance, sees Williams as contaminated by epistemological traces of the classical Marxist problematic.[22] There is perhaps some connection between this dismissing of Williams and the fact that American work in cultural studies simply ignores Williams altogether. He is virtually never cited in *Critical Studies in Mass Communication*. His articulation of "cultural materialism" is acknowledged as a key influence on the American literary-critical movement "the New Historicism," but this movement has largely jettisoned class analysis in a way that Williams hardly would have approved.

  Grossberg identifies Williams's position as different from either classical Marxism or the Frankfurt School.

> The relationship between cultural texts and social reality is always mediated by processes and structures of signification. Thus, texts reveal their social significance, not on the surface of images and representations, but rather, in the complex ways that they produce, transform, and shape meaning-structures.[23]

Where Grossberg, in a sense, goes wrong is in highlighting the term "mediation," which, for Williams at least, perpetuates the assumption that "culture" and "society" are somehow separate things that need to be introduced to one another and reconciled.

Although in practice Williams concentrated far more on imaginative literature than on strictly strategic discourse, his way of looking at culture and communication was profoundly dialectical. He refused both the idealist version of culture as above society and the materialist version of culture as a reflection of society. Instead, "the theory of culture" is "the study of relationships between elements in a whole way of life."[24] The most interesting aspect of studying culture is the most difficult to achieve: a "felt sense of the quality of life at a particular place and time: a sense of the ways in which the particular activities combined into a way of thinking and living."[25] This intangible thing—the "particular sense of life," the "particular community of experience"—is termed a "structure of feeling."

The centrality of the arts in making sense of culture is that the arts of a given period reveal that

> in the only examples we have of recorded communication that outlives its bearers, the actual living sense, the deep community that makes the communication possible, is naturally drawn upon.[26]

Williams illustrates this insight through a close analysis of the communicative forms and stories of the 1840s in England. The analysis reveals a complex interaction between a dominant view of society and its lived experience in literature.

By the 1840s, the dominant social character looked something like this:

> There is the belief in the value of work, and this is seen in relation to individual effort, with a strong attachment to success gained in these terms. A class society is assumed, but social position is increasingly defined by actual status rather than by birth. The poor are seen as the victims of their own failings, and it is strongly held that the best among them will climb out of their class. A punitive Poor Law is necessary in order to stimulate effort. . . . Thrift, sobriety, and piety are the principal virtues, and the family is their central institution. The sanctity of marriage is absolute, and adultery and fornication are unpardonable.[27]

These arguments and "values" make up the "dominant social character" of the period—an abstract of the dominant group, in this case the industrial and commercial middle class. There existed at the same time, however, a residual aristocratic social character insisting that

> birth mattered more than money; that work was not the sole social value and that civilization involved play; that sobriety and chastity, at least in young men, were not cardinal virtues but might even be a sign of meanness or dullness.[28]

These values served as a positive resource in the debate over the Poor Law and over the Reform Bills. The working class itself began to formulate alternative ideals and arguments, in the form of Chartism. England came out of the 1840s better because of the interaction of the three social characters: "the aristocratic ideals tempering the harshness of middle-class ideals at their worst; working-class ideals entering into a fruitful and decisive combination with middle-class ideals at their best."[29]

These arguments are readily accessible from historical documents and subject to verification and revision as is any historical interpretation. What Williams adds to this account is a focus on the structure of feeling that emerges from studying the arts, particularly fiction, of the period. What emerges from the fiction of the 1840s is a recurring theme of loss of fortune, a "pervasive atmosphere of instability and debt."[30] Characters who faced loss of fortune were inevitably rescued by the magical plot device of the unexpected legacy or by emigration to one of the outposts of the Empire. All resolutions, moreover, were conceived as individual ones—"there could be no general solution to the social problems of the time."[31] This latter fact reveals in part a kind of "false consciousness, designed to prevent any substantial recognition; part again a deep desire, as yet uncharted, to move beyond this."[32]

Williams provides at this point a sort of methodological summary.

> We do not now compare the art with the society; we compare both with the whole complex of human actions and feelings. We find some art expressing feelings which the society, in its general character, could not express. They may also be the simple record of omissions: the nourishment or attempted nourishment of human needs not satisfied.[33]

Williams's analysis of the 1840s has some remarkable features, especially in the light of previous Marxist theorizing about culture. First, it keeps the moments of the "ideal" and the "material" in balance. Second, it does not assume that there was one correct consciousness that one must have had at the time. Yes, elements of the middle-class social character were simple evasions or rationalizations—false consciousness, if you will. Unlike later theorists of cultural studies, Williams recognizes that there is a reality that sometimes gets distorted. However (at least during this one particular time in English history), the interaction of different classes had some positive benefits for everyone. To use the jargon that would later infest cultural studies (even in Williams's own work), the political is "relatively autonomous," with class being a determining factor only in the "last instance."

There is a standard account of the evolution of cultural studies in which Williams is seen as caught up in a dilemma: He collapses the difference between encoding and decoding by "simultaneously collapsing the social into the cultural."[34] Grossberg uses Williams's analysis of television to illustrate the concept of structure of feeling. Television was marketed as a privately owned commodity for the home, and this fact is manifest in the structure of feeling, "mobile privatization." The fact that television seemed to capture best an enclosed internal atmosphere, local interpersonal conflict, and private feeling was "homologous" with the interests of capitalism itself. The problem, as Grossberg writes, is that when forms of struggle cease to have any necessary correspondence to class position, this kind of analysis breaks down. The solution? Focus on mediation through appropriation—that is, see how subcultures decode dominant meanings in aberrant ways and incorporate them into their own "style." Subcultures are thus "free" to make what they will of communicative processes but ultimately not free because their very subjectivity is "produced" within "specific discursive formations."[35]

Now the discursive turn in cultural studies has its own problems; I will focus here instead on Grossberg's simple misinterpretation of Williams. First, he does not discuss the work in which Williams first develops the concept of structure of feeling. Second, he turns the concept of structure of feeling into the classical notion of ideology per se as the reflection of class relations and class interests. But the actual passage from Williams does no such thing. The discussion Grossberg quotes is not so much of television as of television *drama,* which carried on the structure of feeling present in naturalistic drama—the sense of being enclosed in a room dealing with private conflict. Williams points out that there were other ways of doing television drama than the strictly naturalistic one. There is no way to interpret Williams accurately and conclude that the structure of feeling is in fact a mediation at all. It is simply one moment in the social and cultural fabric, and it coexists with others different in kind.[36]

I believe that this sort of misinterpretation of Williams has political implications, for it is the very rejection of lived experience itself that is an integral part of the "structure of feeling" of Grossberg's academic generation. Suspended between older ethnic and working-class cultures and an increasingly technocratic dominant culture, the academic postmodernists salve their status anxiety with a celebration of deviance and an exaltation of style above politics. That this structure of feeling is, finally, bound up with something that looks very much like an *aristocratic* social character would probably be no surprise to Williams.

Keywords

If Williams can, finally, escape the charge of being insufficiently radical and of being too Marxist in the classical, reductionist sense, he is vulnerable to charges of privileging the cultural over the political. Or, to be more precise, Williams privileged the fictional moment of the cultural over other elements. Now to say this is to blame a writer for not doing everything. Williams could only work where he was planted, in the thick of the academic practice of literary studies in the United Kingdom. Yet it is finally paradoxical that Williams, who did so much to open up the academic field of literary studies to diverse forms of expression by criticizing the ideological uses of the keyword "literature," should end up leaving other aspects of literature—notably political rhetoric—quite neglected. It was this element of Williams's legacy that Eagleton, students of cultural studies, and proponents of the New Historicism would take up rather uncritically. Like Marx, Williams opened himself up to the charge of celebrating that which he was criticizing.

In *The Long Revolution,* for instance, Williams carefully analyzes the development of new *forms* of communication in the technical sense. He gives us a brilliant reading of the structure of feeling in the popular and serious fiction of the period. But when it comes to defining the social characters of the middle class, the aristocracy, and the working class, he does not examine the specific arguments and symbols used in the political negotiation of the meanings of work, morality, and politics. He does not analyze election campaigns or parliamentary debates.

A similar phenomenon occurs in what is perhaps Williams's greatest work—*The Country and the City.* He traces the theme of the country and the city through pastoral literature, countryhouse poems, and novels from the classical period through the twentieth century. Williams makes good sense not only of a variety of seemingly disparate literary forms but of capitalism and actually existing socialism themselves. He unites his own personal experience—that sense of connection and decency that Williams learned from Orwell (but that seems so much more authentic in Williams)—with what can only be called an ethical defense of socialism and a brief for Green politics *avant-la-lettre.* Yet he does not analyze parliamentary debates over the Corn Laws, agricultural subsidies, or entry into the Common Market. One would not learn from *The Country and the City* about the status of farmers as protected "special interests" in the United Kingdom, Japan, and the United States. Williams's discussion of the possibility of overcoming the division of labor—and, by extension, the division of country and city—would be enhanced by more specifically rhetorical analysis. The trick is to figure out how to retain a sense of the autonomy of the political without giving up a sensitivity to class and a moral revulsion against capitalism.

Just as Eagleton criticized Williams for being a political gradualist, conservatives could criticize Williams for neglecting that social change in Britain had occurred through the hegemony of the Tories: the legalization of trade unions, universal suffrage, and the welfare state itself.[37] If this is true, then it was not the "dominant" or the "emergent" culture that was progressive, but the "residual" one. There is an answer to this question—one that leaves the political and rhetorical more or less autonomous within larger structures determined by the logic of capitalist development. The

Empire was both a rhetorical and economic solution to the political contradictions of nineteenth-century Britain. Still, it is understandable that Williams, in neglecting the analysis of the actual political discourse of the day, is open to the charge of political gradualism on the one hand and the charge of distorting the achievements of the Tories on the other. We still do not have an analysis of the rhetoric of Disraeli. It is a sign of the destructive legacy of romanticism that if such a study were accepted by a major university press today it would still most likely have to focus on his novels more than his speeches.

This is not to say that Williams did not or could not engage in political analysis. His analysis of keywords in the miners' strike of 1984–85 illustrates the sort of criticism I have been advocating throughout this book. He traces both the history and political contradictions of four key terms in the strike: management, economic, community, and law-and-order.[38]

First, "management" made the decision to close certain pits. The very term "management" evades an issue that is at the heart of the Socialist project: "the claim of workers to control not only the wages and conditions, but also the very nature of their work." To deny this claim "is to subordinate a whole class of men and women to the will of others."[39]

In order to realize the claim of the workers, Socialist politics chose the path of nationalization. The result was a confusion between the term "management" and the older terms "master" and "employer." "The claim of the workers to control their own production was set aside, under the presumed priorities of a wider national interest and the most efficient possible production."[40] The Coal Board itself came not to represent the public interest so much as the interests of a technical elite responsive only to the state. Both the unions and the concept of a public sector ceased to be a bulwark against the idea that labor exists at the arbitrary disposal of others. This central principle of Socialist democracy needs to be understood and presented not as a special interest but as

> the general interest: that people working hard at their jobs should not be exposed to these arbitrary operations of capital and the state, disguised as the "right to manage." In a period of very powerful multinational capital, moving its millions under various flags of convenience, and in a period also of rapid and often arbitrary takeover and merger by financial groups of all kinds, virtually everyone is exposed or will be exposed to what the miners have suffered.[41]

The nomadic character of multinational capitalism is also reflected in the reduction of the term "economic" to isolated accounting of short-term costs. The decision to close the pits did not take into account long-term energy policy. Nor could it find a way to calculate the amount "of social capital and continuing social investment in the old coalfields which, under the 'right to manage,' it is proposed to make obsolete. Houses, schools, hospitals, and roads in these areas compose a huge economic investment which dwarfs the trading calculations of any particular industry."[42] Any claims to move beyond Marx into the "discursive" seem to neglect the fact that the Marxist indictment of the uses to which capital puts the term "economic" is if anything more valid now than in the nineteenth century. "Community" is always the victim of the "economic" under capitalism, even if, as in this case, the threat to real, local communities is conducted in the name of an appeal to the interest of the nation-state as a whole.

Finally, the appeal to "order" can be turned around by Socialists. For it is the state itself, responsive only to Market calculations, that is now subversive of national order, "hauling coal, for example, across the seven seas to undercut, reduce or close down any supposedly national industry."[43]

It is not clear, of course, how this analysis of the contradictions of the key terms in the miners' strike will result in an effective alternative to Thatcher's policy. Williams hints that a rhetoric based on appeals to national unity and order might work. As Stuart Hall argues, the success of Thatcherism owed much to its ability to combine the new doctrines of the free market with the traditional emphases of organic Toryism: the old values of "tradition, Englishness, respectability, patriarchalism, family, and nation." It thus became a kind of "authoritarian populism."[44]

What is neglected in Hall's analysis, like Williams's, is the problematic of *persuasion*. They do not consider either the idea that the Left itself might bear some responsibility for the public's lack of trust in its ability to lead or the fact that no major leftist figure possessed the charisma (however contradictory) of Thatcher. Another way of looking at the specific strategy of the Right is to see it as exploiting middle-class fears of falling back into the old working class—whose politics had become at best a kind of quaint curiosity and at worst the recklessness of an Arthur Scargill. It effectively stole class resentment against the old Tory aristocracy and its general lack of competence in management. The fact that Angry Young Men like Kingsley Amis, Labourites through the 1960s, could become rabid Thatcherites by the 1980s suggests that it was the appeal of meritocratic politics and the simultaneous lure and blockage of upward mobility that was a major source of Thatcher's appeal. The recent election victory of Prime Minister John Major reinforces my claim that the lingering ideology of meritocracy combined with fear of Labour incompetence is a better explanation than "authoritarian populism" for the success of Thatcherism.

Yet, attempts by Williams and by Socialists generally to make sense of reactionary politics embrace the contradictions of Marxism itself. The Socialist tradition simply has too few resources for understanding *from within* how ruling classes reproduce themselves. It is unlikely, for instance, that E. P. Thompson, author of the classic *The Making of the English*

Working Class, will ever write "The Making of the English Bourgeois Class." As I noted in the Introduction, John Steinbeck's *The Grapes of Wrath* falls short of being a great novel because it could not represent the structure of feeling of the big growers in the story. Raymond Williams's own ventures into fiction fail precisely at the point where they would need to represent the social totality. *Border Country* works on its own terms as a memory of a working-class boyhood, but when the last novel of the trilogy, *The Fight for Manod,* ventures into the realm of the state and multinational corporations as they parcel out the future of Wales, Williams fails.[45] As he said in a discussion of his fiction in *Politics and Letters,* "I still mainly know the actual ruling class only by reading about it."[46]

The problem faced by any contemporary strategic account of Socialist politics is how to balance out the claims of regional and national community with those of what once was called "proletarian internationalism." Perhaps one of the reasons Williams has been so little used in the United States is that his more explicitly political writings are so tied both to Welsh and British politics. By the end of his life, Williams had become increasingly devoted to Welsh nationalism in the context of the larger emerging European order. It is unclear, given the destructiveness of the nationalisms unleashed after the fall of communism, whether the promise of Williams's reflections on his own nationalism can bear fruit:

> Suddenly England, bourgeois England, wasn't my point of reference any more. I was a Welsh European, and both levels felt different. . . . Through the intricacies of the politics, and they are very intricate indeed, I want the Welsh people—still a radical and cultured people—to defeat, override, or bypass bourgeois England; the alternatives follow from the intricacies. That connects, for me, with the sense in my work that I am now necessarily European; that the people to the left and on the left of the French and Italian communist parties, the German and Scandinavian comrades, the communist dissidents from the East like Bahro, are my kind of people; the people I come from and belong to, and my more conscious Welshness is, as I feel it, my way of learning those connections.[47]

Williams helped us see how the contradictions of nationhood and community are deeply bound up with communicative forms. The mass media of communication itself, like the dominant ideology it reinforces, relies on a cultural power to distance, and it at times seems almost impossible to break through this power. In a discussion of the Falklands/Malvinas War, Williams writes:

> The sovereign power to order war operates within the cultural power to distance. General discussion and voting are replaced by television discussion and opinion polls. The modes interact, for the war is fast or is made to appear fast, and there can be no hanging about when the threat is urgent and

the blood is roused. Modern systems, in television and opinion-polling, alone correspond to this induced urgency.[48]

It is important to see that Williams's own rhetoric became more personal, less distant from the reader as the years went by. Consider the power of the following passage, toward the end of *The Country and the City:*

> I have had the luck to thin a wood and watch the cowslips and bluebells and foxgloves come back; to repair and rebuild old drystone walls; to hedge and ditch, after long neglect, and to see from skilled men how the job should be done.[49]

It is the simultaneous sense of place with a fear of losing it forever that animates Williams's socialism. It is different from the class priorities of American environmental politics in that it recognizes the mutual relationship of the country and the people who work in it. What capitalism is about, finally, is "abstracted economic drives" whose priorities in social relations and "criteria of growth and of profit and loss" have changed the country and created the city.

It is a crucial need at this point in the history of socialism to engage the rhetoric of the environmental movement. It is no accident that the most powerful invective in all of Williams's fiction is reserved for the bourgeois ex-Communist and traitor Sir Norman Braose in *Loyalties,* who retreats into a naive environmentalism.[50] However, a major distortion in the history of communism itself had been conducted in the name of "a confidence in the singular values of modernization and civilization."[51] Orthodox communism and orthodox social democracy were both incorporated into the expanding, centralizing logic of capitalism and imperialism. For Williams, the contribution of the Chinese Cultural Revolution was at least to put the question of country and city back on the agenda of socialism. What for many was a historical embarrassment for Marxism—the fact that it was only in the undeveloped, agricultural nations that the Revolution occurred—is turned by Williams into a manifestation of the larger dialectic of country and city. Now it is possible to see more clearly the significance of the historical division of labor:

> The division and opposition of city and country, industry and agriculture, in their modern forms, are the critical culmination of the division and specialization of labor which, though it did not begin with capitalism, was developed under it to an extraordinary and transforming degree. Other forms of the same fundamental division are the separation between mental and material labor, between administration and operation, between politics and social life.[52]

It is an utterly characteristic Williams touch to conclude this observation not with one more bemoaning of the "iron cage" of industrial society but by pointing out that good work is being done to overcome the division of labor:

> The symptoms of this division can be found at every point in what is now our common life: in the idea and practice of social classes; in conventional definitions of work and of education; in the physical distribution of settlements; and in temporal organization of the day, the week, the year, the lifetime. Much of the creative thinking of our time is an attempt to re-examine each of these concepts and practices. It is based on the conviction that the system which generates and is composed by them is intolerable and will not survive. In many areas of this thinking there is not only analytic but programmatic response: on new forms of decision-making, new kinds of education, new definitions and practices of work, new kinds of settlement and land-use.[53]

Only someone who grew up around rural labor can understand, perhaps, how silly the division of labor is, finally, as a cultural principle. For when rural labor is least alienated it has an egalitarianism (across genders, ages, and class) that makes no sense to, say, a college professor who cannot empty his own wastebasket. As Williams writes, "The last recess of the division of labor is this recess within ourselves, where what we want and what we believe we can do seem impassably divided. We can overcome division only by refusing to be divided."[54]

It is, unfortunately, the logic of a certain kind of leftist cultural politics at the end of the twentieth century to affirm division. This affirmation of division—in the form of identity politics—is conducted in the name of a sort of internationalism, a Benetton Left incapable of devotion to a country wall or cowslip. For the cultural Left is as much bound up with the culture of distance as the capitalist media it simultaneously decries and celebrates.

It is no accident that Theory, with a capital T, has become the international lingua franca of the intelligentsia. The more rarified and specialized the language, the more able Theory is to bridge the vast cultural distances still prevailing even in the Western industrialized world. (It is not surprising that a major review of critical communication research uses as an illustrative device a passenger lounge in an international airport or that airports feature so prominently in that great satire of the academic structure of feeling, David Lodge's *Small World*.)[55] The danger for Socialists in the present moment is that they will become like the nomadic capitalism they criticize—traveling easily across national and subcultural boundaries, bearing no allegiance to traditional languages or institutions, and fixated increasingly on power for its own sake. As Williams notes, "The now rampant politics of the Right, which seeks to substitute . . . individually-shaped desires for the difficult practices of common and sharing provision" is made easier by the reduction of radicalism itself to individual desire.[56]

It is this reduction—in the form—of the second wave of cultural studies, to which I now wish to turn.

Constructing Cultural Studies: Two Paradigms

Stuart Hall has written a by-now standard account of the development of cultural studies and its "two paradigms." It began with the work of Richard Hoggart *(The Uses of Literacy),* Raymond Williams *(Culture and Society),* and E. P. Thompson *(The Making of the English Working Class).* What these texts had in common was a "break" with the assumptions of "technological evolutionism, with a reductive and an organizational determinism" that had characterized both orthodox Marxism and social democracy. These texts instead foregrounded "questions of culture, consciousness and experience," and accented agency.[57]

Williams's contribution was an understanding of "culture" as not simply "the best that has been thought and said" but the interrelationship of social *practices* in a particular period. As I referred to earlier, Hall notes that Williams offers a "radical interactionism" against economic determinism: "The distinctions between practices is overcome by seeing them all as variant forms of praxis—of a general human activity and energy."[58] Williams, Hall writes, was of course handicapped by his "isolated position and the impoverished Marxist tradition he had to draw on," but his study of Gramsci and of Goldmann sent him in the right direction. He retained, however, his characteristic stress on "sensuous human activity, as practice": "No mode of production, and therefore no dominant society or order of society, and therefore no dominant culture, in reality exhausts human practice, human energy, human intention."[59]

Williams also was helped by Thompson's criticism that he had neglected elements of struggle and confrontation in the English past. Thompson's emphasis on "classes as relations, popular struggle, and historical forms of consciousness, class cultures in their historical particularity" served as a corrective to Williams's tendency to "absorb conflicts between class cultures into the terms of an extended 'conversation.'"[60] Thompson insisted on using the base-superstructure metaphor in ways that Williams refused and insisted as well in sharply delimiting the realm of the cultural from the moral and the economic. Thompson seems to use "experience" where Williams uses "culture," but both writers have in common a tendency "to read structures of relations in terms of how they are 'lived' and 'experienced.'"[61] Hall summarizes: "The *experiential pull* in this paradigm, and the emphasis on the creative and on historical agency, constitute the two key elements in the *humanism* of the position outlined."[62]

Even by 1992 Hall's use of quotation marks around "lived" and "experienced" and his pejorative use of the term "humanism" seem dated in ways that the statements of Williams and Thompson do not. It was the arrival of structuralism—and particularly the Althusserian detour—that marks the language of Hall's "second paradigm" of cultural studies. Someone still needs to write the intellectual history of this period in Britain, but (despite the very real intellectual achievement for which *New Left Review* can serve as a representative anecdote) it is somewhat plausible to view the second paradigm both as a kind of Oedipal revenge against the good gray fathers and as a mirror image of nomadic capitalism itself. Socialism had to become *Marxism*—and a Euro-international Marxism with a nod to Third World fashions at that. The characteristic denunciation of English (and Welsh and Scottish and Irish) provincialism and (another rhetorical relic of the time) "empiricism" reflected the experience of subjects no longer rooted in any particular "social formation."[63]

In any case, it was putatively greater sophistication of French modes of thought (France standing to Britain in the late 1960s somewhat as Britain was to stand to the United States circa 1984, at least in communication studies) that helped cultural studies move along—not, perhaps, along some sort of evolutionary tramline, but at least as a "rupture."

Hall identifies two specific ways in which structuralism contributed to the development of cultural studies: a renewed focus on the concept of ideology (a term or problematic largely absent from the "culturalist" paradigm), and the productive use of semiotics as a way of rendering the "human sciences of culture" "scientific and rigorous in a thoroughly new way."[64]

It is possible to acknowledge Williams's critique of the "mediation" metaphor and still recognize the existence of an untheorized "space" in classical Marxism that served as a spur to the development of Marxist theory and politics after Marx and Engels. In this book, I have attempted a history of that untheorized space as it moves from Bernstein to Lenin down to the Frankfurt School. It should be clear by now that Williams and Thompson use "culture" and "experience" as ways of filling in the gap in Marxism. It is not quite clear, however, even in Williams, how *language* itself relates to social practice. The immense prestige of structuralist linguistics in the 1960s (everywhere, of course, except within the science of linguistics itself) seemed to promise the solution to the problem of mediation once and for all. It would henceforth be possible to be scientific without being reductionistic, and to study culture without being tainted by the political failures of Thompson's and Williams's generation.

The idea that cultural forms serve to reconcile contradictions is a classic Lévi-Straussian insight. The structuralist turn sees culture as the categories and frameworks in which a society classifies its conditions of existence, especially the relations between the human and natural worlds. These categories and mental frameworks are produced and transformed largely in the same way that language is. They do not reflect or express an underlying reality, but are, in a sense, reality itself: "The causal logic of determinacy was abandoned in favour of a structuralist causality—a logic of arrangement, of internal relations, of articulation of parts within a structure."[65]

This latter move was crucial to the development of the Althusserian notion of ideology as the representation of "the imaginary relation . . . of individuals to the real relations in which they live."[66] As Hall puts it, "'Ideologies' are here being conceptualized, not as the contents and surface forms of ideas, but as the unconscious categories through which conditions are represented and 'lived.'"[67] This is an advance on classical Marxism because it makes politics and culture more than simple reflections of class relations. It also clarifies a problem in Marxist psychology: How are class (and other) subjects *constituted?* Ideology takes on a central role: "The existence of ideology and the hailing or interpellation of individuals as subjects are one and the same thing."[68] Christianity, for instance, constitutes subjects as children of God. The discourse of Christianity makes possible a dual recognition of self as subject to God as Subject. Althusser writes,

> We observe that the structure of all ideology, interpellating individuals as subjects in the name of a Unique and Absolute Subject is *speculary,* i.e., a mirror-structure, and *doubly* speculary: this mirror duplication is constitutive of ideology and ensures its functioning. Which means that all ideology is *centred,* that the Absolute Subject occupies the unique place of the Centre, and interpellates around it the infinity of individuals into subjects in a double mirror-connexion such that it *subjects* the subjects to the Subject, while giving them in the Subject in which each subject can contemplate its own image (present and future) the *guarantee* that this really concerns them and Him.[69]

This sort of writing is such an easy target that it is possible to miss the significance of what Althusser is doing. There is a strong and a weak way to read Althusser's discussion of ideology. In the strong sense, Althusser is a critical functionalist, to use Alain Touraine's term, who seems to see no way out of the seamless web of ideology. The system seems capable of reproducing itself endlessly. From this standpoint, it is possible to see that it is not class per se, but power—endlessly self-reproducing power in both the macro- and microstructures of human and animal life—that is at the heart of ideological analysis. It is thus possible to read Althusser as a kind of "vanishing mediator," a halfway house for leftist intellectuals on the way to Discourse Theory but not quite ready to abandon the working class or, more precisely, Marxism.[70]

But it is possible to read Althusser in a weaker way, one that allows elements of human agency while still acknowledging the fact that we live our lives through language. The problem is that we cannot see this as long as language is conceived as a system of signs *(langue)* rather than as performance *(parole)*. The absolute incomprehension that exists between discourse-theory-influenced scholars of mass communication and rhetoric-influenced scholars stems from this fundamental fact. Consider another way of stating the earlier Althusserian insight into the structure of ideology.

Language is not stable but changing and . . . it is perpetually remade by its speakers, who are themselves remade, both as individuals and communities, in what they say. . . . Our subject is rhetoric, if by that is meant the study of the ways in which character and community—and motive, value, reason, social structure, everything, in short, that makes a culture—are defined and made real in performances of language. Whenever you speak, you define a character for yourself and for at least one other—your audience—and make a community at least between the two of you; and you do this in a language that is of necessity provided to you by others and modified in your use of it. How this complex process works and can work well, is our concern. As the object of art is beauty and of philosophy truth, the object of rhetoric is justice: the constitution of the social world.[71]

Now there are problems with James Boyd White's approach to texts—the neglect of orality and the neglect of class struggle, to name but two—but note how his summary of his approach gives students of "ideology" work to do, acknowledges our inability to get outside of ideology, recognizes that human beings must act under circumstances "not of their own making," and understands the centrality of language in the reproduction of social processes. The differences are that White uses the "problematic" of rhetoric while Althusser uses the structuralist problematic. Only the former, I will argue, preserves the dialectical character of Marxism. The latter will inevitably fracture into two extremes: seeing everything in terms of power (Foucault) or the free decoding of the audience (Fiske and Grossberg).

But before we turn to this final moment in the development of cultural studies, it is useful to compare the style of the two passages compared earlier. Note how Althusser implicitly constructs two audiences: One is "in the know," properly contemptuous of Christianity as a practice and capable of understanding the heavy irony of the technical structuralist language's similarity to technical theological language. (Surely this is intentional? Perhaps not?) The other audience is absent, the uncomprehending reader still caught in the web of ideology. But note how—no matter if ideology is conceived as relatively autonomous—the impulse to continue the stripping-away-the-veils metaphor of classical Marxism is still present. The heavy trope of irony as well as the heavy jargon constitutes an audience of intellectuals rather than workers.

What function could this sort of writing serve? Fredric Jameson has developed the legacy of Lévi-Strauss and Althusser in a productive direction with his analysis of narrative. Narratives, especially the narratives of mass culture, must be seen "not as empty distraction or 'mere' false consciousness, but rather as a transformational work on social and political anxieties and fantasies which must then have some effective presence in the mass cultural text in order subsequently to be 'managed' or repressed."[72]

The "story" of the appropriation of Althusser (down to the narrative closure provided by his murder of his wife) serves as a kind of encoding of social and political anxieties and fantasies of a New Left caught between an Old Left either politically irrelevant or caught up in Stalinism and a working class bought off by social democracy. Appropriating Althusser reenacts the Burke-Paine debate (with Thompson eventually taking the role of Burke in *The Poverty of Theory*) over the French Revolution. It is thus possible to take a form of Oedipal revenge while feeling legitimate in the pursuit of "theoretical practice" now that "ideology" is itself a "material" force. All this while cultivating the hard, masculine image that a rejection of "humanism" entails.

Now this is unfair, of course, but it illustrates the emotivism that a single-minded focus on ideology will lead to. Without some sort of relatively privileged position of observation—whether it be a class position or the party or even just plain old Right Reason—ideological analysis begins to eat up itself.[73] Foucault's role was to set the table for this auto-cannibalism of Theory.

The Descent into Discourse

Lawrence Grossberg's classic essay "Strategies of Marxist Cultural Interpretation" enacts the narrative I just constructed. "Discourse" becomes the mediator for the transition from Marx to Foucault. Grossberg extracts the lesson of Althusser:

> Experience can no longer be seen as something pregiven, outside of particular cultural or textual practices. It is already inherently implicated with structures of power. Power is no longer outside of culture (in the social) but within the very structures of signifying practices themselves. ... It is the cultural practices themselves which define identities for their producers and consumers by inserting them into the fabric of their discursive spaces.[74]

Once again, there are strong and weak versions of this insight. Grossberg sees Hall as preserving some breathing room for political action. For Hall, "cultural criticism becomes the study of the connotational codes within which a particular term (such as nation or democracy) or a particular point of social identity (such as black, female, or adolescent) are located."[75] The significance of Gramsci for such a project is that he detaches power per se from the economic—that is the contribution of the theory of hegemony:

> One cannot explain particular ideological moments by reducing them to a single contradiction within the real. Rather, such effects are determined by a multiplicity of power relations which can only be identified within the particular context of the articulation.[76]

Race and gender can thus be seen as at least as fundamental as class. These are the three planes on which power is organized, and they may "have different relations to each other at different points within the struggle for hegemony."[77] This assumption, of course, is the great unquestioned assumption of contemporary cultural studies. It ignores the fundamental difference between exploitation and domination—only class is by definition exploitative. It also authorizes the fragmentation of the Left into identity politics.[78]

It is possible, of course, to interpret the above position as a sort of "Rainbow Coalition" of Theory—the common experience of oppression, however it is mediated, will serve to authorize a practical politics. There is, however, a more radical interpretation, that of Foucault, who for Grossberg:

> seeks . . . to locate those voices and practices which have been excluded by the contemporary technologies of power, and to struggle to open a space within which their resistance can be heard. It is then the already existing history and context of struggle which needs to be organized, not as the attempt to develop alternative or counter-hegemonic strategies but as the on-going struggle against all moments of power and domination.[79]

Grossberg sees this stance as authorizing his own investigation of rock and roll as "a set of apparatuses within which a variety of events are empowered as sites of pleasure for youth cultures."[80]

Americans tend to miss the political context in which Foucault's theory was developed. Arguably the political moment of "les Maos," the more or less anarchist activities of the Gauche Proletarienne, was the foundational experience. This militantly anti-hierarchical group was a leftist nomad, wandering through the marginal spaces of French social life lending its aid to factory workers, Arab immigrants, prisoners, and other "marginalized" groups. There was really no equivalent, either politically or intellectually, in the United States or Britain. The Gauche Proletarienne arguably served as a sort of vanishing mediator as well, the last outpost of Marxism before it deconstructed into various forms of gender and ethnic politics—and, in a turn familiar to students of American communism—a French form of neo-conservatism: the Nouveaux Philosophes.[81]

As a number of recent commentators have argued, the American reception of cultural studies, as filtered through structuralism and Foucault, has emerged as a kind of substitute for politics: "Insisting that interpretation is intrinsically political, its writing style largely incapacitates its practitioners for political and intellectual action that extends beyond the protected grazing fields of academe. Wonder of wonders, this subversion requires not the slightest engagement in the polity."[82] Gitlin could have gone on to add that this sort of style especially incapacitated the cultural Left when confronted with the onslaught of the carefully orchestrated "political correctness" campaign by neoconservatives in the early 1990s.

American cultural studies responded to the iron cage of the Reagan era by displacing not the social, but the political into culture. Thus John Fiske was able to define a new paradigm of "British cultural studies" as the notion that all texts are political. But he, like Grossberg, would resist the implication, inevitable to a follower of Althusser or Lévi-Strauss, that all effective spaces of freedom have been eliminated, if they ever existed. Rather, it is now the marginalized social spaces and even the spaces of mass consumption that offer abundant possibilities for aberrant decoding, reading against the grain for one's own pleasure.

It is uncanny—and, I think, so far unnoted by students of academic trends in mass communication—that the final move by Grossberg and Fiske mirrors the move of liberal pluralism itself in the 1950s as it shed the last vestiges of the mass society thesis. As Mike Budd, Robert Entman, and Clay Steinman have written—themselves rewriting a familiar mass society theme: "We suspect that rootedness in a subculture that organizes the lived experience of a community usually provides a firmer basis for the critique of the dominant than the deracinated consciousness promoted by the political economy and the culture of mass advertising."[83]

Put another way, the fixation of the later generation of cultural studies scholars on subculture as style makes it seem as if Marx's *Eighteenth Brumaire* had now reached its second writing, this time as farce. All those lumpen, bohemian elements that Marx saw as the raw material for fascist politics have become the agents of liberation for children of the 1960s anxiously clinging to their memories of sex, drugs, and rock and roll.

Conclusion

Raymond Williams's and E. P. Thompson's insistence on the memory of liberty as preserved in working-class culture serves as a rebuke to those younger writers who sought to dethrone that memory in the name of Theory. What Grossberg rightly identifies as the culturalists' *hermeneutic* mediation of culture and society remains largely a road not taken in American cultural studies, even though (or perhaps because) it is congenial to the peculiarly American defense of the rhetorical tradition.

It remains, however, an open question how much of the culturalist moment of cultural studies can be imported into the United States, where the language of class was itself never articulated as an independent rhetoric but was largely grafted onto a native republican rhetoric that could easily be turned against outsiders, such as immigrants or racial minorities. The American sons and daughters of the working class actually had more opportunities, educational and otherwise, than their counterparts in England and France. It was far different, even through the 1960s, being a "scholarship boy" at Oxbridge and attending City College, a land-grant university, or an ethnic-religious liberal arts college in the United States. Neoconservatism and the "end of ideology" thesis were developed by the children of working-class ethnics who had passed through some form of Socialist politics in the 1940s and 1950s. The political contradictions of the 1980s and the 1990s in the United States seemed to issue in a conflict, largely centered in colleges and universities, between the grateful children of immigrants and their ungrateful grandchildren. It was not surprising that the former would be so scandalized by the insistence of the latter on studying forms of mass communication.

It is, perhaps, the central problem of contemporary critical communication research that so much of it has focused on the cultural dimension of communication, especially television, film, and popular music. There is relatively little critical work in political communication or especially in interpersonal, small group, or organizational communication research. The quest for a general theory of communication remains on the agenda of contemporary research. Its chief proponent is Jürgen Habermas.

❧ 5 ❧

Rhetoric Between System and Lifeworld: A Reconstruction of Habermas's Historical Materialism

SHORTLY AFTER THE FALL of the Berlin Wall, Jürgen Habermas reflected on the debate over the legacy of socialism. The debate exhibits a pattern familiar to students of reactionary rhetoric: "the refrain that utopian thought and philosophies of history necessarily end in subjugation."[1] The non-Communist Left, however, has no reason to "don sackcloth and ashes," since it has always criticized state socialism. Nevertheless, "it must ask itself how long an idea can hold out against reality."[2]

Habermas identifies three types of critical arguments against socialism occasioned by the fall of communism. The first of these he terms the "postmodern critique of reason." In it, "the uneasy dreams of reason, which have produced demons for the last two hundred years, are over. But it is not reason that awakes—reason is itself the nightmare that vanishes as we wake."[3] Of course, Habermas points out—no doubt thinking of Lyotard's critique of "master narratives"—that the facts just did not fit the theory. Spontaneous mass action, a public sphere opened up by international mass media, appeals to universal principles of "sovereignty of the people and human rights"—all these were old-fashioned, "modern" things that caused the dramatic changes. The very fact of radical change "discredited the image of a posthistorical standstill; it also destroyed the picture, painted by postmodernism, of a universal bureaucracy of crystalline rigidity that had torn itself loose of all forms of legitimation."[4]

Habermas also rejects the anti-Communist interpretation, which created a mirror image of Leninism in its idea of a worldwide civil war now at an end. He reserves his major arguments, however, for an assault on the liberal assumption that "the end of ideology" thesis has finally come true. The modernization process—in the form of constitutional democracy, the market economy, and social pluralism—has finally extended into Central and Eastern Europe. As Habermas writes, "The liberal interpretation is not wrong. It just does not see the beam in its own eye."[5]

117

As "capital scrambles into markets corroded by state socialism," it is still worthwhile to ask whether

> a civilization can afford to surrender itself *entirely* to the maelstrom of the driving force of just one of its subsystems—namely the pull of a dynamic, or, as we would say today, recursively closed, economic system which can only function and remain stable by taking all relevant information, translating it into, and processing it in, the language of economic value. Marx believed that any civilization that subjects itself to the imperatives of the accumulation of capital bears the seeds of its own destruction, because it thereby blinds itself to anything, however important, that cannot be expressed as a price.[6]

It is somewhat hard to imagine that this is written by Habermas, whose "reformism" and "liberalism" have been assaulted by the hard Left for the past two decades. Habermas, as this passage indicates, is more complicated than that.

My purpose in this chapter is to provide a sympathetic account of Habermas's effort at the reconstruction of historical materialism. Habermas partly solves (insofar as a dialectical system of thought can "solve"/"resolve" anything) the problem of mediation in historical materialism that has been the subject of this book so far. The central contradiction in Habermas's system, however, lies in the fact that his universalizing discourse contradicts the practical goals of a historical-hermeneutic art of rhetoric.

I will proceed by following Habermas's development of the dialectic of language, labor, and interaction in his early work and by discussing his development of a communicative ethic in the context of a theory of the legitimation crisis of late capitalism. I will defend his theory of the ideal speech situation against assaults by poststructuralists and then discuss what is the most undeveloped part of Habermas's theory: the historical-hermeneutic role of rhetorical practice within a larger theory of communicative action. In the concluding section of this chapter, I will provide an analysis of a concrete case study of political rhetoric informed by Habermas's theory.

A Theory of Multiple Mediations: Language, Labor, and Interaction

Habermas's early work centers on finding a solution to the problem of mediation in Marxism. He found in the Hegel of the Jena *Philosophy of Spirit* a potentially useful regrounding for Critical Theory:

> The categories language, tools, and family designated three equally significant patterns of dialectical relation: symbolic representation, the labor pro-

cess, and interaction on the basis of reciprocity; each mediates subject and object in its own way. The dialectics of language, of labor, and of moral relations are each developed as a specific configuration of mediation; what is involved are not stages constructed according to the same logical form, but diverse forms of construction itself.[7]

Habermas criticizes the later Hegel for exalting the Spirit's self-reflection to the detriment of the material realm in which the Spirit is constituted:

> It is not the spirit in the absolute movement of reflecting on itself which manifests itself in, among other things, language, labor, and moral relationships, but rather, it is the dialectical interconnections between linguistic symbolization, labor, and interaction which determine the concept of spirit.[8]

Habermas is able to trace a significant number of philosophical (and, by extension, political) errors to a featuring of one of the three mediating categories at the expense of the others. Cassirer, for instance, elevates a dialectic of *symbolic representation* as the "chief interpretive principle of the whole." Lukács elevates *labor*. Marx, Habermas argues, grasped the dialectical character of the relationship among the three categories, especially in his understanding of the dialectic of the forces and relations of production. Unfortunately, Marx could not theorize communicative action adequately, and it was easy to interpret his argument in a mechanistic manner:

> Marx does not actually explicate the interrelationship of interaction and labor, but instead, under the unspecific title of social praxis, reduces the one to the other, namely: communicative action to instrumental action. Just as in the Jena *Philosophy of Spirit* the use of tools mediates between the laboring subject and the natural objects, so for Marx instrumental action, the productive activity which regulates the material interchange of the human species with its natural environment, becomes the paradigm for the generation of all the categories; everything is resolved into the self-movement of production.[9]

It is a sign of an appalling lack of ethics in contemporary scholarly controversy that Habermas, who has been so explicit throughout his writings about the need to keep the competing moments of the tripartite dialectic balanced, is so frequently accused of "privileging" communication over class struggle.[10] But there is perhaps a sort of rhetorical inevitability principle that any dialectical thinker who attempts to foreground contradiction by correcting prior tendencies to eliminate it ends up being an easy target for charges of reductionism.

Habermas's next balancing act is an attempt to reconstruct our understanding of different fields of inquiry. Human understanding, as reflected in the empirical-analytic sciences, in the historical-hermeneutic sciences, and in the social sciences, is based on the natural history of the human species as mediated through the categories of social organization: work, language, and power. Knowledge is constituted by the *interests* present in each of these categories.

> The specific viewpoints from which, with transcendental necessity, we appre-
> hend reality ground three categories of possible knowledge: information that
> expands our power of technical control; interpretations that make possible
> the orientation of action within common traditions; and analyses that free
> consciousness from its dependence on hypostasized powers. These view-
> points originate in the interest structure of a species that is linked in its roots
> to definite means of social organization: work, language, and power.[11]

The historical errors of the empirical-analytic sciences are linked to their understanding of human beings as things to be manipulated, thus ignoring communicative action. In much the same way, the historical-hermeneutic sciences have been concerned with the recapturing of the past as a common tradition, with no attention to the constitution of that common tradition in terms of the social category of work.[12] Even a critical, liberating social science such as psychoanalysis ignores the role of social and economic processes in forming mental illness.[13]

The solution to the partial vision of traditional forms of knowledge is critical theory itself. Critical theory is the product of both historical development of social learning capacity (it is thus able to account for its own origins) and of Western philosophy itself. Although it is a product of class struggle, it does not represent the position of a specific class. It professes to speak for the totality. Its regulatory function is to determine when theoretical statements grasp invariant regularities of social action as such and when they express ideologically frozen relations of dependence that are capable of being transformed by collective action.[14]

System, Lifeworld, and the Legitimation Crisis

In *The Theory of Communicative Action,* Habermas unites two traditions of sociological theory that hitherto have been radically separate: those that focus on system and those that focus on lifeworld.[15] Once again we find Habermas arguing that the defects (theoretical and practical) of previous theories of society are an overemphasis on one part of the social totality. Thus, system theorists neglect the historical-hermeneutic task of interpreting and transmitting cultural values, while phenomenologists like Schutz neglect questions of power.

Societies are simultaneously system and lifeworld. The lifeworld is that sphere of human action in which cultural reproduction, social integration, and socialization occur. These three functions correspond to culture, society, and personality, respectively. Ritual practice and religious belief once formed the core of the lifeworld, but these have gradually been replaced by communicative action. As societies evolve there is also a tendency to separate culture, society, and personality.

It is the error of hermeneutic idealism (as represented by Gadamer or by phenomenologists such as Schutz) to assume that there is only lifeworld.[16] There is also system, which consists of the mechanisms that maintain the material base—such as the state and the economy. The story Habermas tells about modernization is one in which lifeworld and system get progressively uncoupled. The lifeworld is "colonized" and becomes just one more subsystem among others. The state apparatus and the market economy penetrate those parts of the lifeworld that are responsible for cultural transmission, socialization, and the formation of personal identity. Habermas's story is thus similar to Marx's story about the accumulation and valorization of capital and about commodity fetishism. The difference is that Habermas theorizes the specifically political elements of the colonization of the lifeworld, something that Marx was unable to do. Habermas is thus able, still within the assumptions of historical materialism, to account for the rise of state intervention in capitalism.

Habermas's theory of the legitimation crisis and of a communicative ethic illustrates the way in which a critical theory of society operates. His theory of the legitimation crisis indicts the partial vision of positivism and systems theory, which focus solely upon the purposive-rational, technical interests of work. He argues that inner nature (human personality) cannot belong to the system environment in the same way as outer nature. The fact that human organisms need to be motivated by a sense of the legitimacy of their social systems makes the steering of such systems contradictory— hence the importance of the historical-hermeneutic sciences in constituting the common understanding of traditions.[17] The "public sphere," which was born in the eighteenth century, has survived in a very limited way in the twentieth century.

Although Habermas never really addresses the problematic entailed by using the term "rhetoric" directly, his discussion of the role of historical-hermeneutic sciences opens up a space for rhetorical concerns. The rhetorical tradition has operated with two different conceptions of the relationship between rhetoric and politics: on one hand, a conception of rhetoric as mythmaking for the masses (a doctrine traceable most clearly to Plato, and best represented in the modern era by Edmund Burke's politics of "presumption, prejudice, and prescription"); on the other hand, the Sophistic and Ciceronian view of rhetoric as a common skill possessed by all citizens in a republic authorizes more participatory sorts of politics. (The historical-hermeneutic role of *ethos* serves as a kind of point of potential cleavage in the tradition.) Stressing the participatory, republican pole of the rhetorical tradition is perfectly consistent with Habermas (and Marx), although the stress on equality may lead to occasional confusions between manipulation and leadership.[18]

Habermas identifies specific elements of late capitalism that have resulted in structural changes in the public sphere. The shift from early to late capitalism required massive state intervention in the economy. This intervention stabilized the economic crisis cycle but ultimately at the expense of inflation and a permanent crisis in public finance.[19] Political leadership has been taken over by an administrative elite: "The citizenry, in the midst of an objectively political society, enjoy the status of passive citizens with only the right to withhold acclamation."[20]

The traditional need for the social order to achieve legitimation is reduced to two residual requirements: the justification of civic privatism and structural depoliticization. Citizens must come to believe in the virtues of career, leisure, and consumption. Democratic elite theories and technocratic systems theories are used to justify such an attitude toward political activity. Cultural impoverishment occurs because of the development of expert cultures.

It is important to note here that Habermas does not make these arguments about privatism in either a conspiratorial or strictly functionalist way. He follows Weber in accepting system tendencies that are autonomous of individual wills or class "intention." Where he does not follow Weber is in Weber's pessimism. Weber, according to Habermas, did not adequately distinguish between the form and the content of rationalization and modernization. The content could have taken a more liberatory form, then and now. Most important, the fact that advanced industrial society is simultaneously system and lifeworld leads to the existence of contradictions. One cannot colonize the lifeworld without exacting a cost. Crime, addiction, lack of political participation, the rise of new social movements from feminism to fundamentalism—all these things are results of a crisis in legitimation stemming from the attempt to "steer" the lifeworld.

None of these new social movements seem to deal directly with the process Marx identified as the motor force of history: class struggle over distribution of the social surplus of production. Almost all deal with cultural questions. What Habermas sees is that the new social movements are not the New Vanguard (contrary to Marcuse and Aronowitz) but are produced by the legitimation crisis of capitalism.[21]

Habermas does not define the future course that the new social movements of the Right or Left will take, nor does he envision a point at which the system will finally cease to be able to reproduce itself. He is, nonetheless, optimistic about human learning capacity. Given these factors, how can we characterize Habermas's relation to the Marxist tradition?

His postmortem on communism has a useful summary of the limitations of Marxism.[22] First, Marx focused narrowly (with good reason, given the economic context of his time) on a productivist concept of labor. This precluded "consideration both of the ambivalences of the increasing domination of nature, and of the potential for social integration within and beyond the sphere of social labor."[23]

Second, Marx oversimplified the nature of capitalism. By emphasizing the illusory aspects of the capitalist system, he himself created an illusion that capitalism could be revealed in its underlying objective form and thus be made subject to rational control:

> Theory in this way blinds itself to the resistance inherent in the system of a differentiated market economy, whose regulative devices cannot be replaced by administrative planning without potentially jeopardizing the level of differentiation achieved in a modern society.[24]

Third, Marx underestimated the complexities of regional, cultural, and social structures in relation to economic substructures. All these structures have logics of their own that only occasionally harmonize with those of the economic substructures.

Fourth, Marx simply could not imagine institutional forms beyond the dictatorship of the proletariat, especially democratic forums for the resolution of conflicts.

Finally, Marx's concept of inevitability had a number of negative results. It left the normative basis of historical materialism unclear. It concealed the margin of contingency within which any revolutionary practice must move. The notion of inevitability reduced the sense of risk and moral responsibility among "vanguards."

Habermas also rejects the idea that socialism can be seen as a "historically privileged form of ethical practice," since the "most a theory can do is to describe the conditions necessary for emancipated forms of life. What concrete shape these take is something for those eventually involved to decide amongst themselves."[25] Insofar as Marxism claimed to view things from the standpoint of the totality, it ran the risk of prescribing how people should live.

Habermas's final verdict on state socialism is that the weaknesses of Marxism he describes represent conditions for abuse, even if they are not necessary or sufficient ones.[26] But, most important, his final verdict on *social democracy* is that it, like "actually existing socialism," staked everything on the development of the productive forces and on a productivist concept of labor, thus sacrificing the prospects for radical democracy in the long run.

Habermas's theory "solves" some key problems in mediation that have plagued Marxism since its inception. On the one hand, he allows a space for audience decision, culture, and communication in ways that no previous Marxist theorist had. On the other hand, his theorizing of communicative action leaves some key questions about political transformation unanswered.

Conversation, Irony, and the Ideal Speech Situation

Habermas's critique of late capitalism centers on the fact that spaces for communicative action have been invaded by the state apparatus and market mechanisms. This critique has a normative basis in the concept of truth as a product of undistorted communication. Truth is what we would rationally agree to in a situation of undistorted communication, one in which manipulation as well as errors of fact, wishful thinking, rationalization, and ideological positioning would not occur. Habermas develops the concept of an ideal speech situation to serve as a clarification of this conception of truth.[27]

Habermas's ideal speech situation is constructed through three steps: an analysis of types of speech acts, a description of the validity claims each implies, and a description of the ideal situation in which the claims could be redeemed.

First, he reconstructs the types of speech acts people can engage in: *communicatives* ("What I am saying is that Habermas said . . ."), which express the meaning of an utterance as an utterance; *constatives* ("Habermas resides in Starnberg"), which explicate the meaning of a statement with reference to the external world; *representatives* ("I wish I were done writing this chapter on Habermas"), which explain the meaning of the self-representation of the speaker to the hearer; and *regulatives* ("Thanks for reading this chapter on Habermas thus far, and please keep going"), which explain the relationship of the speaker and hearer in reference to moral and social rules that can be followed or broken.

Engaging in any of these speech acts carries with it a *promise,* a "validity claim" that can be made good on, given the right set of circumstances. The validity claim of a communicative speech act is *comprehensibility;* that of a constative speech act is *truth;* that of a representative speech act is *truthfulness;* and that of a regulative speech act is *rightfulness.*

Although any given communicative exchange may violate one or more of these claims, the act of entering into communication presupposes a commitment to abide by these standards. If these values are presumed to exist implicitly in all acts of communication, what social situation would most likely guarantee the fulfillment of these values? One in which the following four standards prevail:

1. Each speaker must have an equal opportunity to initiate and perpetuate communication (use communicative speech acts).
2. Each speaker must have an equal opportunity to employ regulative speech acts, without having to obey one-sidedly binding norms.
3. Each speaker must have an equal opportunity to employ constative speech acts—no propositional statements are immune from criticism.

4. Each speaker must have an equal opportunity to employ representative speech acts—to be able to express feelings and attitudes.

Although Habermas does not specify the social requirements for the embodiment of the ideal speech situation, some key prerequisites are obviously these, as Alvin Gouldner points out: No violence, the existence of permeable boundaries between public and private speech, the ability to make traditional symbols and rules of discourse problematic, and an insistence on equal opportunities to speak.[28]

A number of questions remain unanswered by Habermas's account. For instance, what are the similarities and differences between the ideal speech situation and Plato's (or Marcuse's) notion of dialectic? Are there any categories of speech acts Habermas omits? Two potential categories might be "manipulatives," in which the speaker and hearer tacitly agree to play a kind of persuasion game (as in consuming television advertisements) and "imaginatives," which covers aesthetic forms of communication. What is the status of the ideal speech situation within social theory as a whole? Is its function essentially similar to Rawls's "veil of ignorance"? That is, does it serve only as a persuasive or explanatory device within a philosophical system, with no real implications for practice? When are we justified in violating the standards? What are the limits of argument? May we use violence if we have reasonable hope of creating a classless society in which the ideal speech situation may be fulfilled? What politics generally would secure the ideal speech situation? Finally, does Habermas's seeming banishment of metaphysical categories go hand in hand with the scientism he rejects? Does his acceptance of the Durkheimian view of religion and ritual as devices for social integration in traditional societies artificially limit one important source of meaning in the lifeworld and thus radically alter the function of the historical-hermeneutic sciences?

My own view of the ideal speech situation is that it simply serves as a persuasive or explanatory device within his overall system, much like Rawls's veil of ignorance. No one argues against Rawls's system simply because it is impossible to enact that situation. (Although MacIntyre does argue that the veil of ignorance exhibits the same problem Rawls's larger theory of justice has: It ignores the past of the participants and thus evades the question of whether a given person deserves to be treated fairly.[29] I am convinced, too, that Habermas makes his argument in order to be persuasive to as many people (holding many different normative positions) as possible. It would not be too difficult—although considerably beyond the scope of this book—to reconstruct Habermas's argument as a statement about human nature along the lines of Aristotelian virtue ethics. Human beings have a *telos* that is bound up with exercising their communicative capacities. One cannot separate questions of virtue, happiness, and politics. Most critiques of Habermas work within essentially emotivist views of ethics and thus cannot comprehend how ideals can exist at all.

Three influential criticisms of Habermas are worth examining in detail. The first, an essentially conservative argument, centers on the inevitability of self-deception in conversations. The second, an allegedly radical argument, focuses on the exclusion of aesthetic concerns from Habermas's account of speech acts. The final criticism, Richard Rorty's assault on Habermas for being insufficiently ironic, is politically ambiguous.

Critiques of Habermas

Inevitability of Self-Deception

The terms dialectic and communication have their roots, of course, in the idea of everyday conversation. The term "conversation" enjoys considerable prestige in a variety of circles at this point in history. A characteristic critique of Habermas centers on his allegedly limited view of conversation. Conservative political theorist Michael Oakeshott has drawn a useful distinction between two different versions of human interaction. In the first version, a good conversation is one in which, over time, human beings will come to agree on more and more things. In the second version, to which Oakeshott himself subscribes, the whole point of a conversation is that it does not have a point.

In order for the second type of conversation to flourish, tolerance and good manners are essential. There need to be some accepted principles in common so that one or more of the participants do not bully the others. The participants need to possess the virtues of skepticism and humility in order to keep the conversation going.[30]

Oakeshott believes that the first view of conversation is essentially that of John Stuart Mill, although I could add Rousseau and Marx and Habermas to the list. Furthermore, Oakeshott contrasts two forms of politics implied by these two root conceptions of conversation. In the first view, politics becomes a matter of including voices in the conversation to ensure consensus. In the second view, politics is a matter of assuring fair play among participants who may not necessarily come to complete consensus.

Although Oakeshott does not discuss the American political tradition explicitly, it could be argued that "the low, but solid ground" of assuring fair play rather than consensus is the political theory of the American regime. The political theory embodied in *The Federalist Papers* and in Washington's *Farewell Address* is one in which politics is, finally, the aggregation of preferences combined with the assurance that popular passions and particular sectional or economic interests do not become too dominant. There is a consensus on the need for republican virtue, but that consensus is in many ways a minimal one—compared with classical accounts of virtue—but it shares with the classical tradition the assumption that perfect virtue is at best attainable only by a small number of human beings.[31]

Although Marxism shares the "realistic" vision of the Framers in believing in the inevitability of conflict, it assumes that over time people will and must agree on more and more things if we are to have a rational society. As Jon Elster writes, Marx's commitment (shared by Hegel, Rousseau, Habermas, and Arendt) is to a standard of public rationality in which private preferences are subordinate to the common good. This standard implies, as Elster writes, that

> the goal of politics should be unanimous and rational consensus, not an optimal compromise between irreducibly opposed interests. The forum is not to be contaminated by principles that regulate the market, nor should communication be confused with bargaining.[32]

One could add here, following Gouldner's analysis of the culture of critical discourse, that the forum should not be contaminated with claims to authority based on tradition or greater experience (the classical notion of *ethos*). Rational consensus is thus also the product of individual autonomy, not a heteronomous imposition, although—paradoxically, perhaps—making the individual the locus of rational decisionmaking suggests a greater continuity with classical liberalism than might initially be apparent. (Oakeshott's attribution of his first type of conversation to Mill suggests how contradictory these matters become after a while.)

Elster's critique of Marxism (as well as Habermas's ideal speech situation) centers on the following problems. First, collective rationality requires a suppression of merely private interest. It also requires the elimination of the passions—those things that may lead people to give up autonomy or else deceive themselves about their long-term interests. Elster catalogues a number of ways in which people deceive themselves: simple inferential error, wishful thinking, and the fascinating phenomenon of "sour grapes," or "adaptive preference formation," in which wants are adjusted to possibilities, stemming from the drive to reduce tension or frustration that one feels in having wants that one cannot possibly satisfy.

There are other problems besides self-deception that a quest for universal consensus may fall into. The system must be strategy-proof—both communication and the distribution of resources must work so that it does not pay to express false preferences. The system obviously must have a long period of time in which to arrive at consensus. It must have ways of preventing the phenomenon of groupthink. Elster summarizes:

> First, one cannot assume that one will get closer to the good society by acting as if one had already arrived. If, as suggested by Habermas, free and rational

discussion will only be possible in a society where political and economic domination have been abolished, it is by no means obvious that abolition can be brought about by rational argumentation. Perhaps irony, eloquence, and propaganda will be needed—assuming that the use of force to end domination would be self-defeating. Secondly, even in the good society the process of rational discussion could be fragile and vulnerable to individual and collective self-deception. To make it stable there would be a need for structures—political institutions—that could easily reintroduce an element of domination.[33]

The contradiction (in the logical rather than dialectical sense) is thus that a communication theory based on the possibility of consensus leads to measures for enforcing consensus either (a) at the origins of the system, in which case audiences must be persuaded on the basis of self-interests or of claims to authority (ethos) or of force, all of which violate the conditions of the central premises; or (b) that for system maintenance make privacy impossible, because individual tendencies for self-deception continually must be rooted out.

The substance of Elster's critique makes sense when lodged against classical Marxism—in fact, it is easily recast in a form sympathetic to the rhetorical tradition, as I did in the previous paragraph. However, it hardly seems fair to accuse Habermas of being some sort of crypto-Leninist simply for having a normative principle for his theory. The ideal speech situation has become an easy target mainly, I think, because of a larger lacuna in Habermas's writing. The universalizing quality of Habermas's work is necessary in order to defend the role of philosophy as guardian of reason, but this necessarily leads to an inadequate discussion of the historical-hermeneutic space at the level of individual social formations or subcultures. It is hard to imagine using the ideal speech situation as a motivational device for a political movement. No one is going to hold up a sign saying, "Free Constative Speech Acts for Everyone." But Habermas never said that anyone should, and besides, the "bourgeois" freedoms of speech, press, and religion still serve vital rhetorical functions, and they are embodied in Habermas's ideal. Because Habermas's political analyses are, understandably, related to the German cultural context, he will necessarily seem to have little to say to residents of the United States or the United Kingdom. For one thing, he may overemphasize the incorporation of labor into the system simply because of the tremendous power of the German labor movement. And, as a philosopher, it is simply not his *job* to construct a rhetoric. That is a specific historical-hermeneutic "science" directed at particular social formations. But Elster is right to note the gap in Habermas's theory.

Habermas does, however, "privilege" the concept of communication, and that has led to criticisms from the Left. Alvin Gouldner, for instance, made several interesting arguments that center on the problem of violence. Gouldner argues that violence may actually remove distortions of communication. Torture of captured enemy personnel is one example. Violence also indicates what is *not* open to discussion. *Real* politics, Gouldner writes, involves killing. Adolf Hitler presumably would not be admitted to the ideal speech situation. Additionally, absolutely free expression of feelings hardly leads to undistorted communication, but may lead to a situation in which everything is problematic at the same time and thus is utterly incapable of leading to action. The ideal speech situation sounds like government by encounter group, but Habermas seems unable to put his theory into "politically manageable focus." Finally, in a point similar to Elster's, Gouldner poses the questions: What if some people in some ideal speech situations develop faster than others? Would some sort of "speech busing" be necessary to impose equality? The ghost of Leninism thus intrudes into a theory intended to banish it for good.

Habermas's "Exclusion of Aesthetic Concerns"

Lenin is invoked also by Michael Ryan, who attempts to construct a Derridean Marxism. Some of the steps in Ryan's argument are missing, and the following is an attempt to reconstruct them. Recall that Habermas seems to have left out the realm of the aesthetic in his discussion of speech acts. A deconstructive reading of Habermas would then focus, first, on his acceptance of Austin's binary opposition between "serious" and "nonserious" speech acts. "Writing poems and telling jokes" are secondary to authentic illocutionary acts. Habermas further differentiates "communicative action" from "strategic" and "symbolic" action—the first of which we would probably call "rhetoric" and the second "poetic." Nevertheless, in an utterly predictable deconstructive move, Habermas can be shown to use language that subverts itself: "We know that institutionalized actions do not as a rule fit this model of pure communicative action, although we cannot avoid proceeding as if the model were really the case—on this unavoidable fiction rests the humanity of intercourse among men who are still men."[34] Elsewhere he writes that the ideal speech situation "even when counterfactual . . . is a fiction that is operatively effective in communication."[35] The figurative choice here thus would betray a certain anxiety at the heart of the theory of ideal speech: perhaps it is just like writing a poem or telling a joke.

Because "real" communication is more like writing a poem or telling a joke, Michael Ryan argues that fulfilling the ideal speech situation would require a Leninist politics.

> A speech in which error and misunderstanding, the possibility of nontruth, are purged entirely could function only by establishing absolute univocal

meanings for words and by rigorously determining contexts so that a displacement of truthful meaning by a contextual shift would no longer be possible.[36]

Ryan, in keeping with his own "autonomist" Marxist politics—really a sort of Marxist anarchism—wants to argue that there are only distorted communication situations:

> If there are only distortional communication situations, unregulated by any ideal situation and structured by forces that are prelinguistic or preconscious, then the politics that addresses them cannot be univocal or homogeneous, that is, it cannot operate in pursuit of a single goal (restored communication) that mirrors the ground of the theory (the model of an ideal speech situation).[37]

Ryan is thus in the position of giving reasons for rejecting rationality—but that is, within the confines of deconstruction's satin cage, as sensible a move as any. The political problem with Ryan's position is that the charge of Leninism can be lodged against it as easily—more easily in fact—as against Habermas. By eliminating any rational, universal moral or epistemological basis for socialism, Ryan makes politics into an emotional exercise of identity politics—so instead of a Communist vanguard, we more likely will have gay, lesbian, African-American, or Irish-American vanguards. Not only does such a politics lack any realistic hope of overthrowing the power of White Males, but it presents a world in which the White Male perspective (whatever it is that, say, George Bush and Eugene Debs have in common) is as *valid* as any other.

Habermas's "Insufficient Irony"

A more subtle version of Ryan's position is Richard Rorty's argument that Habermas lacks the cardinal intellectual virtue of irony. Rorty picks up Oakeshott's distinction between two types of conversation in making a distinction between hermeneutics and epistemology:

> Hermeneutics sees the relations between various discourses as those of strands in a possible conversation which preupposes no disciplinary matrix which unites the speakers, but where the hope of agreement is never lost so long as the conversation lasts. This hope is not a hope for the discovery of antecedently existing common ground, but *simply* hope for agreement, or at least exciting and fruitful disagreement. Epistemology sees the hope of agreement as a token of the existence of common ground which, perhaps unbeknown to the speakers, unites them in a common rationality. For hermeneutics, to be rational is to be willing to refrain from epistemology—from thinking that there is a special set of terms in which all contributions to the conversation should be put—and to be willing to pick up the jargon of the interlocutor rather than translating it into one's own.[38]

Rorty, of course, wants to eliminate epistemology entirely in the name of a hermeneutic ideal. This passage, however, illustrates unwittingly a contradiction at the heart of the hermeneutic ideal. "Picking up the jargon of the interlocutor" can mean either surrendering oneself to the other or else "praising Athens among Athenians." There is a fundamental question of the definition of communicative action itself that underlies Rorty's opposition, a question not easily eliminated by the supposedly pragmatist liquidation of it as uninteresting.

Habermas's problem, according to Rorty, is that he lacks a sense of irony. Rorty's liberal utopia is one in which everyone could

> see one's language, one's conscience, one's morality, and one's highest hopes as contingent products, as literalizations of what once were accidentally produced metaphors. ... That is why the ideal citizen of such an ideal state would be someone who thinks of the founders and the preservers of her society as ... poets, rather than as people who had discovered or who clearly envisioned the truth about the world or about humanity.[39]

Habermas wants to defend the idea of truth, and he bases it in an ideal of a domination-free communication. However, Rorty says there is no real political difference between himself and Habermas:

> We do not disagree about the worth of traditional democratic institutions, or about the sorts of improvements these institutions need, or about what counts as "freedom from domination." Our differences concern *only* the self-image which a democratic society should have, the rhetoric which it should use to express its hopes.[40]

Rorty then, on the verge of calling for a new rhetoric, in a move utterly characteristic of his era, wants to exalt literature—in the strictly imaginative sense—to the central position in his utopia. Further, Rorty wants to preserve the distinction between public and private spheres. He writes that people like Derrida and Heidegger, positively dangerous as public philosophers, can help develop the ironist's private sense of identity. Rorty summarizes:

> Habermas wants to preserve the traditional story (common to Hegel and to Peirce) of asymptotic approach to *foci imaginarii*. I want to replace this with a story of increasing willingness to live with plurality and to stop asking for universal validity. I want to see freely arrived at agreement as agreement on how to accomplish common purposes (e.g., prediction and control of the behavior of atoms or people, equalizing life-chances, decreasing cruelty), but I want to see these common purposes against the background of an increasing sense of the radical diversity of private purposes, of the radically poetic character of individual lives, and of the merely poetic foundations of the "we-consciousness" which lies behind our social institutions.[41]

Rorty thus proposes a radical uncoupling of system and lifeworld, in which the lifeworld itself is split into unbridgeable private and public spheres. The "irony," of course, is that this split is precisely what the logic of capitalism has entailed all along.

Rorty is right in criticizing Habermas for remaining at the level of universalizing discourse, but Rorty's own choice of literature as mediation repeats Habermas's error. Rorty closes his chapter on Habermas by quoting John Dewey's *Art as Experience*. It would have made more political sense to quote the Dewey of *The Public and Its Problems*: "No government by experts in which the masses do not have the chance to inform the experts as to their needs can be anything but an oligarchy managed in the interests of the few. . . . The essential need . . . is the improvement of the methods and conditions of debate, discussion and persuasion. That is *the* problem of the public."[42] Rorty's only real program is a technocratic Mondale liberalism combined with an academic project that involves extending even further the paralyzing grip of the English department on liberal education. Students who once learned the arts of citizenship by speaking and debating public issues will now only learn the passive pleasures of liberal irony from Nabokov.

I have maintained in this section that Habermas's notion of ideal speech can withstand criticisms, but only at a price. By remaining a universal ideal, it runs into difficulties when guiding practice. The tension between being a citizen of the world—which is seemingly the ultimate goal of philosophical discourse—and being a citizen of a nation (or member of a culture, which is, of course, not always the same thing) is inscribed at the heart of Habermas's theory. What sorts of messages will motivate someone who cannot understand the elegant theorizing of the ideal speech situation? Gadamer's response to Habermas indicates that the Kantian residue in Habermas's communicative ethic prevents him from seeing the significance of the classical concepts of rhetoric, ethos, and political judgment.[43] Critics' customary indictments of Habermas—for lacking a politics or an ability to identify collective agencies for social change—stem from Habermas's insistence on the absolute autonomy of communicative action.

It is possible to reconstruct critical theory along more strictly rhetorical lines. This is not to say that a descent into discourse is called for. Like Habermas and Palmer, I want to insist on the significance of the world of outer nature, system, and forces and relations of production. The study of rhetoric is simply one part of the science of politics—the understanding of the historical-hermeneutic space in which the relationship between system and lifeworld is reproduced and negotiated by human actors.

Work, Place, and Space

My purpose in this concluding section is to demonstrate how a strictly rhetorical analysis informed by Habermas's theory can illuminate the contradictory relationship between system and lifeworld in the United States. Habermas's idea of a legitimation crisis can explain the rhetorical appeal of Ronald Reagan, while preserving a sense of contradiction and political possibility.

A thorough account of the rhetoric of the conservative ascendancy in the United States in the past twelve years requires an understanding of how lifeworld and system interrelate. The first step is an understanding of how the lifeworld is constituted rhetorically and ideologically. The central points of tension in American rhetoric, at least, are between citizenship as constituted in space versus time, and between liberal and republican political languages.

In an unusually fair and perceptive documentary, CBS's *48 Hours* covered the conflicting points of view in the United Mine Workers strike against Pittston Coal in Virginia and West Virginia. The company president, the scabs, the miners and their families, and the state police were interviewed. The contested issue in the strike was the now commonplace one of the need for competitiveness in the global marketplace versus the workers' need for security of jobs and benefits.

An interesting pattern emerged in the conflicting accounts of the strike. Those who supported the company repeatedly invoked a different sense of time than those who supported the strikers. The company side made much of the fact that "times have changed," that the old social contract between labor and management has to give way to the flexibility required by America's entry into a global marketplace. On the other side, the miners themselves repeatedly invoked the long and bloody history of class war in the coalfields. One retired miner even spoke nostalgically of the 1920s and the "Matewan massacre," when the owners' Pinkerton men were gunned down on the streets of Matewan, West Virginia.

The different configurations of argument in this incident are illustrative of a larger pattern of conflict between system and lifeworld in the United States during the Reagan-Bush era. The rhetoric of the mine-owners is space-binding—that is, their community is not "in place but in space, mobile," and connected over vast distances. The rhetoric of the miners and their families, however, is time-binding—it is rooted in place rather than space, and its symbols are more "oral, mythopoetic, religious, and ritualistic."[44] In more Habermasian terms, the conflict is between a rhetoric of system integration and a rhetoric of social integration of the lifeworld. The logic and rhetoric of the system is extension in space with simultaneous elimination of the past. Such elimination is, of course, contradictory because the destruction of memory has serious motivational and intellectual costs among the citizenry. I will argue that it was the rhetorical job of Ronald Reagan to resolve this contradiction.

There has been relatively little effort by the Left to make sense of the rhetoric of Ronald Reagan. (Left-cultural critics spent more time studying television and rock and roll in the 1980s than Reagan.)[45] I draw together here the scattered discussions of rhetoric from throughout this book and apply them to an exemplary piece of Reagan rhetoric: his response to proposed plant closing legislation in 1988. I will demonstrate that Reagan, like the mine owners in the Pittston strike, chose to locate his arguments in internal space rather than communal time and memory (place), a rhetorical choice that reveals the instability of the conservative rhetorical idiom at this point in the history of the republic. Before reading Reagan's response closely, I will provide some definitional work on a theoretical concept, that of a "rhetorical idiom," which will be useful in making sense of the former president's choices.

If we return to Erik Olin Wright's discussion of levels of abstraction in Marxist analysis that I provided at the beginning of Chapter 2, we see that Habermas's discussion of the colonization of the lifeworld by the demands of system integration occurs at the highest level of abstraction: the mode of production. What Habermas does not theorize is what happens at the level of the social formation, in this case the United States. How are the positive and negative moments of mediation—between structure and struggle, between system and lifeworld, and in turn between the public and private spheres—accomplished? These moments are accomplished through political languages or rhetorics that have some features in common with the system of capitalism itself, but which are nonetheless often culture-specific. It is one of the tasks of rhetoric as a historical-hermeneutic science to trace the development and fragmentation of political languages over time.

American public discourse has tended to operate within two different "languages" since before the American Revolution. The language that prepared the way for the Revolution was that of eighteenth-century republicanism, a language in which political debates were conducted, featuring such terms as "virtue," "the public" or "common" good, and "corruption." These terms were anchored in a few core tenets: human beings are essentially political animals; they can fulfill their natures only by participating in self-government; and the function of government is to promote virtue among the citizenry. Because republics require constant vigilance, republican rhetoric is time-binding, insisting upon historical memory as a foundation for civic virtue. As Bruce Smith writes, republics are mnemonic structures; they are founded "upon the injunction: remember."[46]

Liberalism, however, insists that individuals are the ultimate definers of moral value, that consensus on what would constitute civic virtue is not only impossible but dangerous, that politics is as much an arena for the oppression of others as one of self-fulfillment, and that government must devise a system that recognizes and protects individual rights, especially, but not exclusively, property rights.

The contrast between liberalism and republicanism has emerged in a conflict over the meaning of the U.S. Constitution. Some interpreters see the Constitution and its framers as displacing a republican paradigm with a liberal one, with allegedly dire consequences for the subsequent history of the United States. This position not only makes political language completely autonomous from economic forces but it tends to reify the categories liberalism and republicanism in ultimately untenable ways. How, for instance, is one to explain the simultaneous presence of both "paradigms" in the rhetoric of the *Federalist Papers*?

It is possible to argue that liberalism is a characteristic (but not inevitable—since an authoritarian capitalism is possible, Milton Friedman's arguments notwithstanding) mediating political language under capitalism. It has been a relatively stable political language in the United States for some time. It is primarily spatial in configuration and individualistic in its audience appeals. It is "progressive" in its ability to break through various provincialisms—especially those related to race and gender. But it has a rhetorical deficit. It is difficult to motivate people with a concept of wholly negative liberty unless there is a clearly identifiable oppressor, and even then the old republican language of patriotism and civic virtue gets dusted off and called in to do its work.

This fluid and contradictory character of the two political languages is captured well in Isaac Kramnick's essay on "rhetorical idioms." This term heightens the way in which the political languages are not all-constraining paradigms so much as strategic resources in public debate. Kramnick illustrates how the defenders of the U.S. Constitution skillfully employed the idioms of classical republicanism and Lockean liberalism as well as the idioms of work-ethic Protestantism and state-centered power and sovereignty.[47] Anyone who has ever engaged in the practice of advocacy for an extended period of time, whether in political or legal settings, knows that the fundamental rule is usually a striving for effectiveness rather than consistency with a paradigm. However, there is a productive tension between the requirements of rhetorical practice and the long-term survival of a rhetorical idiom. Looking at Reagan from within the framework of postwar American conservatism illustrates how this tension works in practice.

The major historians of American conservatism, George Nash, Paul Gottfried, and Thomas Fleming, have identified at least four strains in postwar conservative thought: (1) the traditionalist wing (now sometimes called the "palaeo-cons"), represented above all by Russell Kirk and including Southern regionalists Richard Weaver and M. E. Bradford; (2) the libertarian wing, with its roots in the thought of Albert Jay Nock and Frank Chodorow, which has spun off into more radical versions by Ayn Rand and Murray Rothbard, and is represented most popularly by Milton Friedman; (3) the fusionist wing—so called because of its desire to fuse cultural conservatism with a celebration of capitalism—represented by Frank S. Meyer, William F. Buckley, Jr., and *National Review;* and, finally, (4) the neoconservative wing, distinguished from the others by its more social-scientific focus, secular outlook (or, more accurately, its Jewishness), internationalism, and acceptance of the welfare state—represented by Irving Kristol and Norman Podhoretz. The so-called New Right, much less self-reflexive than the other perspectives, seems to borrow elements of each, although it is more hospitable to populist themes and more appealing to blue-collar voters than the others.[48]

Despite differences of emphasis, most people would agree that a "conservative" political position embodies elements of the following propositions: Something called "Western culture" and its institutions are under assault by both liberal relativists and "politically correct" partisans of various radical causes; individual liberty, especially property rights, are under assault by an ever more intrusive state; and the United States possesses a unique position in the world, namely as the defender of Western culture and institutions against communism.

Now the problem, of course, with these propositions is that they are not necessarily compatible. The defense against communism may require substantial intrusions into civil liberties. Enlightenment liberalism, with its emphasis on individual property rights, has been as great a threat to established institutions, such as the church, as communism itself. Marx and Engels's observation that under capitalism "all that is solid melts into air" finds echoes in the writings of Kirk and Weaver, who when read out of context can sound just like E. P. Thompson. Perhaps the best way of describing the situation in which contemporary conservatism finds itself is the right-wing Socialist Daniel Bell's characterization of the "cultural contradictions of capitalism": capitalism, in order to survive as an economic system, requires that self-discipline and deferral of gratification known (rather misleadingly) as the Protestant work-ethic; yet it also requires massive consumption of commodities and stimulation of desire for them, which tends to undermine that ethic.[49] Another contradiction is more recent, but bears even more directly on the conservative collapse over economic policy. With the end of the Cold War, the normative basis of American conservatism has disappeared. Hatred and fear of the Soviet Union and its client states could serve as the rhetorical glue that united figures as otherwise different as Patrick Buchanan, William F. Buckley, and Norman Podhoretz. Not surprisingly, perhaps, if my space-time theory of rhetorical mediation is correct, the place at which conservatism threatens to fly apart is over the question of "America First."

The inconsistencies I have identified do not in and of themselves justify a rejection of "conservatism" per se, nor do they authorize the observation that it is the "ideology" of the "ruling class." As I have maintained throughout this book, all political paradigms, even and especially Marxism, involve contradictions and evasions of reality. The major purpose of rhetorical practice is, through a sense of timing and taste, to glue together the contradictory arguments, symbols, and narratives of a political tradition. Because rhetorical time is rather short, individual acts of cut-and-paste tend to split apart eventually under the weight of historical events. At other times, however, particularly strong rhetorical acts by individuals or collectivities will come to stand as relatively autonomous paradigms of discourse—rhetorical idioms—that will remain more or less constant resources in political argument. These resources, however, will always strain against elements of system integration. Put more simply, rhetorical practice as a means of social integration of the lifeworld is constrained by the logic of system integration. Contemporary rhetorical theorists tend to emphasize the autonomy of rhetoric over the logic of system integration. Contemporary cultural theorists tend to emphasize system integration over social integration. Prudential politics requires a sort of Aristotelian mean between the two positions.

Returning to the disparate wings of postwar American conservatism, we find familiar rhetorical idioms of Lockean liberalism, the Protestant ethic, and patriotism. The traditionalism of Russell Kirk is hardly recognizable as a rhetorical idiom at all, at least in the United States. One can hear it occasionally in Britain, as in Harold Macmillan's eloquent defense of the miners strike, or in some of the Tory "wets," but never in authentically *public* discourse in the United States. Even the widespread dissemination of the neoconservative critique of American education (Bennett, Bloom) has more to do with the fear that students are losing some of their educational capital in an increasingly competitive global marketplace than with any authentic desire to restore the traditional humanities curriculum, whatever that was. Even the centrality of virtue in the discourse of the New Right has more to do with the restoration of sexual virtue than with the civic virtue of the classical republicans. The labor movement has argued exclusively in liberal terms since the 1940s, and the civil rights and women's movements seem forced by the realities of public debate into liberal modes of argument despite their natural affinities with classical republicanism. The problem there, of course, is that framing equal rights arguments in liberal terms always opens such groups up to charges of being a "special interest."

It is only possible to make sense of the enduring popularity and political success of Ronald Reagan in terms of his ability to glue together the contradictions in Lockean liberalism, the Protestant ethic, and traditional conservatism both by the force of his personality and with his use of the rhetorical idiom of national glory. Ethos again makes sense less as an embodiment of a cultural tradition than as a masterful reconciliation or evasion of contradictions in that tradition.

Now, what happens when the rhetorical idiom of national glory becomes so widespread that it can be turned upon its chief proponent? The rhetorical glue begins to melt, and the contradictions of the cut-and-paste job begin to emerge. This is precisely what happens in the plant-closing debate. President Reagan, so fond of using time-binding rhetoric when speaking of foreign policy or education, reverts to space-binding rhetoric when speaking of work or economics.

The United States, until recently, was the only Western industrialized nation without a law requiring some sort of advance notice for workers in the event of a plant closing. Walter Mondale and William Ford had introduced such legislation in 1974. By 1988 it had

> lost much in substance but acquired a political life. Gone were mandates for consultations with workers before plant closings, authorization for extensive court and government intervention in closing disputes, payoffs for communities hit by major shutdowns, and continuing health coverage and severance pay for out-of-work employees.[50]

The legislation became simply a requirement for firms with more than 100 employees to give workers and communities 60 days' notice in the event of a closing or else pay workers for each day of notice missed. There were exemptions in cases of strikes or particularly precarious financial circumstances.

Predictably, the Reagan administration came out against the legislation and vetoed the trade bill in which it was included. Also predictably, the U.S. Chamber of Commerce and the National Association of Manufacturers opposed it. Less predictably, James J. Kilpatrick, the *Wall Street Journal,* and Paul Weyrich's (the founder of the Moral Majority) Institute for Cultural Conservatism came out for it. Many Republican senators and representatives, including Dole and Simpson, urged Reagan not to fight the bill once it was offered as a single piece of legislation detached from the trade bill, and the Bush campaign reportedly urged the same, especially in light of public opinion polls indicating a high level of public support (80–86 percent) of the legislation, including 70 percent support among Republican males. Articles in the conservative *American Spectator* and *National Review* supported the bill as well, although William F. Buckley, Jr., opposed it.[51]

The Senate approved the bill on July 6, 1988, by 72–23. The House approved it by 286–138 on July 13. On August 2, President Reagan sent a message to Congress in which he explained his decision to let the bill become law without his signature.

Reminding his audience that his chief priority as president had been "to reduce the intrusion of the Federal government into the lives of all Americans," he first reviews the economic accomplishments of his administration: "17 million new jobs—mostly high quality and full-time," with the unemployment rate the lowest in 14 years, and "more people ... at work in America than ever before." Despite this record of success, Congress "has taken a step in the wrong direction by passing the plant closing legislation." The standard for judging such legislation is "flexibility": "If we are to be competitive, America must be able to adapt to changing conditions here and abroad. We cannot stand still. We must be flexible enough to meet the challenges of the future." He then characteristically appeals to letters from workers and businessmen warning him against the legislation, although he only cites one from a businessman.

Arguing from analogy, he warns against going down the same slippery slope as the Western European countries:

> We should not go down the road of European labor policy—a policy that has resulted in no net job growth in the last decade. The European experience has proven that notification mandated by law does not create or save one job. Nor does it assist those who find themselves without work—it does just the opposite. Plant closing restrictions have resulted in fewer plant openings.

Finally, he explains the real reason why the legislation is being pushed through, the desire to score "political points with organized labor." Those in Congress who supported him were able to see beyond "the parochial interest" and vote for the "national interest." Yet, the national interest now dictates that the congressional majority stop being able to play politics. He will allow the bill to become law without his signature in order to stop these "political shenanigans."[52]

This speech is interesting not so much for its effect on Congress or public opinion as for the way in which it reveals the tension of conservative rhetoric under conditions of strain. All of Reagan's arguments are space-binding. Americans must be united across the vast space of the continent and across groups. He alone speaks from the general—as opposed to the special—interest. The United States itself exists in a vast world with many competitors. We are better than our competitors because of our flexibility, our inability to "stand still."

If we move Reagan's arguments up one step on the ladder of abstraction we find the characteristic theme of liberalism: Reduce the intrusion of government. This is the only actual principle invoked in the speech. It might have been possible for him to appeal more directly to the principle of avoiding intrusion into the private right of contract, as in the Lochner case, but he did not do so. William F. Buckley, Jr., however, did make this appeal in his last column on the subject: "Suppose one were to take the complementary position, and pass a law stipulating that no American can quit his job without serving sixty days' notice? Interesting thought, except it's unconstitutional. Section One of the Thirteenth Amendment proscribes involuntary servitude. Well, Section Two of the Thirteenth Amendment should proscribe involuntary employment."[53] But here even the agile Buckley strikes a strained rhetorical note: Surely an invocation of neutral principles is inappropriate here given the lack of equality in power between a multinational corporation and a worker.

Richard Weaver, the great conservative rhetorical theorist, points out that true conservatives always argue from general principle *(argument from definition)* while liberals (by which he meant anything from nineteenth-century laissez-faire to the New Deal) always argue from expediency *(argument from circumstance)*.[54] Weaver's distinction fits in neatly with the space-binding, time-binding distinction. Liberal argument does not place itself in historical time, except perhaps future time. It does not know the past as resource; the historical-hermeneutic aspects of the lifeworld are displaced by the demands of the system as it extends itself in space. Any claim on the past or on the unique histories of particular groups such as organized labor is translated into the charge of "playing politics." Also, in keeping with the perversity thesis identified by Albert O. Hirschman, Reagan contends that any attempt to benefit the workers, however well-intentioned, will have the perverse effect of creating economic stagnation.

The problem with liberal argument in times of crisis is that it has a motivational deficit. Reagan simply lacks a substantial argument from principle to counter the principle of "common decency" invoked repeatedly by the bill's proponents. Weyrich's Institute for Cultural Conservatism did justify the legislation strictly on the basis of conservative principle: the need to preserve local traditions and communities against the rootless rapacity of large corporations with no regional, or even national, ties.

This attack on business interests is echoed by the traditionalist Chilton Williamson, Jr., in a review of a book by Anthony Harrigan and William R. Hawkins. Williamson attacks the American Right's "fetish" of free trade and praises Harrigan and Hawkins for developing the outline of a new mercantilism for America. He attacks the "American business interests wishing to profit by sale to America's enemies and Pollyannish intellectuals who rejoice at the coming of the 'globalized' world economy."[55] If one were to add Pat Robertson's rejection of usury on biblical principles—an issue that seems to have been ignored in the 1988 presidential campaign—one finds another time-binding argument from principle against free-market capitalism. One can see a similar split between business interests and sound conservative principle in the Bush administration's refusal to punish the Chinese government after the events of May and June 1989. The candidacy of Patrick Buchanan in the 1992 election and the protest by evangelicals against the Bush administration's abandonment of Israel represent other points of fracture among conservatives.

Those conservatives who refused to go along with Reagan's view of the plant-closing legislation were perhaps neither "playing politics" nor somehow misguidedly serving the European social-democratic conspiracy. They were simply taking the idea of national glory and communal stability—the republican strain in Reagan's rhetoric—more seriously than Reagan himself. The defense of plant-closing legislation is easily reconcilable with the notion of "societal property rights" proposed by one New Right theorist.[56]

The contradictions of traditionalism itself are revealed in this notion of societal property rights. It sounds like a form of socialism, but it was first developed in the context of an argument for legislation restricting immigration. The coexistence of Patrick Buchanan's anticapitalist arguments (themselves funded by American textile manufacturers) with barely disguised forms of racism and anti-Semitism suggest that a very different political language, that of fascism, has some significant, if limited, appeal after the conservative division.

These signs of a split in American conservatism indicate that President Reagan was able to emphasize the threats to civic virtue and republican stability caused by rapid social change. If nothing else, Reagan introduced a sense of stability and predictability into our national life. His eloquent appeal to time-binding historical memory in his farewell address, with his references to Jimmy Doolittle and "thirty seconds over Tokyo," was remarkably effective. It is all the more curious that when faced with the opportunity to reinforce the conservative virtues of stability and predictability in a discussion of the national economy and to reach out to his blue-collar supporters, Reagan reverted to a standard, space-binding liberal rhetoric. As Paul Auerbach writes, even the latter represents a "new contradiction" in capitalism, for it requires a level of national education that undercuts capitalism: "Underlying competitive pressures in the most advanced forms of competitive capitalism engender a need for a flexible, educated workforce that has broad autonomy in decision-making."[57]

One could argue a left-wing version of the perversity thesis against Reagan. If Reagan's rhetoric worked because he was able to link the idioms of Lockean liberalism with peculiarly American forms of republicanism, it is no accident that Reagan's legacy should be most vulnerable where he was most effective in the short term. Reagan's own ethos (as well as an expanding economy) helped gloss over contradictions, but with the recession of the late 1980s and increased racial tension, the antirhetorical presidency of George Bush was unable to keep Reaganism going. The only things that seemed to raise George Bush to Reagan-style eloquence were the Gulf War, a capital-gains tax cut, and the free trade agreement with Mexico. What the rhetoric of the Gulf War did—just or unjust—for Americans was to reveal a deep-seated hunger, not so much for domination over others, but for a sense of community at home.[58] That the sense of community was so powerful and so fleeting is perhaps the root of Bush's political failure.

The larger problem revealed by both sides in the plant-closing debate is how remarkably impoverished our public language is for talking about *work*. I have tried to demonstrate in this chapter that Habermas's arguments about communicative action and the colonization of the lifeworld solve a number of problems in classical Marxism. Like the Marxist tradition, however, he seems unable or unwilling to spend much time theorizing the historical-hermeneutic space between lifeworld and system that is occupied by rhetorical action.

I also have tried to deliver on my argument that a rhetorical analysis of what the Left usually calls "ideology" may have some strategic benefits. Without being too overtly Leninist, an understanding of the "weak links" in the rhetoric of the class adversary opens up hope for change. An ideology is not a transparent reflection of interests, nor is it a monolithic force with an all-powerful life of its own. An ideology is simply an unstable stitching together of the disparate rhetorical idioms in which a social formation tries to make sense of an ever-inscrutable history.

To discuss the rhetorical aspects of ideology, however, is not to give up Marxism. As Perry Anderson has written, although the working class in the West and the Socialist movement throughout the world are in disarray, Marxism is in many ways less "defeated and dispersed" than it was during the Great Depression. There is no reason for Marxism

> to abandon its Archimedean vantage-point: the search for subjective agencies capable of effective strategies for the dislodgement of objective structures. But amidst pervasive changes within world capitalism today, those three terms [agencies, strategies, structures] can only be successfully combined if they have a common end that is at once desirable and believable for millions who are now hesitant or indifferent to them.[59]

It is the function of a critical theory of rhetoric to help formulate strategies to make socialism a desirable and believable end and to call into being publics who will implement them.

Conclusion:
Toward a Red Rhetoric

MARXISM, AS KENNETH BURKE HAS WRITTEN, is "unsleepingly rhetorical." Burke tells the (surely autobiographical?) story of a Marxist who got "soundly rebuked by his comrades for the suggestion that leftist critics collaborate in a study of 'Red Rhetoric.'" The comrades would not allow such talk because "for them, 'Rhetoric' applied solely to the persuasiveness of capitalist, fascist, and other non-Marxist terminologies (or 'ideologies')."[1]

My argument in this book has been that Burke's experience was inevitable, given the historical development of both Marxism and the capitalist system it sought to displace. Classical Marxism adopted an implicit theory of language and communication that was an unstable mixture of romantic expressionism and a positivist dream of perfectly transparent communication. The lack of a theory of rhetoric and political judgment led to considerable confusion among later Marxists about how to relate subjective agencies and objective structures. There was in principle no difficulty in Marx and Engels's asserting that people make history, but not under circumstances of their own choosing. Yet history itself would tend to force people to emphasize either the first or second half of that sentence.

The flexibility and open-endedness of classical Marxism is apparent in this quotation from the *Eighteenth Brumaire*:

> Proletarian revolutions criticize themselves constantly, interrupt themselves continually in their own course, come back to the apparently accomplished in order to begin it afresh, deride with unmerciful thoroughness the inadequacies, weaknesses and paltrinesses of their first attempts, seem to throw down their adversary only that he may draw new strength from the earth and rise again, more gigantic, before them.[2]

But only part of Marx's prediction was true. Capitalism did draw new strength from the earth and rise again, ever more gigantic. Yet proletarian revolutions were marked above all by their failure to criticize themselves constantly. The failure of communism was *in part* a failure to allow spaces for political deliberation outside the confines of the vanguard party. I say

143

"in part" because we will never know how much of the political pathology of communism stemmed from the relentless efforts of the capitalist nations to encircle it and stamp it out, even in its most humane forms.

The more humane forms of Marxism themselves possess contradictions that are connected to the problematic of rhetoric. The reformism of Bernstein possesses a motivational deficit in direct proportion to its humane, universalizing rhetoric. Lukács's theory of reification authorizes both Leninist elitism and the political quietism of the Frankfurt School because of its denial of rhetorical possibilities among a public deformed by capitalism. Gramsci's theory of hegemony resolves the classical contradiction between structure and struggle—but at the price of authorizing a rampant culturalism in Western Marxism. Marcuse and Williams inherit and extend these contradictions of Lukács and Gramsci. Habermas attempts to resolve them from within the framework of a theory of communicative action, but his refusal of rhetoric—as strategic action that violates the ethical autonomy of the subject—blocks political application of his theory. Alec Nove presents a workable model for market socialism yet proclaims that he has no idea how to build popular support for it. Analytic Marxists, such as G. A. Cohen, Erik Olin Wright, John Roemer, and Jon Elster make Marxist social science as rigorous as mainstream economics, sociology, and analytic philosophy, but, like Nove, are unable to develop political strategies.

Virtually the only place where Marxism today possesses unquestioned prestige is in the literature departments of universities in the Western democracies. As Perry Anderson writes, the final days of Western Marxism exhibit a "virtual hypertrophy of the aesthetic—which came to be surcharged with all the values that were repressed or denied elsewhere in the atrophy of living socialist politics."[3] Hundreds of thousands of dollars are spent each year in the United States alone on Marxist analyses of literary works and works of popular culture, while analysis of Marxist discourse, the rhetoric of the labor movement, and the rhetoric of capitalist institutions occurs only in a few, usually marginalized places. Even those rhetoricians who take a leftist political perspective have largely jumped on the postmodern theory train that leaves the working class behind.[4]

Despite my aim of criticizing Marxism from a rhetorical standpoint, it is even more important to criticize rhetorical theory and practice from a Marxist standpoint. One purpose of my book has been to isolate those key knots, or points of contradiction, in the Marxist tradition that have left it open to argument from the Right or from liberals. My goal has been to use concepts from the rhetorical tradition to "confront the internal obstacles, aporias, blockages of [Marxist] theory in its own attempt to approximate to a general truth of the time."[5] Any attempt to construct a Marxist rhetoric—both as a theory of revolutionary communicative practice and as a practical handbook for the management of discourse—must begin with a guide to chief arguments against Marxism.

My analysis of Marxist rhetoric has revealed seven key enduring moments in the argument against Marxism. First, those arguments that stem from a definition of *human nature*. Hirschman's perversity, futility, and jeopardy arguments stem from a conception of human nature—in religious or social-scientific terms—as unable to learn from mistakes. The religious critique of communism that emerged with Reinhold Niebuhr in the 1940s emphasized the significance of original sin as a political principle.

Marxists need to be able to defend the notion of learning and progress against its reactionary and postmodern opponents. Even a defense of market mechanisms as feedback devices under socialism need not capitulate to the reigning assumption that all incentives are economic. The reality is that those nations and regions in the West in which class struggle and Socialist politics have been strong exhibit higher educational and health levels than in those regions in which such factors have not been as strong. From the standpoint of Grand Theory, the difference between Minnesota and Virginia or between Norway and South Africa may not be great, but from the standpoint of those who would care for an autistic child or battered woman the difference is quite literally worth killing and dying for. One wonders, too, if without revolutionary movements, capitalist states and regions would have had the "incentive" to provide even minimum standards of social welfare.

A second argument against Marxism is its mechanistic conception of human motivation, politics, and culture. This rhetorical contradiction of Marxism stems from the fact that it emerged in a rhetorical situation in which the idealism of German philosophy and Christianity were dominant. Even classical Marxism was far less deterministic than is usually depicted by its opponents. It will be the enduring legacy of Western Marxism to have opened up discussions of freedom and culture within the Marxist tradition. Yet today, when the reduction of politics to language and spectacle is an article of faith on the Left, it is more crucial than ever to insist upon the existence of material needs.[6]

A third recurring argument against Marxism relates to the problem of inevitability. What Gouldner called "the nuclear contradiction in Marxism" stemmed from the difficulty in reconciling determination by modes of production and the existence of agents who would struggle against these modes. The revolution simply did not happen in the West, and where the revolution did occur it was a moral and economic failure. So-called postmodern theory has emerged as a strategy for making sense of the collapse of the "master narratives" of liberal progress and Marxist revolution that emerged in the nineteenth century.

Marxism needs to rethink its concept of temporality. The space-binding characteristics of nineteenth-century capitalism and liberalism were taken up more or less uncritically by Marxism. Only Raymond Williams has spoken significantly for the need of a sense of place in Marxist theory. The preservation of local and national traditions and practices in the face of the corrosive leveling by nomadic capitalism may make a kind of Marxist conservatism possible. Similarly, the prospect of ecological catastrophe may be the best argument for democratic control of the economy since the Great Depression—although democratic control will require substantial rethinking of the productivist assumptions that communism and capitalism shared.

Perhaps the most crucial aspect of a Marxist theory of temporality would be the revival of the republican sense of the fragility of the public sphere. As Hannah Arendt has taught us, modernity in both capitalist and Communist forms has tended to collapse the political into the economic. Where Marx in the *Eighteenth Brumaire* could see only "the poetry of the past" in eighteenth-century republicanism, Marxists after the fall of communism can see an enduring rhetoric for the future. Capitalism still has a cycle of boom and bust, and that cycle creates opportunities for reform and revolution. But that moment of revolutionary time, like the moment of the republic in classical theory, is fleeting. Careful planning and a sense of political and rhetorical judgment are needed in order to make a revolution. Classical republicanism recognized the need for leadership and rhetoric—a theme that may be missed by an uncritical defense of participatory democracy. A vanguard party is not in principle a violation of the republican spirit. Preventing the corrupting influence of centralized power and a taste for luxury—common themes in eighteenth-century republicanism—require constant vigilance and free spaces for deliberation, discussion, and debate.

A fourth argument against Marxism relates to its systemic character. Why jeopardize the achievements of the Western democracies in the name of a revolutionary leap into the void? How can systemic indictments be persuasive to audiences who have a stake in the survival of the system? Classical Marxism, even Leninism, made it clear that socialism would build on the achievements—cultural, political, and economic—of capitalism. Somehow by the late twentieth century, leftism had mutated into a rejection of the system that was so total that all past achievements in science and art and politics had become suspect. When Walter Benjamin wrote that there is no document of civilization that is not simultaneously a document of barbarism, he was right, but the contemporary academic Left, in its rejection of the possibility of truth and rational deliberation, sees only barbarism and not the vital *contradiction* that Benjamin, as a Marxist, grasped so clearly.[7]

Fifth, the tendency of Marxism to label as reformist and opportunist any party or movement to the right of itself is perhaps the worst legacy of its system-thinking. Such thinking—in the form of the Stalinist doctrine of "social fascism"—was directly responsible for the rise of the Third Reich. As Roy Medvedev writes, "Communists must find a way of maintaining their organization and revolutionary spirit while crediting the long-scorned democratic institutions of Western society with far greater value than they have ever done before. Meanwhile, Socialists must, for their part, become more radical in their demands for the reform of capitalism."[8] The division between the two is responsible for the continued survival of capitalism.

Sixth, what about the uncertainty of the memory of communism itself? Why even bother preserving the names of Marx and Engels and Lenin after the universal triumph of the Market? One response, of course, is that capitalism's relentless effacement of its own past and the absence of historical memory in the Western democracies, especially in the United States, may make any of the demonic connotations of Marxism or communism disappear in about the same time that it takes a successor to, say, Madonna to come before the popular consciousness. A more sensible response is to preserve the memory of Communist terror while refusing to let the equivalent terror of Western imperialism and militarism pass out of memory as well. If American schoolchildren must learn about Stalin and Babi Yar and the Gulag, they must also learn about Peterloo and Ludlow and El Salvador.

Finally, the persuasiveness of Marxism rises or falls with a commitment to the centrality of class as a factor in history. Does not race or gender possess an equivalent if not greater claim? The appalling success of the recent political correctness campaign by the Right illustrates the vulnerability of the Left on this question. The proliferation of "special interest" groups jockeying for most-favored-victim status has undercut the possibility of solidarity with those groups—the white working and middle classes—who, like it or not, have the greatest chance of affecting change in public policy. The need to sell one's labor power, increasingly under physically and psychologically degrading conditions, is the one unifying experience across age, ethnic, gender, and status lines. That was Marx's insight into capitalist alienation. It remains the moral basis for socialism. But it also possesses a practical, rhetorical, and political basis. As Perry Anderson writes in response to the feminist critique of Marxism:

> Universal though the cause of women's emancipation may be, one so radical that men too will be freed from their existing selves by it, it is insufficiently operational as a collective agency, actual or potential, ever to be able to uproot the economy or polity of capital. For that, a social force endowed with another strategic leverage is necessary. Only the modern "collective labourers," the workers who constitute the immediate producers of any industrial society, possess that leverage—by reason of their specific 'class capacity,' or structural position within the process of capitalist machinofacture as a whole, which they alone can paralyze or transform; just as they alone, by

reason of their potential cohesion and mass, can furnish the central contin-
gents of the organized army of popular will and aspiration required for any
decisive confrontation with the bourgeois state.[9]

To argue, however, for the recovery of class-based politics and a concentration on the workplace as a site of oppression is not to dismiss the significance of feminism for socialism. As the new feminist labor history is beginning to demonstrate, both socialism and the labor movement have been
deeply caught up in the contradictions of gender. The centrality of "man-
hood" as an ideological term in the rhetoric of craft unionism, the rhetorical configuring of the Great Depression as a crisis of masculinity, and the
recent attempt to make feminism responsible for increased poverty rates
among women and children suggest that gender-based oppression, rather
than being a holdover from feudalism, may in fact be the central social site
in which the contradictions of capitalist development are mediated and resolved.[10] It is in tracing the symbolic relationship between gender and work
that students of practical rhetoric have the greatest contribution to make to
the development of Marxism.

Studying the rhetorical significance of gender and work will especially
help us understand how the Right has stolen the language of class from the
Left. A significant force in that theft has been the class-ridden character of
the American Left. As Paul Cowan writes, at some time during the 1960s
the Left lost its ability to speak for the working class. When Agnew railed
against the "educated bums" who opposed the Vietnam War, "he sought to
fashion a 'silent majority' out of class envy. He was particularly effective in
second- or third-generation Polish or German or Italian communities in cit-
ies like Milwaukee or Indianapolis. . . . There, he'd paint his half-accurate,
half-lurid portraits of the upheavals in the ghettos or on the campuses.
Then, in his flat, nasal voice he'd ask—with no visible reference—'Did we
come all that way for this?'"[11]

From the standpoint of a factory worker in Lawrence, Massachusetts,
hippies and student radicals were well-to-do young people from Andover,
Beacon Hill, and Harvard, the "off-spring of families that had always mis-
treated Lawrence millhands."[12] It is no accident that the same pattern is
repeated over twenty years later, when academic radicals provide easy opportunities for right-wing caricature. Messrs. Bush, Bennett, Kimball,
Bloom, D'Souza, and others can ask middle- and working-class taxpayers,
"We worked hard to send our children to this?" and thus justify one more
set of budget cuts for higher education.

As Elizabeth Fox-Genovese and others have argued, the American Left's
primary problem is its inheritance of a rhetoric and ideology of individualism from classical liberalism and 1960s radicalism.[13] Rather than, in the
spirit of classical republicanism, seeing human beings as political animals
who can best fulfill their natures only by participating in self-government,

and who require a sense of communal virtue to sustain republican institutions, much of the academic Left still defines human beings as individuals first, who must be freed from the oppressive chains of family, religion, and national loyalty whether they like it or not. As American workers, even those who do not fall within the classical Marxist definitions of the working class, experience the dislocations imposed by the increased movement of capital across state and national boundaries, it is high time to revive a political language that speaks of the fragility of republics, the importance of national unity and patriotism, and the importance of the historical memory of liberty. The rhetoric alone will not do it, but it is at least a start.

Notes

Preface

1. Kenneth Burke, *A Rhetoric of Motives* (Berkeley: University of California Press, 1969), p. 101.

2. Ibid., p. 101.

3. Bryan D. Palmer, *Descent into Discourse* (Philadelphia: Temple University Press, 1991).

Introduction

1. For a useful discussion of this form of rhetorical action, known as epideictic oratory by the classical theorists, see Celeste Michelle Condit, "The Functions of Epideictic: The Boston Massacre Orations as Exemplar," *Communication Quarterly* 33 (1985), 284–299.

2. Richard Rorty, "The Intellectuals at the End of Socialism," *Yale Review* 80 (1992), 1–16.

3. Ibid., p. 1.

4. Ibid., p. 2.

5. Ibid., p. 3.

6. Ibid., p. 4.

7. Ibid., p. 5.

8. Ibid., p. 10.

9. Ibid., p. 16.

10. On Marx's "ceremony of status degradation" of Weitling, see Alvin W. Gouldner, *Against Fragmentation: The Origins of Marxism and the Sociology of Intellectuals* (New York: Oxford University Press, 1985), pp. 93–100. Regarding Engels's attack on Dühring, see Frederich Engels, *Herr Eugen Dühring's Revolution in Science (Anti-Dühring),* tr. Emile Burns (New York: International Publishers, 1939).

11. Rorty, "The Intellectuals at the End of Socialism," p. 11.

12. The fairer comparison might be to John F. Kennedy. Compare Rorty's argument to Kennedy's address at Yale in 1962: "What is at stake in our economic decisions today is not some grand warfare of rival ideologies which will sweep the country with passion, but the practical management of a modern economy. What we need are not labels and cliches, but more basic discussions of the sophisticated and technical questions involved in keeping a great economic machinery moving ahead" (cited in Alvin W. Gouldner, *The Dialectic of Ideology and Technology* [New York: Seabury, 1976], p. 250n). One might add, given Kennedy's love for Ivy League intellectuals, if Rorty's call for the banalization of politics is not: (a) ulti-

mately another form of Kennedy nostalgia after six more or less militantly anti-intellectual administrations, and (b) another way of trying to shore up the position of intellectuals over the masses, something he criticizes partisans of Grand Theory for doing. That is, intellectuals tend to benefit when social problems are redefined as "technical" problems.

13. John Dewey, *The Public and Its Problems* (Athens, OH: Swallow Press, 1980), p. 208.

14. See, for instance, Donald C. Bryant, "Rhetoric: Its Functions and Scope," *Quarterly Journal of Speech* 39 (1953), 401–424, and Douglas Ehninger, "On Systems of Rhetoric," *Philosophy and Rhetoric* 1 (1968), 131–144.

15. See Larry Arnhart, *Aristotle on Political Reasoning* (DeKalb, IL: Northern Illinois University Press, 1981); John S. Nelson, Allan Megill, and Donald N. McCloskey, eds., *The Rhetoric of the Human Sciences* (Madison: University of Wisconsin Press, 1987); Frank Lentricchia, *Criticism and Social Change* (Chicago: University of Chicago Press, 1983).

16. Terry Eagleton, *Walter Benjamin or Towards a Revolutionary Criticism* (London: Verso, 1981), p. 101.

17. Paolo Valesio, *Novantiqua: Rhetorics as a Contemporary Theory* (Bloomington: Indiana University Press, 1980).

18. Gareth Stedman Jones, *Languages of Class* (Cambridge: Cambridge University Press, 1983).

19. Michael Denning, *Mechanic Accents: Dime Novels and Working-Class Culture in America* (London: Verso, 1987), p. 217n1.

20. On the "poverty of strategy" in contemporary Marxism, see Perry Anderson, *In the Tracks of Historical Materialism* (Chicago: University of Chicago Press, 1984), pp. 27–28. See also Anderson's criticism of the structuralist/linguistic paradigm in Marxism, p. 64. Anderson rightly criticizes both the French structuralist Marxists and Habermas, but, of course, lacks a theory of rhetoric as an alternative view of language and communication.

21. Hans-Georg Gadamer, *Truth and Method,* tr. Garrett Barden and John Cumming (New York: Crossroad, 1975), pp. 10–39.

22. John Angus Campbell, "Hans-Georg Gadamer's Truth and Method," *Quarterly Journal of Speech* 64 (1978), 103.

23. Ronald Beiner, *Political Judgment* (Chicago: University of Chicago Press, 1983), p. 87.

24. Paul Ricoeur, *Freud and Philosophy: An Essay on Interpretation,* tr. Denis Savage (New Haven: Yale University Press, 1970), pp. 32–36.

25. Alvin W. Gouldner, *The Future of Intellectuals and the Rise of the New Class* (New York: Oxford University Press, 1979), pp. 28–37.

26. Gouldner clarifies this point in his discussion of Marx's degradation of Weitling: "The culture of critical discourse is thus a rhetorical strategy that appeals to younger persons who are commonly the less prominent and less accomplished. It is useful against those who are older and more prestigious, by in effect declaring that the latter's claims—even when grounded in their achievements—are irrelevant to the discussion" (*Against Fragmentation,* p. 98). CCD thus can function as *a* rhetoric, but is an essentially antirhetorical *stance* toward communication.

27. See Cicero on Socrates, "the source from which has sprung the undoubtedly absurd and unprofitable and reprehensible severance between the tongue and the

brain" (*De Oratore* III.xvi59–61, in *Cicero IV,* tr. Horace Rackham [Cambridge: Harvard University Press, 1942]).

28. See Christine Oravec, "The Democratic Critics: An Alternative American Rhetorical Tradition of the Nineteenth Century," *Rhetorica* 4 (1986), 395–421; and "The Sublimation of Mass Consciousness in the Rhetorical Criticism of Jacksonian America," *Communication* 11 (1990), 291–314. My indebtedness to Oravec's work will become obvious in Chapters 1 and 2, which focus largely on the construction of audiences by Marxist rhetoric.

29. See Chaim Perelman and Lucie Olbrechts-Tyteca, *The New Rhetoric: A Treatise on Argumentation,* tr. John Wilkinson and Purcell Weaver (Notre Dame, IN: University of Notre Dame Press, 1969), especially pp. 398–410.

30. There may have been political reasons for this fact. Whether it was the moral collapse of communism or the pressures of domestic McCarthyism or both, what could have been a "red rhetoric" was never written, although it survives in spots in *A Rhetoric of Motives* (Berkeley: University of California Press, 1969); see especially pp. 101–110 and 189–197. My work could be read as an elaboration of one sentence in Burke: "The Marxist persuasion is usually advanced in the name of no-rhetoric" (p. 102). Where I differ with Burke is in having had the advantage of studying the tradition of "Western Marxism," something Burke was never able to engage. On the very complicated issue of Burke's relationship to Marxism, see Lentricchia, and especially the articles in a special section of *Communication Studies* 42 (1991) edited by Edward Schiappa: Edward Schiappa and Mary F. Keehner, "The 'Lost' Passages of *Permanence and Change,*" 191–198; Philip C. Wander, "At the Ideological Front," 199–218; Don M. Burks, "Kenneth Burke: The Agro-Bohemian 'Marxoid,'" 219–233; and James Arnt Aune, "Burke's Palimpsest: Re-reading *Permanence and Change,*" 234–237.

31. Albert O. Hirschman, *The Rhetoric of Reaction* (Cambridge: Harvard University Press, 1991).

32. Ibid., p. 11.

33. Ibid., pp. 35–42.

34. Ibid., p. 170.

35. Ibid., p. 45.

36. See Alain Touraine, "An Introduction to the Study of Social Movements," *Social Research* 52 (1985), 749–789.

37. Hirschman, *The Rhetoric of Reaction,* p. 158.

38. Ibid., p. 80.

39. Ibid., p. 132.

40. Hirschman does not really deal with the theological roots of the futility thesis, probably because he is rightly more concerned with its manifestation in secular social science. The argument from radical evil was a staple of cold-war theologizing both in government and in the churches, and its primary representative was Reinhold Niebuhr.

41. Without defending the Soviet regime, it is nonetheless essential to keep pointing out that this was a *fundamental* and *wrong* dogma of both traditional and neo-conservatism. See especially Jeane Kirkpatrick, *Dictatorships and Double Standards: Rationalism and Reason in Politics* (New York: Simon and Schuster, 1982).

42. Karl Marx and Friedrich Engels, *The Communist Manifesto* (Harmondsworth: Penguin, 1967), p. 83.

43. Kenneth Burke, *A Grammar of Motives* (Berkeley: University of California Press, 1969), pp. 59–61.

44. Karl Marx, *Grundrisse,* tr. Martin Nicolaus (New York: Vintage, 1973), p. 611.

45. Alvin W. Gouldner, *The Two Marxisms* (New York: Oxford University Press, 1980), pp. 15–16. Theories move forward (or die) when inherent contradictions (research-driven anomalies) or external circumstances (event-driven anomalies) demand revisionary work.

46. This crucial point is developed by John Roemer, *A General Theory of Exploitation and Class* (Cambridge: Harvard University Press, 1982) and *Free to Lose: An Introduction to Marxist Economic Philosophy* (Cambridge: Harvard University Press, 1988). See also Erik Olin Wright's discussion of exploitation in *Classes* (London: Verso, 1985), pp. 64–104. It could be argued that the labor theory of value survived so long because of its rhetorical usefulness (it is one Marxist economic concept that anyone can understand fairly quickly), but there is probably no point in trying to make a case for it on those grounds.

47. Alan Sinfield, *Literature, Politics, and Culture in Postwar Britain* (Berkeley: University of California Press, 1989), p. 300.

48. Hirschman, *The Rhetoric of Reaction,* pp. 158–159.

49. Karl Marx, *Capital,* Vol. I, tr. Ben Fowkes (New York: Vintage, 1977), p. 92.

50. Although, arguably, this is the purpose of Karl Marx's *The Eighteenth Brumaire of Louis Bonaparte* (New York: International Publishers, 1963).

51. See David M. Gordon, Richard Edwards, and Michael Reich, *Segmented Work, Divided Workers: The Historical Transformation of Labor in the United States* (Cambridge: Cambridge University Press, 1982). The long-wave scheme provides an answer to Aileen Kraditor's charge that the system-orientation of Marxists ignores the fact that workers "chose" trade unions and the welfare state rather than "socialism"—the latter being simply an elitist obsession. The response is that the system was in crisis, and that it seemed reasonable to the vast majority of Western workers to select the moderate alternative. Other crises and other political movements in the future may provide other alternatives. See Aileen S. Kraditor, *The Radical Persuasion* (Baton Rouge: Louisiana State University Press, 1981). Every Marxist or Socialist needs to engage this work by the former Marxist who now writes for the far-Right newspaper *Human Events.*

52. Hirschman, *The Rhetoric of Reaction,* p. 148.

53. On this point see Gouldner, *The Dialectic of Ideology and Technology,* p. xv.

54. Gouldner, *The Two Marxisms,* p. 32.

55. Alec Nove, *The Economics of Feasible Socialism Revisited* (London: HarperCollinsAcademic, 1991), p. x.

Chapter 1

1. Karl Marx and Friedrich Engels, *Collected Works,* Vol. I (New York: International Publishers, 1975), p. 11.

2. Ibid., pp. 18–19.

3. John Durham Peters, "John Locke, the Individual, and the Origin of Communication," *Quarterly Journal of Speech* 75 (1989), 392.

4. See James W. Carey, "A Cultural Approach to Communication," *Communication as Culture: Essays on Media and Society* (Boston: Unwin Hyman, 1989), pp. 13–36.

5. See Thomas De Quincey, *The Logic of Political Economy and Other Papers* (Edinburgh: A. C. Black, 1863); Richard Whately, *Introductory Lectures on Political Economy* (London: J. W. Parker and Son, 1855). No one seems to have explored the connections between the economic and rhetorical writings of Smith, De Quincey, and Whately. Smith's lectures on rhetoric seem to be singularly unimaginative, although their connection to other aspects of Smith's social philosophy is explored in J. Michael Hogan, "Historiography and Ethics in Adam Smith's Lectures on Rhetoric, 1762–1763," *Rhetorica* 2 (1984), 75–91.

6. See Chaim Perelman and Lucie Olbrechts-Tyteca, *The New Rhetoric: A Treatise on Argumentation,* tr. John Wilkinson and Purcell Weaver (Notre Dame, IN: University of Notre Dame Press, 1969), p. 1; Wayne Booth, *Modern Dogma and the Rhetoric of Assent* (Notre Dame, IN: University of Notre Dame Press, 1974), pp. 133–134; Richard Weaver, *Ideas Have Consequences* (Chicago: University of Chicago Press, 1948), pp. 3–17; Richard McKeon, "The Use of Rhetoric in a Technological Age: Architectonic Productive Arts," in Lloyd F. Bitzer and Edwin Black, eds., *The Prospect of Rhetoric* (Englewood Cliffs, NJ: Prentice-Hall, 1971), p. 49; and Karl Wallace, "The Fundamentals of Rhetoric," in Bitzer and Black, eds., *The Prospect of Rhetoric,* p. 10.

7. John Gunnell, in *Political Theory: Tradition and Interpretation* (Cambridge, MA: Winthrop, 1979), makes a persuasive case for calling this story "the myth of the tradition," a "*recherche de temps perdu* that seeks to probe the political psyche of the West and isolate that point, or points, when its derangement began. Usually it is argued that the tradition developed to a certain stage of knowledge but then degenerated or was fundamentally diverted. The specification of this critical juncture is a matter of particular importance" (p. 35). A Marxist would point out that the similarity of the basic narrative structure—despite the widely varying politics of these writers—verifies that the rise of capitalism is central to the story. A rhetorician would also point out that Marxism was unable to free itself from all the derangements produced by capitalism. Also, it is possible to argue that the decline of rhetoric was a kind of derangement without committing to a restoration of, say, Roman republican politics. Michael Calvin McGee, for instance, argues for a restoration of the study of rhetoric as a practice without necessarily restoring any particular classical theory or pedagogical system of rhetoric. See "A Materialist's Conception of Rhetoric," in Ray E. McKerrow, ed., *Explorations in Rhetoric: Studies in Honor of Douglas Ehninger* (Glenview, IL: Scott, Foresman and Company, 1982), pp. 23–48. As will perhaps become obvious by the end of this book, my commitment to the uses of historical narratives of decline and fall is similar to that of Alasdair MacIntyre, *After Virtue* (Notre Dame, IN: University of Notre Dame Press, 1981), although I am more optimistic about rehabilitating Marxism as a critique of liberal individualism. MacIntyre places greater value on the Greek conception of virtue than the Roman one and thus does not adequately come to terms with the centrality of rhetoric in public life or with civic republicanism. See the brief discussion in *After Virtue,* pp. 236–238.

8. Terry Eagleton, *The Ideology of the Aesthetic* (Oxford: Basil Blackwell, 1990), p. 366. Eagleton, on the verge of recovering rhetoric in earlier work, seems to abandon this project in his major statement of aesthetic theory. It was in rhetorical education and oratorical practice that these three "mighty regions" were most often connected.

9. Other recent rehabilitations of rhetoric tend to focus on the epistemic function of tropes or narrative, or on practical reasoning. The line of work starting from Wayne Booth, *The Rhetoric of Fiction* (Chicago: University of Chicago Press, 1961), and continuing through the work of reception-aesthetics and reader-response theory provides a clearer link to audiences, although often at the price of political analysis and practical reasoning. See John Rodden, *The Politics of Literary Reputation* (New York: Oxford University Press, 1989), pp. 53–100, for a clarification of the differences between a rhetoric and an aesthetic of reception.

10. S. M. Halloran, "Tradition and Theory in Rhetoric," *Quarterly Journal of Speech* 62 (1976), 235–236.

11. See Albert O. Hirschman, *The Passions and the Interests* (Princeton: Princeton University Press, 1981).

12. Richard H. Fallon, Jr., "What Is Republicanism and Is It Worth Reviving?" *Harvard Law Review* 102 (1989), 1697.

13. See Gordon S. Wood, *The Creation of the American Republic 1776–1787* (Chapel Hill: University of North Carolina Press, 1969); Bernard Bailyn, *The Ideological Origins of the American Revolution* (Cambridge, MA: Harvard University Press, 1967); J.G.A. Pocock, *The Machiavellian Moment* (Princeton: Princeton University Press, 1975). This research is applied in a broader way by socialist legal scholar Mark Tushnet in *Red, White, and Blue: A Critical Analysis of Constitutional Law* (Cambridge, MA: Harvard University Press, 1988); for a critique, see Richard H. Fallon, Jr., "What Is Republicanism and Is It Worth Reviving?" *Harvard Law Review* 102 (1989), 1695–1735. A feminist version of the republican revival is provided by Suzanna Sherry, "Civic Virtue and the Feminine Voice in Constitutional Adjudication," *University of Virginia Law Review* 72 (1986), 543–560.

14. Charles Taylor, *Hegel* (Cambridge, MA: Cambridge University Press, 1975), pp. 17–18.

15. Ibid., p. 18.

16. As Martin Bernal has demonstrated, the rise of romantic expressionist views of language also was deeply linked to German racism and anti-Semitism: "Real communication was no longer perceived as taking place through reason, which could reach any rational man. It was now seen as flowing through feeling, which could touch only those tied to each other by kinship or 'blood' and sharing a common 'heritage.'" *Black Athena, Vol. I: The Fabrication of Ancient Greece, 1785–1985* (New Brunswick, NJ: Rutgers University Press, 1987), p. 28. This same dynamic is bound up with the rise of "literature" as a distinct field of inquiry, as Terry Eagleton documents in *Literary Theory: An Introduction* (Minneapolis: University of Minnesota Press, 1983), pp. 17–54. One may reasonably ask, if Bernal is correct, how *capitalism* and racism interrelate. If it is clear that racism is a relatively modern, "scientific" invention (quite distinct from slavery), how does it relate to the otherwise universalizing tendencies of capitalism? The way in which

the rhetorical tradition was received and reinterpreted by Hegel is discussed by John H. Smith, *The Spirit and Its Letter: Traces of Rhetoric in Hegel's Philosophy of Bildung* (Ithaca, NY: Cornell University Press, 1988).

17. Edwin Black, "The Second Persona," *Quarterly Journal of Speech* 55 (1970), 113.

18. I recognize that I am taking considerable liberty with Chaim Perelman's concept of the universal audience. Compare Perelman and Olbrechts-Tyteca, *The New Rhetoric*, pp. 13–62.

19. Hayden White, *Metahistory: The Historical Imagination in Nineteenth-Century Europe* (Baltimore: Johns Hopkins University Press, 1973), p. 37.

20. Ibid., p. 38.

21. Philip Wander, "The Third Persona: An Ideological Turn in Rhetorical Theory," *Central States Speech Journal* 35 (1984), 209.

22. John Gardner, *The Art of Fiction* (New York: Vintage, 1985), p. 10.

23. See Robert Heilbroner's useful summary of dialectical thinking in *Marxism For and Against* (New York: W. W. Norton, 1980), pp. 29–39.

24. Marx and Engels, *Collected Works,* Vol. I, p. 11.

25. See Richard Rorty, "Philosophy as a Kind of Writing: An Essay on Derrida," *Consequences of Pragmatism* (Minneapolis: University of Minnesota Press, 1982), p. 94.

26. Karl Marx, "For a Ruthless Criticism of Everything Existing," in Robert C. Tucker, ed., *The Marx-Engels Reader,* 2nd ed. (New York: W. W. Norton, 1978), pp. 13–15.

27. Karl Marx and Friedrich Engels, "Manifesto of the Communist Party," *Collected Works,* Vol. 6, p. 505.

28. Alvin W. Gouldner, *Against Fragmentation: The Origins of Marxism and the Sociology of Intellectuals* (New York: Oxford University Press, 1985), p. 107.

29. Ibid., p. 108.

30. The classic statement in defense of the break is Louis Althusser, *For Marx,* tr. Ben Brewster (London: New Left Books, 1977). Gouldner tries to resolve the problem of the "break" by positing the existence of "two Marxisms," one based on science and the other on critique: *The Two Marxisms* (New York: Oxford University Press, 1980). I am more or less persuaded by Gouldner's argument; my purpose here is to demonstrate that whether one adheres to a humanist, an Althusserian, or a Gouldnerian version of the "break," there is remarkable continuity in Marx and Engels's view of discourse.

31. Jerrold Seigel, *Marx's Fate: The Shape of a Life* (Princeton: Princeton University Press, 1978), documents the centrality of the inversion metaphor and strategy in Marx's work.

32. The links between alienation and Freud's concept of the uncanny might be worth pursuing, continuing the discussion begun by Jeffrey Mehlman, *Revolution and Repetition: Marx/Hugo/Balzac* (Berkeley: University of California Press, 1977), in the context of the uncanny in the *Eighteenth Brumaire.*

33. See Raymond Williams, *Culture and Society, 1780–1950,* new ed. (New York: Columbia University Press, 1983), for a discussion of the conservative critique of capitalism.

34. The following interpretation of the concept of alienation is influenced by

Jon Elster, *Making Sense of Marx* (Cambridge, MA: Cambridge University Press, 1985), pp. 74–92; Catharine A. MacKinnon, *Toward a Feminist Theory of the State* (Cambridge, MA: Harvard University Press, 1989), especially p. 15; and Nancy Hartsock, *Money, Sex, and Power: Toward a Feminist Historical Materialism* (Boston: Northeastern University Press, 1985).

35. V. I. Lenin, *What Is to Be Done?* tr. George Hanna and Victor J. Jerome (New York: International Publishers, 1969), pp. 31–32.

36. See Elster, *Making Sense of Marx*, p. 77; and John Elster, *Sour Grapes* (Cambridge, MA: Cambridge University Press, 1983), especially Chapter III.

37. Perry Anderson notes "the notorious absence of anything approaching . . . ethics within the accumulated corpus of historical materialism" and its "regular displacement by either politics or aesthetics," in *In the Tracks of Historical Materialism* (Chicago: University of Chicago Press, 1984), pp. 82–83. See also Richard W. Miller, *Analyzing Marx: Morality, Power, and History* (Princeton: Princeton University Press, 1984).

38. Elster, *Making Sense of Marx*, p. 465.

39. Marx and Engels, "The German Ideology," *Collected Works,* Vol. 5, p. 36.

40. Ibid., p. 92.

41. Karl Marx, "Contribution to the Critique of Hegel's Philosophy of Law: Introduction," *Collected Works,* Vol. 3, p. 174.

42. Marx and Engels, "The German Ideology," p. 59.

43. Ibid., pp. 60–61.

44. The parody will probably annoy some people, but as precedents, see Rosa and Charley Parkin, "Peter Rabbit and the *Grundrisse,*" *Archives Europiennes de Sociologie* 15 (1974), 181–183, and Terry Eagleton, "The Revolt of the Reader," in *Against the Grain* (London: Verso, 1986), pp. 181–184.

45. See Dallas Smythe, "Communications: Blindspot of Western Marxism," *Canadian Journal of Political and Social Theory* 1, 2 (1977), 1–27.

46. See, for instance, John Fiske, "Television: Polysemy and Popularity," *Critical Studies in Mass Communication* 3 (1986), 391–408.

47. See Elster, *Making Sense of Marx,* pp. 27–37.

48. Ibid., p. 28.

49. Marx and Engels, "The German Ideology," pp. 43–44.

50. Christopher Caudwell, *Illusion and Reality: A Study of the Sources of Poetry* (London: Lawrence and Wishart, 1977), p. 81.

51. See Perelman and Olbrechts-Tyteca, *The New Rhetoric,* p. 413.

52. Karl Marx, *Capital,* Vol. II (New York: International Publishers, 1967), p. 315.

53. G. A. Cohen, *Karl Marx's Theory of History: A Defence* (Princeton: Princeton University Press, 1978), p. 343. Cohen goes on to suggest that current understandings of linguistics and communication render this dream futile (p. 344).

54. Marx and Engels, "Manifesto of the Communist Party," pp. 486–487.

55. Ibid., p. 494.

56. And a staple of neoconservative critiques of "new class" involvement in politics—that is, any new class involvement other than their own. See Peter Steinfels, *The Neoconservatives* (New York: Simon and Schuster, 1979).

57. See Carey, "A Cultural Approach to Communication," *Culture as Communication*, pp. 13–36. Carey goes on to discuss the connection between the transmission view and Harold Innis's idea of space-binding communication media ("Space, Time, and Communications: A Tribute to Harold Innis," pp. 142–172). Communication, for Marx and Engels, is simply transmission across space. The binding of communities through time (traditionally the function of oral forms such as ritual and rhetoric) is neglected or even explicitly rejected, as we shall see later in the case of Marx's *Eighteenth Brumaire*.

58. Robert Paul Wolff, *Moneybags Must Be So Lucky: On the Literary Structure of Capital* (Amherst: University of Massachusetts Press, 1988), p. 81. Wolff's point about the centrality of irony in Marx is influenced by Ludovico Silva, *El Estilo Literario de Marx* (Mexico: Siglo XXI Editores, 1971).

59. There seems to be emerging consensus among Marxist economists that the notion of exploitation of labor, rather than the labor theory of value, is central to the critique of capitalism, mainly because of certain difficulties created by the latter. In a nutshell, equilibrium prices are not generally proportional to embodied labor values, mainly because of differential ownership of the capital stock used in producing goods for consumption. See John Roemer, *Free to Lose: An Introduction to Marxist Economic Philosophy* (Cambridge, MA: Harvard University Press, 1988), pp. 47–51.

60. Karl Marx, *Capital,* Vol. I, tr. Ben Fowkes (New York: Vintage, 1977), pp. 163–164.

61. Ibid., p. 166.

62. Alec Nove, *The Economics of Feasible Socialism Revisited* (London: HarperCollinsAcademic, 1991), p. 41.

63. Ibid., p. 37.

64. Ibid., p. 107.

65. To be fair, Trotsky did address this problem in his Transitional Program. Prices would be set by committees with delegates from factories, unions, farms, cooperatives, and consumers. See Leon Trotsky, *The Transitional Program for Socialist Revolution,* 2nd ed. (New York: Pathfinder, 1974). It is, of course, unclear how this could work on a large scale.

66. See Roberto Unger, *The Critical Legal Studies Movement* (Cambridge, MA: Harvard University Press, 1986), especially pp. 22–27. It is not entirely clear how free this model finally is from liberal individualism. The contemporary revival of the Sophists often seems to coexist with a sort of anarchistic political philosophy. But there are traditions of rhetoric other than the Sophistic one.

67. Jeffrey Mehlman, *Revolution and Repetition.*

68. See Dominick LaCapra, "Reading Marx," *Rethinking Intellectual History* (Ithaca: Cornell University Press, 1983), p. 283.

69. Karl Marx, *The Eighteenth Brumaire of Louis Bonaparte* (New York: International Publishers, 1963), p. 75.

70. LaCapra, "Reading Marx," p. 284.

71. Marx, *The Eighteenth Brumaire,* p. 15.

72. Ibid., pp. 16–17.

73. Ibid., p. 18.

74. Ibid., p. 25.

75. Richard Weaver, *Life Without Prejudice* (Chicago: Henry Regnery, 1965), p. 2.

76. Perry Anderson, *Considerations on Western Marxism* (London: Verso, 1976), p. 104.

77. Alvin W. Gouldner, *The Future of Intellectuals and the Rise of the New Class* (New York: Oxford University Press, 1979), p. 105n21.

78. Aileen S. Kraditor, *The Radical Persuasion* (Baton Rouge: Louisiana State University Press, 1981), pp. 320–321. Kraditor also insists that Marxist historians inevitably follow a "system" rather than "society" model, thus rendering persuasion and rational choice problematic (pp. 55–85).

79. Stuart Hall, "The Problem of Ideology—Marxism Without Guarantees," *Journal of Communication Inquiry* 10 (1986), 28–44.

Chapter 2

1. Karl Marx, *Capital,* Vol. III (New York: International Publishers, 1967), p. 886.

2. Erik Olin Wright, *Classes* (London: Verso, 1985), pp. 6–18.

3. To be fair, the space I am trying to theorize is perhaps captured by Andrew Levine and Erik Olin Wright as a notion of class capacity as opposed to class interest: "Rationality and Class Struggle," *New Left Review* 123 (1980), 47–68. They criticize G. A. Cohen's idea that the motivating force behind development of the forces of production is simple human rationality, the impulse to avoid scarcity. Cohen's idea is another way to talk about the mediation problem, but it shares with Wright—and "analytic Marxism" generally—a lack of interest in problems of language and communication.

4. This paragraph draws heavily on the article "Mediation," in Tom Bottomore et al., eds., *A Dictionary of Marxist Thought* (Cambridge, MA: Harvard University Press, 1983), pp. 329–330.

5. V. I. Lenin, "Conspectus of Hegel's Science of Logic," *Collected Works,* Vol. 38 (Moscow: Foreign Languages Publishing House, 1961), p. 226.

6. Or, rather, something that serves the function of a concept of mediation. I want to use the term in a fairly loose sense to refer to the social space in which messages and other institutional practices permit and encourage the exchange of energies between historical actors and the mode of production that constrains those actors. Raymond Williams rejects the concept of mediation as unnecessarily retaining a division between base and superstructure and wants to place language and signification as parts of the material social process itself: *Marxism and Literature* (Oxford: Oxford University Press, 1977), p. 99. Lawrence Grossberg uses the term to refer to signifying practices as they construct power relations: "Strategies of Marxist Cultural Interpretation," *Critical Studies in Mass Communication* 1 (1984), 399. He criticizes Williams for allowing experience to mediate between the cultural and the social. I discuss Grossberg's criticism of Williams in Chapter 4. What I share with Grossberg is a concern with "signifying practices," although I reject the semiotic vocabulary in favor of a rhetorical one. The concept of mediation as used in this chapter also includes institutional practices such as party orga-

nization that, although they do not exist apart from "signifying practices," are something more than those.

7. Kenneth Burke, *A Rhetoric of Motives* (Berkeley: University of California Press, 1969), p. 22.

8. Ibid., pp. 19–46.

9. Robert Bellah et al., *Habits of the Heart: Individualism and Commitment in American Life* (Berkeley: University of California Press, 1985).

10. Celeste Condit [Railsback], "Beyond Rhetorical Relativism: A Structural-Material Model of Truth and Objective Reality," *Quarterly Journal of Speech* 69 (1983), 362.

11. Leszek Kolakowski, *Main Currents of Marxism,* Vol. II (Oxford: Oxford University Press, 1978), p. 98.

12. Thomas B. Farrell, "Political Communication: Its Investigation and Praxis," *Western Journal of Speech Communication* 40 (1976), 91–103.

13. For a summary of this approach, see John Louis Lucaites and Celeste Michelle Condit, "Reconstructing 'Equality': Culturetypal and Counter-Cultural Rhetorics in the Martyred Black Vision," *Communication Monographs* 57 (1990), 7–8.

14. Ibid., p. 7.

15. Ibid., pp. 7–8.

16. The term "ideograph," of course, comes from Michael Calvin McGee, "The 'Ideograph': A Link Between Rhetoric and Ideology," *Quarterly Journal of Speech* 66 (1980), 1–16.

17. Cited in Peter Gay, *The Dilemma of Democratic Socialism: Eduard Bernstein's Challenge to Marx* (New York: Columbia University Press, 1952), p. 250.

18. Eduard Bernstein, *Evolutionary Socialism,* tr. Edith C. Harvey (New York: Schocken, 1961).

19. Ibid., p. viii.

20. Ibid., p. xiii.

21. Ibid., p. 9.

22. Ibid., pp. 200–201.

23. See Wayne C. Booth, *Modern Dogma and the Rhetoric of Assent* (Notre Dame, IN: University of Notre Dame Press, 1974), pp. 2–40.

24. Bernstein, *Evolutionary Socialism,* p. 166.

25. Ibid., p. 170.

26. See Ernesto Laclau and Chantal Mouffe, *Hegemony and Socialist Strategy: Towards a Radical Democratic Politics* (London: Verso, 1985), pp. 29–36. They write that Bernstein discovered the relative autonomy of the political but was locked within an evolutionary model of social development that eventually made the political irrelevant. It is not clear to me that Bernstein is as narrowly "evolutionary" in his thinking as Laclau and Mouffe allege.

27. Bernstein, *Evolutionary Socialism,* p. 17.

28. Ibid., p. 197.

29. Ibid., p. 146.

30. Ibid., p. 151.

31. Ibid., p. 221.

32. The character of the "roving proletarian" also seems to be situated in a

narrative in which the male worker is to be civilized by the feminine realm of the family. It is important not to lose sight of the importance of primary group institutions, but it is also important to recognize the way in which this sort of talk has made women workers invisible to much of the Socialist tradition. See the important study by Elizabeth Faue, *Community of Suffering and Struggle: Women, Men, and the Labor Movement in Minneapolis, 1915–1945* (Chapel Hill: University of North Carolina Press, 1991).

33. Bernstein, *Evolutionary Socialism,* p. 223.

34. See Robert J. Dostal, "Kant and Rhetoric," *Philosophy and Rhetoric* 13 (1980), 223–244.

35. Alexander Cockburn, "Radical as Reality," in Robin Blackburn, ed. *After the Fall: The Failure of Communism and the Future of Socialism* (London: Verso, 1991), pp. 168–169.

36. Robin Blackburn, "Fin de Siècle: Socialism After the Crash," in Blackburn, *After the Fall,* p. 189.

37. Ibid., p. 199.

38. See Alec Nove, *The Economics of Feasible Socialism Revisited* (London: HarperCollinsAcademic, 1991).

39. Cited in Hannah Arendt, "Bertolt Brecht: 1898–1956," *Men in Dark Times* (New York: Harcourt, Brace, and World, 1968), p. 225.

40. V. I. Lenin, *What Is to Be Done?* tr. George Hanna and Victor J. Jerome (New York: International Publishers, 1961).

41. Ibid., p. 8n.

42. Ibid., p. 11.

43. Ibid., p. 13.

44. Alvin W. Gouldner, *Against Fragmentation: The Origins of Marxism and the Sociology of Intellectuals* (New York: Oxford University Press, 1985), p. 181.

45. Ibid., p. 181.

46. Ibid., p. 181.

47. Lenin, *What Is to Be Done?* p. 11.

48. Ibid., p. 25.

49. Ibid., p. 32.

50. Ibid., p. 32.

51. Robert Hariman, "Rhetoric and World Order: Henry Kissinger's Realism," paper presented at Northwestern University, September 1990, p. 4.

52. Ibid., p. 5.

53. Ibid., p. 6.

54. V. I. Lenin, "Report on the Attitude of the Proletariat to Petty-Bourgeois Democrats Delivered at the Moscow Party Workers' Meeting (November 27, 1918)," in Lenin, *On Culture and Cultural Revolution* (Moscow: Progress Publishers, 1970), p. 57.

55. V. I. Lenin, "The Achievements and Difficulties of the Soviet Government," *On Culture and Cultural Revolution,* p. 64.

56. V. I. Lenin, "Report on the Foreign and Home Policy of the Council of People's Commissars at the Session of the Petrograd Soviet," *On Culture and Cultural Revolution,* pp. 61–62.

57. V. I. Lenin, "The Immediate Tasks of the Soviet Government," *Collected Works*, Vol. 27 (Moscow: Progress Publishers, 1965), p. 259.

58. François George, "Forgetting Lenin," *Telos* 18 (1973–74), 55.

59. Roy Medvedev, *Leninism and Western Socialism*, tr. A.D.P. Briggs (London: Verso, 1981), p. 35.

60. Ibid., pp. 39–41. In the Roman Republic, a dictator was an official, usually a consul, invested with extraordinary powers by the Senate for a specific, limited time period.

61. Ibid., p. 293.

62. See Williams, *Marxism and Literature*, p. 98.

63. Georg Lukács, *Record of a Life: An Autobiographical Sketch*, tr. Rodney Livingstone (London: Verso, 1983), p. 53.

64. Arendt, "Bertolt Brecht," p. 236.

65. Lukács, *Record of a Life*, p. 63.

66. Georg Lukács, *History and Class Consciousness*, tr. Rodney Livingstone (Cambridge: Massachusetts Institute of Technology Press, 1971), p. 84.

67. "Reification," *A Dictionary of Marxist Thought*, p. 411.

68. Lukács, *Record of a Life*, p. 164.

69. Fredric Jameson, *Marxism and Form* (Princeton: Princeton University Press, 1971), p. 185.

70. Lukács, *History and Class Consciousness*, pp. 50–51.

71. On Mann, see Lukács, *Record of a Life*, pp. 93–94. See also Lucien Goldmann, *Lukács and Heidegger* (London: Routledge and Kegan Paul, 1977).

72. Lucien Goldmann, *The Hidden God* (London: Routledge and Kegan Paul, 1967).

73. Fred Pfeil, "Makin' Flippy-Floppy: Postmodernism and the Baby-Boom PMC," in Mike Davis, Fred Pfeil, and Michael Sprinker, eds., *The Year Left: An American Socialist Yearbook* (London: Verso, 1985), pp. 268–295. There are, of course, problems with this sort of explanation. Blocked ascendancy and status anxiety can become an all-purpose form of explanation—Gouldner uses it to explain the appeal of Leninism, for instance. Non-Marxists like Richard Hofstadter used it to discount American radicalism.

74. See Georg Lukács, "Realism in the Balance," in *Aesthetics and Politics* (London: New Left Books, 1977), pp. 28–59.

75. See, for instance, Lukács's citation of Lenin in the "Realism in the Balance" essay: "Marxism attained its world-historical importance as the ideology of the revolutionary proletariat by virtue of its refusal to reject the most valuable achievements of the bourgeois era. Instead, it appropriated and assimilated all that was valuable in a tradition of human thought and human culture stretching back over 2000 years" (p. 55).

76. Aniko Bodroghkozy, "A Gramscian Analysis of Entertainment Television and the Youth Rebellion of the 1960s," *Critical Studies in Mass Communication* 8 (1991), 217.

77. Ibid., 228.

78. M. S. Piccirillo, "An Isocratean Rhetoric of Television," *Communication* 12 (1990), 1–18.

79. Laclau and Mouffe, *Hegemony and Socialist Strategy,* p. 18.
80. Ibid., p. 21.
81. Ibid., pp. 32–33.
82. Ibid., p. 82.
83. Ibid., p. 67.
84. The precise nature of Gramsci's relationship to Lenin is hard to determine. He does not seem to have had Lenin's *What Is to Be Done?* available to him, for instance, even though the English translation of the notebooks says that he did. See Paul Piccone, *Italian Marxism* (Berkeley: University of California Press, 1983), p. 193.
85. Antonio Gramsci, *Selections from the Prison Notebooks,* tr. Quintin Hoare and Geoffrey Nowell Smith (New York: International Publishers, 1971), p. 418.
86. Ibid., p. 97.
87. Antonio Gramsci, *Selections from Political Writings, 1910–1920,* tr. Quintin Hoare (New York: International Publishers, 1977), pp. 34–37.
88. See Piccone, *Italian Marxism,* p. 191.
89. Gramsci, *Selections from the Prison Notebooks,* p. 133.
90. John M. Murphy, "Domesticating Dissent: The Kennedys and the Freedom Rides," *Communication Monographs* 59 (1992), 64.
91. Todd Gitlin, "Prime Time Ideology: The Hegemonic Process in Television Entertainment," in Horace Newcomb, ed., *Television: The Critical View,* 3rd ed. (New York: Oxford University Press, 1982), p. 428. Gitlin retains the essentially *contradictory* character of hegemony in a way that later theorists do not.
92. Gramsci is very similar to Raymond Williams in this respect.
93. Gramsci, *Selections from the Prison Notebooks,* p. 395.
94. Piccone, *Italian Marxism,* p. 178.
95. Gramsci, *Selections from the Prison Notebooks,* pp. 366–367. Gramsci's examples of actual transformation (pp. 272–275, for instance) seem to point to the need to *personalize* class hatred. As long as the peasant confronts only a generic enemy, he does not have class consciousness. See Walter L. Adamson, *Hegemony and Revolution: A Study of Antonio Gramsci's Political and Cultural Theory* (Berkeley: University of California Press, 1980), pp. 152–155.
96. Frantz Fanon, *The Wretched of the Earth,* tr. Constance Farrington (New York: Grove Press, 1968).
97. Laclau and Mouffe, *Hegemony and Socialist Strategy,* p. 191.
98. Piccone, *Italian Marxism,* pp. 196–197.
99. Another way to infer the implications of Gramsci for rhetorical studies is to realize that Gramsci's theorizing of the cultural was overly influenced by Croce, whose rejection of rhetoric was explicit. See Benedetto Croce, *Aesthetic,* tr. Douglas Ainslie (Boston: David R. Godine, 1978), pp. 422–436.

Chapter 3

1. Christopher Lasch, *The Culture of Narcissism: American Life in an Age of Diminishing Expectations* (New York: W. W. Norton, 1979).
2. A thorough discussion of the climate surrounding the malaise speech, includ-

ing Caddell's interpretation of Lasch, is in Elizabeth Drew, "Phase: In Search of a Definition," *The New Yorker,* August 27, 1979, pp. 45–73.

3. This influence, and the extent to which Lasch is faithful to or different from the Frankfurt School, is discussed extensively in a special symposium on narcissism in *Telos* 44 (1980), including essays by Russell Jacoby, Stanley Aronowitz, Paul Piccone, and Jean Elshtain. Lasch responds to his critics and discusses the Carter administration in "Narcissism and the Problem of 'Morale,'" pp. 122–125.

4. I recognize the fact that Theodor Adorno possesses, perhaps, equal claim to consideration. My choice of Marcuse has more to do with the fact that his presentation of the Frankfurt School's position is more accessible (and influential, at least in the United States) than Adorno's. For more sophisticated discussions of the relationship of Marcuse to the Frankfurt School than I am able to present here, see Douglas Kellner, *Herbert Marcuse and the Crisis of Marxism* (Berkeley: University of California Press, 1984), Barry Katz, *Herbert Marcuse and the Art of Liberation* (London: Verso, 1982); and Martin Jay, *The Dialectical Imagination: A History of the Frankfurt School and the Institute of Social Research, 1923–1950* (Boston: Little, Brown, 1973). Adorno seems to have been the only member of the Frankfurt School to discuss rhetoric directly. He captures the contradictions of rhetorical practice rather deftly in a fragmentary passage of *Negative Dialectics,* tr. E. B. Ashton (New York: Seabury, 1973): "In philosophy, rhetoric represents that which cannot be thought except in language. It holds a place among the postulates of contents already known and fixed. Rhetoric is in jeopardy, like any substitute, because it may easily come to usurp what the thought cannot obtain directly from the presentation. It is incessantly corrupted by persuasive purposes—without which, on the other hand, the thought act would no longer have a practical relation" (p. 55). The notion of corruption by persuasive purposes is a representative Frankfurt School position—as is the sense of *aporia* induced by the nostalgia for practice. Where Adorno (and Max Horkheimer) differ from Marcuse is in their differing senses of hope. Adorno can only look to the past: "Philosophy, which once seemed obsolete, lives on because the moment to realize it was missed" (p. 3). Marcuse's project treats the past differently: "Time loses its power when remembrance redeems the past" (*Eros and Civilization* [Boston: Beacon Press, 1962], p. 213).

5. See *Time,* March 22, 1968, p. 38; "Marcuse: Cop-Out or Cop?" In: *Progressive Labor,* February 1969, pp. 61–66; Pope Paul VI denounced Marcuse's work as "the theory that opens the way to license cloaked as liberty," *Vatican Bulletin,* October 1, 1969; the Soviet statement is "Taking Marcuse to the Woodshed," *Atlas,* September 1968, pp. 33–35; on Reagan and the American Legion's attempt to buy out Marcuse's contract, see "Legion vs. Marcuse," *Nation,* October 28, 1968, p. 421. For a thorough discussion of this period in Marcuse's life, see Barry Katz, *Herbert Marcuse and the Art of Liberation,* pp. 162–192.

6. The next two paragraphs draw heavily on Richard McKeon, "Dialectic and Political Thought and Action," *Ethics* 65 (1954), 3–16.

7. See Karl Marx, *Capital,* Vol. I, tr. Ben Fowkes (New York: Vintage, 1977), p. 103.

8. See W. S. Howell, "Renaissance and Modern Rhetoric: A Study in Change,"

in Joseph Schwartz and John A. Rycenga, eds., *The Province of Rhetoric* (New York: Ronald, 1965), pp. 292–308.

9. Herbert Marcuse, "On the Problem of the Dialectic," *Telos* 27 (1976), 33.

10. Herbert Marcuse, *Reason and Revolution* (Boston: Beacon Press, 1960), p. vii. See Fredric Jameson, *Marxism and Form* (Princeton: Princeton University Press, 1971) for a discussion of Marcuse in terms of his development of a "new hermeneutics" in the "form of a profound and almost Platonic valorization of memory, anamnesis, in human existence" (p. 112).

11. Marcuse, *Reason and Revolution,* p. ix.

12. Cited in Herbert Marcuse, *One-Dimensional Man* (Boston: Beacon Press, 1964), p. 120.

13. Ibid., p. 134.

14. Marcuse, "On the Problem of the Dialectic," 17.

15. Ibid., 17–22.

16. Ibid., 16.

17. Marcuse, *Reason and Revolution,* p. 114.

18. Marcuse, *One-Dimensional Man,* pp. 108–114.

19. Ibid., pp. 114–120.

20. Ibid., pp. 196–197.

21. Ibid., p. 199.

22. Herbert Marcuse, "On Hedonism," *Negations: Essays in Critical Theory* (Boston: Beacon Press, 1968), pp. 196–197; the Hegel quotation is from the lectures on the philosophy of history.

23. Ibid., p. 195.

24. Marcuse, *One-Dimensional Man,* p. 199. It is interesting that the major contemporary philosopher most committed to reviving classical notions of happiness and ethics, Alasdair MacIntyre, should have written what can only be called a hatchet job on Marcuse, *Herbert Marcuse: An Exposition and a Polemic* (New York: Viking Press, 1970). Kellner does a fine job of responding to MacIntyre's criticisms. It could be argued, however, that Marcuse is trying to revive classical doctrines of knowledge and ethics without a conception of the *virtues.*

25. Herbert Marcuse, *One-Dimensional Man,* pp. 56–83. See also John David Ober, "On Sexuality and Politics in the Work of Herbert Marcuse," in Paul Breines, ed., *Critical Interruptions: New Left Perspectives on Herbert Marcuse* (New York: Herder and Herder, 1972), pp. 101–135.

26. Mimesis became a central concept in Critical Theory during the 1940s. Imitation, according to Horkheimer, is the primary means of learning during childhood. It is replaced, however, in subsequent socialization by rational, goal-directed behavior. In the history of civilization there is a corresponding replacement of ritual activity by scientific calculation; see Max Horkheimer, *Eclipse of Reason* (New York: Seabury, 1982), p. 115. However, the human need to engage in mimetic behavior, and the gratifying memory of childhood mimesis cannot be repressed completely, and it has "returned" in contemporary civilization in the form of the ritual discipline and hypnotic chanting of Nazism and in the repetition of commercial slogans; see Max Horkheimer and Theodor W. Adorno, *Dialectic of Enlightenment,* tr. John Cumming (New York: Seabury, 1973), pp. 168–208. Only

in a critical mimesis through the language of art and philosophy, a representation of reality through the language that subverts the meanings of ordinary speech, can the faculty of childhood mimesis be put to socially beneficial purposes; see Herbert Marcuse, *The Aesthetic Dimension* (Boston: Beacon Press, 1977), p. 45. The Frankfurt School's discussion of mimesis thus illustrates the double movement of negative and positive mediation I described in the previous chapter. The root of the concept of mimesis is both the classical notion of representation in art and its "material" basis in developmental psychology, a union of the erotic and the aesthetic that is so characteristically Marcusean.

27. Marcuse, *One-Dimensional Man*, p. 84.

28. Ibid., p. 94.

29. Ibid., p. 90.

30. Ibid., p. 92.

31. Ibid.

32. Ibid., pp. 93–94.

33. "One-Dimensional Philosopher," *Time*, March 22, 1968, p. 38; "The Revolution Never Came," *Time*, August 17, 1979, p. 19.

34. Marcuse, *One-Dimensional Man*, p. 95.

35. Herbert Marcuse, "Repressive Tolerance," in *Critique of Pure Tolerance* (Boston: Beacon Press, 1968), p. 90.

36. Ibid., p. 83.

37. Ibid., pp. 83–84.

38. Ibid., p. 123.

39. Albert O. Hirschman, *The Rhetoric of Reaction* (Cambridge, MA: Harvard University Press, 1991), pp. 147–148.

40. Hans-Martin Sass, "Ideational Politics and the Word Tolerance," *Philosophy and Rhetoric* 11 (Spring 1978), 111n10.

41. MacIntyre, *Herbert Marcuse: An Exposition and a Polemic*, p. 102.

42. Ibid., p. 102; the line about Stalinism is on p. 105.

43. Alain Touraine, "An Introduction to the Study of Social Movements," *Social Research* 52 (1985), 767.

44. Ibid., 768.

45. For a more optimistic appraisal of Marcuse's reconcilability with the rhetorical tradition, focusing on Marcuse's concept of "memory," see J. Robert Cox, "Memory, Critical Theory and the Argument from History," *Argumentation and Advocacy* 27 (1990), 1–13. My problem with Cox is that, like Marcuse and Habermas, his focus on argumentation leads to a neglect of strategic elements of rhetorical practice and of the responses of actual audiences.

46. Marcuse, *One-Dimensional Man*, p. 257. There is some debate over the relative influence of Lukács and Weber on Marcuse's work. Morton Schoolman, *The Imaginary Witness* (New York: Free Press, 1970), emphasizes the role of Weber, while Kellner (rightly, I think) emphasizes the role of Lukács. The important issue for our purposes is the constraining effect of the theory of reification/capitalist rationalization upon Marcuse.

47. Herbert Marcuse, *Eros and Civilization* (Boston: Beacon Press, 1962), pp. 158–159.

48. Ibid., p. 162.

49. Friedrich Schiller, *On the Aesthetic Education of Man,* tr. E. M. Wilkinson and L. A. Willoughby (Oxford: Oxford University Press, 1967), pp. 33–35.

50. See Fredric Jameson, *Marxism and Form* (Princeton: Princeton University Press, 1971), pp. 90–94.

51. Herbert Marcuse, *An Essay on Liberation* (Boston: Beacon Press, 1969), p. 26.

52. Immanuel Kant, *Critique of Judgment,* tr. J. H. Bernard (New York: Hafner Press, 1951); the first sentence is on p. 165; the rest of the quotation is from p. 172n50. Note especially Kant's contrast of individual quiet reflection and rhetoric. See Beiner's discussion of Kant and rhetoric, *Political Judgment* (Chicago: University of Chicago Press, 1983), pp. 97–101.

53. Herbert Marcuse, *The Aesthetic Dimension* (Boston: Beacon Press, 1978), p. xiii.

54. Ibid., p. 14.

55. See Marcuse, *One-Dimensional Man,* p. 84.

56. Marcuse, *The Aesthetic Dimension,* p. 24.

57. See Paul Piccone and Alexander Delfini, "Herbert Marcuse's Heideggerian Marxism," *Telos* 6 (1970), 45.

58. Marcuse, *The Aesthetic Dimension,* pp. 63–64.

59. See Susanne K. Langer, *Feeling and Form* (New York: Charles Scribner's, 1953), pp. 13–15.

60. Christopher Lasch, "Recovering Reality," *Salmagundi* 42 (1978), 47. Lasch is responding to and agreeing with an essay by Gerald Graff, "The Politics of Anti-Realism," in the same issue (4–43). Graff writes about Marcuse, "Defined as sensuous 'experience' severed from conceptual correspondence with reality, art has no more basis than the technocratic language of one-dimensional society for transcending existing reality. It becomes an aspect of what it rebels against" (29).

61. See Thomas B. Farrell, "Validity and Rationality: The Rhetorical Constituents of Argumentative Form," *Journal of the American Forensic Association* 13 (1977), 142–149.

62. See Kenneth Burke's discussion in *A Rhetoric of Motives* (Berkeley: University of California Press, 1969), pp. 73–74.

63. See Harold Pepinsky, *The Geometry of Violence and Democracy* (Bloomington: Indiana University Press, 1991). Based on his analysis of crime data, Pepinsky concludes that unresponsiveness at any level is what makes people violent: "Firm intergenerational class lines and enduring power imbalances of gender or age heighten social tension. The higher the geocentric concentration of intergenerational class division, the higher the voltage, and the more highly charged and concentrated the discharges of violent power" (p. 20). Violence in a given locality is "generated by the concentration of unresponsiveness in the area and by the availability of victims too weak to resist" (p. 21). Pepinsky's empirical data provide a hopeful alternative both to the neoconservatives' futility arguments and to the system arguments of the Frankfurt School. The decentralization and democratization of institutions seems to reduce violence—as in Norway's reduction of incarceration rates by 70 percent in the latter half of the nineteenth century after political

power devolved on localities. Pepinsky writes, "Our survival for some hundred thousand generations must mean that cooperation, nurture, compassion, and responsiveness are the overwhelming reality of human existence. The corollary fact—that so many notice only that 'human nature' entails violence, competition, and paying one's own way—must mean that we are highly sensitive to our own unresponsiveness, not that violence and competition are a dominant characteristic. We are so sensitive to this threat that the sound of our 'unresponsiveness alarm' can drown out our awareness of our own compassion" (pp. 29–30).

Chapter 4

1. The story of the relationship of administrative and critical research has been told in a number of places. Perhaps the most readily accessible is George Gerbner, ed., "Ferment in the Field," *Journal of Communication* 33 (1983). The debate over audience as commodity begins with Dallas W. Smythe, "Communications: Blind-spot of Western Marxism," *Canadian Journal of Political and Social Theory* 1 (1977), 1–27. See also Graham Murdock, "Blindspots about Western Marxism: A Reply to Dallas Smythe," *Canadian Journal of Political and Social Theory* 2 (1978), 109–119, and Smythe's reply, 120–129. I recognize that I am slighting the contributions of the radical tradition in mass media studies in this chapter and in this book as a whole. I have no quarrel with much of the radical institutional analysis done by Smythe and others. I am simply arguing that the ways in which the communication process has been conceived philosophically by radical students of the media are flawed.

2. There was also an economic basis. The fiscal crisis of the state affected American universities significantly from the late 1970s onward. Rock and roll and television studies had the advantage of being well-suited to mass lecture courses and to the preoccupations of American undergraduates. The use value of cultural studies was deeply involved with full-time-equivalent value.

3. John Fiske, "British Cultural Studies and Television," in Robert C. Allen, ed., *Channels of Discourse: Television and Contemporary Criticism* (Chapel Hill: University of North Carolina Press, 1987), p. 254.

4. Ibid., p. 255.

5. Ibid.

6. Ibid., p. 286.

7. What follows is not an intellectual biography. It is possible, of course, to argue that there are two Williamses—the Left-Leavisite of the 1950s and 1960s and the committed Marxist radical up until his death. I am glossing over genuine shifts of emphasis during Williams's career, although I believe his career must be seen as a unified one.

8. Terry Eagleton, "Resources for a Journey of Hope: The Significance of Raymond Williams," *New Left Review* 168 (March/April 1988), 3–11.

9. Ibid., 9.

10. Ibid., 10.

11. Raymond Williams, *Culture and Society, 1780–1950* (New York: Columbia University Press, 1983).

12. Raymond Williams, *The Country and the City* (New York: Oxford University Press, 1973), pp. 302–306.

13. Raymond Williams, "Marx on Culture," *What I Came to Say* (London: Hutchinson Radius, 1989), p. 203.

14. Ibid.

15. Ibid.

16. Ibid., p. 214.

17. Ibid., p. 220.

18. Raymond Williams, *Marxism and Literature* (New York: Oxford University Press, 1977), p. 99.

19. Williams, "Marx on Culture," p. 222.

20. Eagleton, "Resources for a Journey of Hope," 9.

21. Ibid., 27.

22. Lawrence Grossberg, "Strategies of Marxist Cultural Interpretation," *Critical Studies in Mass Communication* 1 (1984), 392–421.

23. Ibid., 399.

24. Raymond Williams, *The Long Revolution* (New York: Columbia University Press, 1983), p. 46.

25. Ibid., p. 47.

26. Ibid., p. 48.

27. Ibid., pp. 60–61.

28. Ibid., pp. 61–62.

29. Ibid., p. 63.

30. Ibid., p. 65.

31. Ibid., p. 67.

32. Ibid., p. 69.

33. Ibid., p. 70.

34. Grossberg, "Strategies of Marxist Cultural Interpretation," 401.

35. Ibid., 402–404.

36. See Raymond Williams, *Television: Technology and Cultural Form* (New York: Schocken, 1974), p. 56.

37. See Roger Scruton, *The Meaning of Conservatism* (Totowa, NJ: Barnes and Noble, 1980), especially p. 117.

38. Raymond Williams, "Mining the Meaning: Keywords in the Miners' Strike," *Resources of Hope* (London: Verso, 1989), pp. 120–127.

39. Ibid., p. 120.

40. Ibid., p. 121.

41. Ibid., p. 122.

42. Ibid., p. 123.

43. Ibid., p. 126.

44. Stuart Hall, "The Toad in the Garden: Thatcherism Among the Theorists," in Lawrence Grossberg and Cary Nelson, eds., *Marxism and the Interpretation of Culture* (Urbana: University of Illinois Press, 1988), p. 39.

45. Raymond Williams, *Border Country* (London: Chatto and Windus, 1960); *The Fight for Manod* (London: Chatto and Windus, 1979). The second novel of the trilogy, *Second Generation* (London: Chatto and Windus, 1964), takes place in a working-class and academic setting.

46. Raymond Williams, *Politics and Letters* (London: Verso, 1981), p. 289.

47. Ibid, p. 296.

48. Williams, "Distance," *What I Came to Say*, p. 42.

49. Williams, *The Country and the City*, p. 302.

50. See Raymond Williams, *Loyalties* (London: Chatto and Windus, 1985), pp. 357–366. The invective—surely "Gwyn" is speaking for Williams himself—could stand as an epigraph for the present book: "'You have been a class of betrayers,' Gwyn said angrily. 'You have always fought your internal battles by recruiting and using genuine popular interests or by lining up with some alien power. Or, as in your case, both. And then all that is new is that you damaged something authentic, something that had grown under the weight of you and in your own soil. You betrayed your own countrymen, but always and everywhere your class had been doing that, to serve its own interests. Your special betrayal was that you involved and damaged the only substance, the only hope, of our people. You involved and damaged socialism: our own kind of hope but converted by people like you to a distant and arbitrary and alien power. You say you carry the cost. A whole people is carrying the cost. And this makes it more than an error. It makes it an assault, on good people. It can never be forgiven. It will not be forgiven'" (p. 359).

51. Williams, *The Country and the City*, p. 303.

52. Ibid., pp. 304–305.

53. Ibid., p. 305.

54. Ibid., p. 306.

55. See Michael Real, "Demythologizing Media: Recent Writings in Critical and Institutional Theory," *Critical Studies in Mass Communication* 3 (1986), 460.

56. Williams, "Desire," *What I Came to Say*, pp. 33–34.

57. Stuart Hall, "Cultural Studies: Two Paradigms," *Media, Culture, and Society* 2 (1980), 57–72.

58. Ibid., 60.

59. Ibid., 61.

60. Ibid., 62. It is not immediately clear to me that Thompson's and Williams's positions are irreconcilable. A genuinely dialectical (*and* rhetorical) view of the social totality does not rule out moments of reconciliation or at least compromise between contending classes.

61. Ibid., 63.

62. Ibid.

63. For a useful discussion of general cultural trends in Britain, see Alan Sinfield, *Literature, Politics, and Culture in Postwar Britain* (Berkeley: University of California Press, 1989). His chapter on left-culturalism (pp. 232–252) has a particularly interesting account of Williams. Although Sinfield does not discuss the structuralist moment in cultural studies specifically, he points out that one liability of left-culturalism was its refusal to engage the possibility of politicizing mass commercial culture such as rock and roll (p. 250). It may be that some sort of Thompsonian "experience" of the heady days of the 1960s by the second generation of cultural studies is at the root of its rejection of the Thompson/Williams positions. I cannot resist adding that Sinfield's book, which contains the term "politics" in its title, does not address political discourse as explicitly as it does "literature."

64. Hall, "Cultural Studies," 64.

65. Ibid., 65.

66. Louis Althusser, "Ideology and Ideological State Apparatuses," *Essays on Ideology* (London: Verso, 1984), p. 39.

67. Hall, "Cultural Studies," 66.

68. Althusser, "Ideology and Ideological State Apparatuses," p. 49.

69. Ibid., p. 54.

70. I allude here to Fredric Jameson, "The Vanishing Mediator; or, Max Weber as Storyteller," *The Ideologies of Theory, Vol. 2: The Syntax of History* (Minneapolis: University of Minnesota Press, 1988), pp. 3–34.

71. James Boyd White, *When Words Lose Their Meanings* (Chicago: University of Chicago Press, 1984), pp. x–xi.

72. Fredric Jameson, "Reification and Utopia in Mass Culture," *Social Text* 1 (1979), 141.

73. I beg the reader to notice the term "relatively" above.

74. Grossberg, "Strategies of Marxist Cultural Interpretation," p. 409.

75. Ibid., p. 412.

76. Ibid., p. 413.

77. Ibid.

78. See Bryan D. Palmer, *Descent into Discourse: The Reification of Language and Writing of Social History* (Philadelphia: Temple University Press, 1990), for a thorough criticism of the link between discourse theory and the fragmentation of the Left's politics.

79. Grossberg, "Strategies of Marxist Cultural Interpretation," p. 416.

80. Ibid.

81. See A. Belden Fields, *Trotskyism and Maoism: Theory and Practice in France and the United States* (New York: Autonomedia, 1988). Perhaps the most representative work of the "New Philosophers" is Bernard Henri-Levy, *Barbarism with a Human Face* (New York: Free Press, 1978).

82. Todd Gitlin, "Who Communicates What to Whom, in What Voice and Why, About the Study of Mass Communication?" *Critical Studies in Mass Communication* 7 (1990), 188–189.

83. Mike Budd, Robert M. Entman, and Clay Steinman, "The Affirmative Character of U.S. Cultural Studies," *Critical Studies in Mass Communication* 7 (1990), 180. It is unclear, however, if an insistence on reintroducing economic analysis into media studies will solve the problem Budd and others identify. There is the ghost of Frankfurt School elitism and the antirhetorical spirit of Marx's letter to Ruge in their citation of Christopher Lasch in their conclusion: "There is only one cure for the malady that afflicts our culture, and that is to speak the truth about it" (180). If it were that simple, the revolution would have occurred in 1848.

Chapter 5

1. Jürgen Habermas, "What Does Socialism Mean Today? The Revolutions of Recuperation and the Need for New Thinking," in Robin Blackburn, ed., *After the Fall: The Failure of Communism and the Future of Socialism* (London: Verso, 1991), p. 25.

2. Ibid., p. 33.
3. Ibid., p. 29.
4. Ibid., p. 30.
5. Ibid., p. 31.
6. Ibid., p. 32.

7. Jürgen Habermas, *Theory and Practice,* tr. John Viertel (Boston: Beacon Press, 1973), p. 142.

8. Ibid., p. 143.

9. Ibid., pp. 168–169.

10. See, for instance, the early comment of Gøran Therborn: "Hence Habermas's popularity among young Anglo-Saxon reformist academics. He combines an apparently left-wing pedigree, conventional humanism and a notion that the basic political problems are problems of communication," in "The Frankfurt School," *Western Marxism: A Critical Reader* (London: Verso, 1978), p. 139; or Stanley Aronowitz's astonishingly obtuse review of Habermas's *The Theory of Communicative Action,* Volume I, in which Aronowitz calls Habermas the "Norman Vincent Peale" of social theory. See "The Power of Positive Thinking," *Village Voice (Literary Supplement),* May 1984, pp. 16–17. Where Habermas is most vulnerable to a critique from the Left is in his neglecting a potential feminist interpretation of interaction's roots in the *family.* See Nancy Fraser, "What's So Critical About Critical Theory? The Case of Habermas and Gender," *Unruly Practices: Power, Discourse, and Gender in Contemporary Social Theory* (Minneapolis: University of Minnesota Press, 1989), pp. 113–143.

11. Jürgen Habermas, *Knowledge and Human Interests,* tr. Jeremy J. Shapiro (Boston: Beacon Press, 1971), p. 313.

12. It is in light of the three moments of Habermas's dialectic that the Habermas-Gadamer "debate" is best read. See Jürgen Habermas, "A Review of Gadamer's *Truth and Method,*" in Fred R. Dallmayr and Thomas A. McCarthy, *Understanding and Social Inquiry* (Notre Dame, IN: University of Notre Dame Press, 1977), pp. 335–363. Habermas's characterization of hermeneutic understanding fits well with contemporary views of rhetoric: "Hermeneutic understanding is structurally oriented toward eliciting from tradition a possible action-orienting self-understanding of social groups. It makes possible a form of consensus on which communicative action depends" (p. 353). Gadamer's hermeneutics, however, neglects the reality of the human struggle against nature and the problem of domination. Gadamer's response is "On the Scope and Function of Hermeneutical Reflection," *Philosophical Hermeneutics,* tr. David Linge (Berkeley: University of California Press, 1976), pp. 18–43. Gadamer argues that Habermas sees no middle ground between blind acceptance of prejudice and autonomously derived consent. This middle ground was present in the tradition of rhetoric. Although Habermas had found a Kantian residue in Gadamer (p. 361), Gadamer is quite right to argue that Habermas is the true Kantian, because he cannot account for communal authority and persuasion.

13. Habermas, *Knowledge and Human Interests,* p. 347n20.

14. Ibid., p. 310.

15. Jürgen Habermas, *The Theory of Communicative Action,* Vols. I and II, tr. Thomas McCarthy (Boston: Beacon Press, 1984 and 1987).

16. Habermas, *The Theory of Communicative Action,* Vol. II, pp. 113–152.

17. Jürgen Habermas, *Legitimation Crisis,* tr. Thomas McCarthy (Boston: Beacon Press, 1975), pp. 13ff.

18. The exact relationship between the bourgeois public sphere and the rhetorical tradition is (not surprisingly) a contradictory one. As Gouldner has written, the bourgeois public sphere depended heavily on print (and freedom of the press), a technology that tended to erode traditional authority claims. See Alvin W. Gouldner, *The Dialectic of Ideology and Technology* (New York: Seabury, 1976), pp. 39–44. See also Habermas, *The Theory of Communicative Action,* Vol. II, p. 184. Habermas seems to celebrate the context-freeing aspect of mass communication.

19. Habermas, *Legitimation Crisis,* p. 61. See also Claus Offe, *Contradictions of the Welfare State* (Cambridge: Massachusetts Institute of Technology Press, 1984). Habermas, of course, did not predict the reversion of capitalism to more brutal forms in the United States and the United Kingdom with the rise of monetarism and the New Right. Reagan and Thatcher were able to control inflation— largely because of a *recoupling* of system and lifeworld.

20. Habermas, *Legitimation Crisis,* pp. 36–37.

21. Habermas, *The Theory of Communicative Action,* Vol. II, pp. 392–394.

22. Habermas, "What Does Socialism Mean Today?" pp. 33–35.

23. Ibid., p. 34.

24. Ibid.

25. Ibid., p. 35.

26. Ibid.

27. Habermas, *The Theory of Communicative Action,* Vol. I, pp. 273–337. This chapter expands on the most influential formulation of the theory, "What Is Universal Pragmatics," *Communication and the Evolution of Society,* tr. Thomas McCarthy (Boston: Beacon Press, 1979), pp. 1–68.

28. Gouldner, *The Dialectic of Ideology and Technology,* pp. 142–152.

29. Alasdair MacIntyre, *After Virtue,* 2nd ed. (Notre Dame, IN: University of Notre Dame Press, 1984), pp. 246–252. See Thomas McCarthy's useful discussion of the relationship between Habermas's communicative ethics and Kantian ethics: *The Critical Theory of Jürgen Habermas* (Cambridge: Massachusetts Institute of Technology Press, 1978), pp. 325–333.

30. Michael Oakeshott, *Rationalism in Politics and Other Essays* (London: Methuen, 1962).

31. There is, of course, considerable debate over just how Lockean-liberal the American Founding really is, but both Straussians and partisans of Pocock and Wood would surely agree on this characterization of the *Federalist;* see the Straussian account in David F. Epstein, *The Political Theory of the Federalist* (Chicago: University of Chicago Press, 1984).

32. Jon Elster, *Sour Grapes* (Cambridge, MA: Cambridge University Press, 1983), pp. 37–42.

33. Ibid., p. 42.

34. Jürgen Habermas, "Vorbereitende Bemerkungen zu einer Theorie der Kommunikativen Kompetenz," *Theorie der Gesellschaft oder Sozialtechnologie* (Frankfurt: Suhrkamp, 1971), p. 120. Translated and cited in Thomas McCarthy, "Translator's Introduction," *Legitimation Crisis,* pp. xiv–xv.

35. Jürgen Habermas, "Wahrheitstheorien," *Wirklichkeit und Reflexion* (Pfull-

ingen: Neske, 1973), p. 258. Translated and cited in McCarthy, "Translator's Introduction," *Legitimation Crisis,* p. xviii.

36. Michael Ryan, *Marxism and Deconstruction: A Critical Articulation* (Baltimore: Johns Hopkins, 1982), p. 113.

37. Ibid., p. 115.

38. Richard Rorty, *Philosophy and the Mirror of Nature* (Princeton: Princeton University Press, 1979), p. 318.

39. Richard Rorty, *Contingency, Irony, Solidarity* (Cambridge, MA: Cambridge University Press, 1979), p. 61.

40. Ibid., p. 67.

41. Ibid., pp. 67–68.

42. John Dewey, *The Public and Its Problems* (Athens, OH: Swallow, 1980), p. 208.

43. See Gadamer, "On the Scope and Function of Hermeneutical Reflection"; and Ronald Beiner, *Political Judgment* (Chicago: University of Chicago Press, 1983), pp. 25–30.

44. James W. Carey, "Space, Time, and Communications: A Tribute to Harold Innis," *Communication as Culture: Essays on Media and Society* (Winchester, MA: Unwin Hyman, 1989), pp. 160–161.

45. An exception to this general trend is Stephen Mailloux, *Rhetorical Power* (Ithaca: Cornell University Press, 1989); see especially pp. 170–181, the analysis of the ABM treaty debate.

46. Bruce Smith, *Politics and Remembrance* (Princeton: Princeton University Press, 1985), p. 7; cited in Carey, "Space, Time, and Communications," p. 4.

47. Isaac Kramnick, "The 'Great National Discussion': The Discourse of Politics in 1787," *William and Mary Quarterly* 45 (1988), 3–32.

48. See George H. Nash, *The Conservative Intellectual Movement in America* (New York: Basic Books, 1976); Paul Gottfried and Thomas Fleming, *The Conservative Movement* (Boston: Twayne, 1988).

49. Daniel Bell, *The Cultural Contradictions of Capitalism* (New York: Free Press, 1976). Bell identifies much the same dynamic that Habermas does, although where Habermas wishes to continue the rationalization project of modernity by displacing religion into a communicative ethic, Bell believes that religion needs to be restored to solve capitalism's legitimation crisis.

50. Elizabeth Wehr, "Trade, Plant-Closing Bills Win Strong House Backing," *Congressional Quarterly Weekly Report,* July 16, 1988, p. 1991.

51. The following historical narrative draws on the *New York Times,* July 2, 1988, I:1:6; July 7, IV:13:1; July 12, I:24:1; July 14, I:1:1 and IV:1:3; on Dole, Simpson, and the Bush campaign, see July 27, I:1:1 and August 2, II:4:3. For the conservative response, see the book published by Weyrich's new institute: *Cultural Conservatism: Toward a National Agenda* (Washington, DC: Institute for Cultural Conservatism/Free Congress Research and Educational Foundation, 1988). See also *The American Spectator,* July 1988, pp. 29–30; *Human Events,* July 25, 1988, pp. 5–6. William F. Buckley, Jr.'s, responses to the debate are in *National Review,* August 19, 1988, p. 61 and September 16, 1988, p. 64.

52. Ronald Reagan, "Statement," in *Congressional Quarterly Weekly Report,* August 6, 1988, p. 2226.

53. William F. Buckley, Jr., "Plant-Closings and Humanitarian Delusions," *National Review,* August 19, 1988, p. 61.

54. Richard Weaver, *The Ethics of Rhetoric* (Chicago: Henry Regnery, 1953), p. 57.

55. Chilton Williamson, Jr., "The Right Books," *National Review,* July 30, 1989, p. 54.

56. See Robert W. Whitaker, "Social Property Rights," in Whitaker, ed., *The New Right Papers* (New York: St. Martin's Press, 1982), pp. 170–179.

57. Paul Auerbach, "On Socialist Optimism," *New Left Review* 192 (1992), 5–35.

58. See Russell A. Berman's eloquent essay, "The Gulf War and Intellectuals, in Germany and the United States," *Telos* 88 (1991), 167–179.

59. Perry Anderson, *In the Tracks of Historical Materialism* (Chicago: University of Chicago Press, 1984), pp. 105–106.

Conclusion

1. Kenneth Burke, *A Rhetoric of Motives* (Berkeley: University of California Press, 1969), p. 101.

2. Karl Marx, *The Eighteenth Brumaire of Louis Bonaparte* (New York: International Publishers, 1963), p. 19.

3. Perry Anderson, *In the Tracks of Historical Materialism* (Chicago: University of Chicago Press, 1984), p. 17.

4. See, for instance, Raymie E. McKerrow, "Critical Rhetoric: Theory and Praxis," *Communication Monographs* 56 (1989), 91–111; and Kent A. Ono and John M. Sloop, "Commitment to Telos—A Sustained Critical Rhetoric," *Communication Monographs* 59 (1992), 48–60. Additionally see Robert Hariman's important criticism of McKerrow's project in "Critical Rhetoric and Postmodern Theory," *Quarterly Journal of Speech* 77 (1991), 67–70.

5. Perry Anderson, *In the Tracks of Historical Materialism,* p. 14.

6. On the idea of shifting from rights talk to needs talk, see Nancy Fraser, "Women, Welfare, and the Politics of Need Interpretation," *Unruly Practices: Power, Discourse, and Gender in Contemporary Social Theory* (Minneapolis: University of Minnesota Press, 1989), pp. 144–160.

7. Walter Benjamin, "Theses on the Philosophy of History," *Illuminations,* tr. Harry Zohn (New York: Schocken, 1969), p. 256.

8. Roy Medvedev, *Leninism and Western Socialism,* tr. A.D.P. Briggs (London: Verso, 1981), p. 293.

9. Anderson, *In the Tracks of Historical Materialism,* pp. 92–93.

10. I am chiefly influenced here by Elizabeth Faue, *Community of Suffering and Struggle: Women, Men, and the Labor Movement in Minneapolis, 1915–1945* (Chapel Hill: University of North Carolina Press, 1991). See also Joan Wallach Scott, "On Language, Gender, and Working-Class History," *International Labor and Working-Class History* 31 (1987), 1–13, 39–45.

11. Paul Cowan, "Whose America Is This?" *Village Voice,* April 2, 1979, p. 11.

12. Ibid., p. 1.

13. See Elizabeth Fox-Genovese, *Feminism Without Illusions: A Critique of Individualism* (Chapel Hill: University of North Carolina Press, 1991).

About the Book and Author

THIS BOOK IS THE FIRST extended study about the relationship between Marxism and the rhetorical tradition. Aune suggests that the classical texts of Marx and Engels wavered incoherently between positivist and romantic views of language and communication—views made possible by the decline of the rhetorical tradition as a cultural force. Though Western Marxism attempted to resolve this incoherence, it lacked a satisfactory theory of its own. Aune argues that the liberating impulse of Marxist tradition, ultimately, would be better served if we paid closer attention to the rhetorical history of the labor movement and to the role of public discourse in arousing or quieting revolutionary consciousness.

James Arnt Aune is associate professor of communication at the University of St. Thomas in St. Paul, Minnesota.

Index

1. problem of mediation (68